HOWARD W. HUNTER

HOWARD W. HUNTER

ELEANOR KNOWLES

Deseret Book Company
Salt Lake City, Utah

Photographs on the following pages are used by permission of the Idaho State Historical Society: page 27, ISHS #73-80.7; page 45, ISHS #75-177.6; page 58, ISHS #75-177.4; page 60, ISHS #80-94.40.

Photographs on pages 187, 196, and 227, courtesy *Deseret News*.

Library of Congress Catalog Card Number 94-13988

ISBN 0-87579-862-4

Printed in the United States of America

10   9   8   7   6   5   4   3

Contents

Acknowledgments

PRESIDENT HOWARD W. HUNTER is a modest man, a person who rarely talks about or draws attention to himself, even with close associates, friends, and family members. Thus, the challenge in writing his biography has been to ferret out pieces of information from many individuals and written sources and to weave these facts together into a whole that reveals the man beloved by those who know him best as well as the millions of Latter-day Saints throughout the world who have been touched by his spirit and messages. I am deeply grateful to the many individuals who so willingly shared their experiences with and observations of him and who encouraged me in my research and writing.

I am especially grateful to President Hunter, who, despite a reluctance to have his story written, allowed me to read a transcript of the diary he kept for a few months around his eleventh birthday; the journal he kept during the year when he went to the Orient on a cruise ship and subsequently moved to Southern California; the history he wrote of his life up to the time he became a General Authority; the nearly three thousand pages in the four-volume set of journals chronicling his life since 1959; and many scrapbooks of newspaper and magazine articles, photographs, and other memorabilia. Because of illnesses, travel assignments, and many demands on his time and energy, he has not been available for long, in-depth interviews. However, because he has always been a meticulous record keeper, genealogist, and historian, these materials became the primary source for his biography. Without them, it could not have been written.

Others who assisted me and provided valuable help and insights include the following:

Members of the First Presidency and the Quorum of the Twelve, and Elders F. Burton Howard and Jeffrey R. Holland of the Seventy.

John J. and Louine Berry Hunter and Richard A. and Nan Greene Hunter, President Hunter's sons and daughters-in-law; Inis E. Hunter, his wife; Dorothy Hunter Rasmussen, his sister; Lee Waldman Child, Claire Hunter's niece; and Corey Child, Lee's son.

Alicebeth Ashby, Leda Duncomb, Elva Hellings, Lael Littke, Loraine Major, Claron L. Oakley, Ernest H. Reed, Claire Smith, Richard S. Summerhays, and Daken K. Broadhead, longtime friends and fellow workers in the Pasadena Stake.

William H. Cravens, a former associate of President Hunter at the Polynesian Cultural Center; Daniel H. Ludlow and Fred J. Schwendiman, friends and associates with his assignments in the Middle East and Jerusalem; Gordon L. Lund, his law partner in Los Angeles; Dorothy and Talmage Nielsen, his former home teachers and longtime neighbors in Salt Lake City; Donna Dain Snow, his former legal secretary, and her husband, Karl Snow; Gary Gillespie, secretary to President Ezra Taft Benson; and Thomas E. Daniels, who served for many years in the Genealogical (now Family History) Department.

R. W. and Naomi Christensen, who drove me to places in the Boise area where President Hunter grew up, and the staff at the Idaho State Historical Society library in Boise.

Carole O. Cole, who tracked down old documents and newspaper articles in libraries and archives and helped to organize President Hunter's messages and talks; and Elizabeth L. Nichols of the Family History Department, who helped to find and verify genealogical records.

Dorene Beagles, President Hunter's secretary and my dear friend, who helped me find photographs, talks, articles, and other sources, answered dozens of questions, and gave me constant support and encouragement in my research and writing.

Elder Marvin J. Ashton, chairman of the board of directors at Deseret Book and a longtime associate of President Hunter in the Quorum of the Twelve, who had a special interest in this biography and was invaluable in opening doors so that it could be written and published.

Ronald A. Millett, president of Deseret Book Company, and Sheri Dew, vice president and director of publishing, who gave me the opportunity to write this book; and Kent Ware, design director, and Patricia Parkinson, typesetter, who contributed their special talents to the final product.

1

Born of Goodly Parents

ON MAY 2, 1374, Scotland's King Robert II signed a piece of parchment confirming a royal charter of land to William Hunter, the laird (lord, or owner) of Hunterston Castle, "for his faithful service rendered and to be rendered to us." William, the tenth Hunter of Hunterston, descended from a Norman family who left Normandy after Duke William of Normandy conquered England in 1066. A history of Hunterston explains that the family "came to Scotland, probably at the invitation of David I, who was brought up with his sister at the Norman Court, early in the 12th century and were given the lands of Arnele-Hunter, which eventually became known as Hunter's Toune [town]."[1] There, on their thousand-acre estate, the Clan Hunter built an impressive castle in the thirteenth century.

On October 20, 1987, Charles Hunter, the man who was in line to become thirtieth laird of Hunterston, visited in Salt Lake City, Utah, to honor a descendant of the family, Howard William Hunter, president of the Council of the Twelve Apostles in The Church of Jesus Christ of Latter-day Saints. At a luncheon in the Lion House, one of Utah's most historic homes, Charles Hunter presented to President Hunter a framed certificate recognizing him as a life member of the Clan Hunter and referred to him as "one of the noblest scions of a noble race, and one of the greatest Hunters of them all."[2]

Never, in their wildest dreams, would John William (Will)

and Nellie Rasmussen Hunter have foreseen this honor coming to Howard, their first child and only son, when he was born in their humble home in Boise, Idaho, nearly eighty years earlier. In a way, it was remarkable that Will and Nellie had even met, for they came from widely different backgrounds. And though their son would not characterize himself as "one of the greatest Hunters of them all," he certainly would echo the words of Nephi, "having been born of goodly parents," for he was a descendant of faithful, diligent individuals who followed the dictates of conscience to leave their ancestral homes in distant places and settle in the frontier West.

The Hunters from Scotland

JOHN HUNTER, Howard W. Hunter's great-grandfather, was born in Paisley, Renfrewshire, Scotland, not far from Hunterston Castle. As a young man he became a manufacturer of dress goods and textile products, many featuring the distinctive paisley designs characteristic of that area. He and his wife, Margaret Carse (or Carss), had three sons: John (Howard's grandfather), James (who died at age five), and Robert.

In 1860 missionaries of The Church of Jesus Christ of Latter-day Saints brought the message of the restored gospel to Paisley, and among those whom they baptized were John and Margaret Hunter. At the time the Church was encouraging new converts to gather with the Saints in the Salt Lake Valley, and the missionaries urged John and his family to emigrate. This presented a difficult problem, for John would have to give up a prosperous business, and the family, a comfortable home.

Many years later their son John wrote that for his father, the decision rested on "the many inducements and bright future for his class of business awaiting him in Utah, which was manifested beyond doubt by the higher-ups who claimed to have fully investigated this great undeveloped domain set apart for the Mormons to dwell in peace and harmony."[3] The family decided to emigrate.

Pedigree chart of Howard W. Hunter's Father, John William Hunter

John HUNTER
Born: Dec 1797
  Paisley, Scotland
Died: 4 Jan 1888
  Paisley, Scotland

John HUNTER
Born: 27 Aug 1825
  Paisley, Scotland
Marr: 11 Aug 1849
  Paisley, Scotland
Died: 30 Aug 1903
  Ogden, UT

Jean (Jane) MURCHIE
Born: Abt 1799
  Paisley, Scotland
Died: Feb 1849
  Paisley, Scotland

John HUNTER
Born: 8 Jul 1850
  Paisley, Scotland
Marr: 2 May 1878
  Salt Lake City, UT
Died: 10 Aug 1941
  San Francisco, CA

James CARSS
Born: 1796
  Glasgow, Scotland
Died: 1840

Margaret CARSE (CARSS)
Born: 27 Jul 1823
  Glasgow, Scotland
Died: 3 Jul 1909
  Ogden, UT

Marion CLELAND

John William HUNTER
Born: 16 Apr 1879
  Salt Lake City, UT
Marr: 3 Dec 1906
  Mt Pleasant, UT
Died: 1 Feb 1963
  Huntington Park, CA

Silas NOWELL
Born: 20 Jan 1798
  North Berwick, ME
Died:

William NOWELL
Born: 22 Nov 1828
  Maine
Marr: 9 Oct 1860
  St Joseph, MO
Died: 14 Nov 1882
  Salt Lake City, UT

Nancy F HATCH
Born: 28 Feb 1805
  Pittston, ME
Died: 13 Jul 1902
  Salt Lake City, UT

Josephine May NOWELL
Born: 2 May 1860
  St Joseph, MO
Died: 7 Jun 1934
  Oakland, CA

Adam CRITES

Rebecca CRITES
Born: 16 Dec 1836
  Pennsylvania
Died: 16 Mar 1916
  Salt Lake City, UT

Mary STROUSE

The voyage across the Atlantic Ocean was a sad one, for Margaret gave birth to a son who died shortly after birth and was buried at sea. Moreover, when they reached the Salt Lake Valley in late September 1860, John soon became disenchanted and, as his son John described it, "finally detached himself and family from the Church, . . . leaving the family in a strange country without a guide."

With the money John got from the sale of his property in Scotland, the family had financial resources until he could become reestablished. A few months after they arrived, he purchased two wagons and four yoke of oxen and hired a driver to help him take produce and other food items to Montana. His family remained at Camp Douglas in Salt Lake City, where Margaret and her two sons, John and Robert, were employed by the U.S. government. John made two successful trips to Montana, but during the third one he was caught in a freezing snowstorm and lost his cattle and the produce.

In the spring of 1866 the family moved to Fort Bridger, Wyoming, where John found employment with the government as a stonemason and began building a home. That August Margaret gave birth to a daughter, Margaret, who died one week later.

About two years later the family moved to South Pass City, Wyoming, where they built a large log home on the Washakie Indian reservation. Soon after the house was completed, they were ordered off the reservation, with no compensation for their home. From there they went to the Wind River Valley and built another home—with "portholes" upstairs large enough for rifles to protect them from hostile Sioux Indians. Because of the constant threat to their lives (they had to carry guns whenever they left home, even to work in the fields), they returned to South Pass City and eventually to Fort Bridger. There they remained for several years before moving to Ogden, Utah, sometime in the 1880s. John died in Ogden in 1903, at age seventy-eight, and Margaret died six years later, a few weeks before her eighty-sixth birthday.

Their son John, who was sixteen when the family moved to Wyoming, was employed by the government that fall as a teamster. He moved with his parents to South Pass City and the Wind River Valley, and when they returned to Fort Bridger, he again became a teamster. Once he was ordered to deliver seventy-five pack mules to General Custer's command at Fort Russell. When he arrived, he was asked to go on to Fort Fetterman, about one hundred miles north. After turning the animals over to one of Custer's officers, he returned to Cheyenne, where he learned that he had narrowly missed the massacre that became known as "Custer's last stand."

In 1876 the owners of the hotel at Fort Bridger visited some friends in Salt Lake City and invited the friends' daughter, Josephine (Josie) Nowell, to return to Wyoming with them for a visit. John, now twenty-six years old, drove the government ambulance that met the Union Pacific trains. Knowing that a pretty young woman was coming to Fort Bridger (where there were few single women to date), he spruced up the wagon and made it shine.

After that initial meeting, John courted Josie for two years, primarily through letters. In the meantime he entered into a business agreement with a Judge Carter to build large cattle yards at Hampton Station on the Union Pacific line and ship thousands of cattle to Chicago. "We built a large two-story house to accommodate cattle drivers," he wrote, "and I had in mind a part to be arranged for our comfort, which Miss Nowell and I had anticipated just prior to our marriage." They were married by an Episcopal bishop on May 2, 1878, at the home of her parents in Salt Lake City.

The Nowell Family

WILLIAM NOWELL, Josie's father, descended from English immigrants who were among the earliest settlers in New England. His Nowell ancestors settled in the Massachusetts Bay

Colony at Salem, and by the mid-1600s they were living in North Berwick, Maine. His maternal Hatch ancestors were in Falmouth, Massachusetts, by the 1700s, and then moved to Pittston, Maine. William's parents, Silas Nowell and Nancy Hatch, married in 1825 in North Berwick. William, the eldest of their seven children (some of whom died in infancy) and the great-grandfather of Howard W. Hunter, was born three years later.

In the mid-1830s Silas and Nancy Nowell moved to Lapeer, a small village east of Flint, Michigan. There Silas tried to eke out a living as a farmer, but his efforts were often stymied by heavy winter snows and bitterly cold weather that lasted until late spring. Within a few years he was thinking about moving south to Ohio.

Nancy, a deeply spiritual woman and devout Methodist, kept a diary from January 1840 to September 1842 in which she poured out feelings about her relationship to the Lord, her gratitude for his favors, her desires to learn what was expected of her, and her search for the pure gospel of ancient days, as these entries indicate:

> [Saturday, July 25, 1840] Being convinced that much, very much depends upon personal effort, I believe it to be a binding and responsible duty of every child of God to labor and do all in their several capacities, and to the utmost in their power for the upbuilding and promotion of God's cause of the universal spread of the glorious gospel throughout the world.
>
> [Saturday, April 2, 1842] The mercy of God has spared me to see the close of another week. I am often led to wonder what I am spared for; why is my unprofitable life prolonged from week to week and from year to year?
>
> [Monday, April 4, 1842] The present view that I have of the church of God universally causes me to weep. It appears to me that it has fallen from its primitive holiness and purity as a body, though it may be enjoyed by individuals as far as the light of God's spirit can bear upon the soul through the dark mist of unbelief. . . . It has not only lost its holiness and purity,

but its power and strength. Where do we find that mighty, powerful faith, with all the gifts of the Spirit, that was once enjoyed under the gospel dispensation?

[Saturday, April 9, 1842] Have felt to rejoice in the spirit today while meditating upon the latter-day glory, which I believe to be drawing very near.

[Tuesday, September 13, 1842 (Nancy's final entry)] I have appealed my cause to the great Judge of all the earth by committing myself and all into his hand, therefore I should be silent and patiently submit, knowing that he is omnipotent, omnipresent, and omniscient, and that he is my friend. I feel a sense of God's love.[4]

About the time Nancy wrote that last entry, a Mormon missionary came to Lapeer from Nauvoo, Illinois. After listening to his message, praying about it, and receiving "a testimony that he spoke truth," Nancy decided to go to Nauvoo to learn more about the Church. In her journal she wrote: "I went to hear the Mormon preacher [Joseph Smith] with great caution, hoping not to be deceived. His subject was the second coming of Christ. I had a testimony that he spoke the truth, and that Joseph Smith was a true prophet, called and ordained of God to do a great work, because he had brought forth the truth as it was taught by Jesus Christ. I asked to be baptized."

Nancy and Silas, with their family, moved to Nauvoo in 1843, and she gave birth to a son, Oliver, in January 1844. Late that June, after the Prophet and his brother Hyrum were martyred, she viewed their bodies laid out in the Mansion House. Little is known about the Nowell family's experiences in Nauvoo, but apparently Silas joined the Church also, for, according to Nauvoo Temple records, the couple both received their temple endowments on January 28, 1846. Soon afterwards, he and Nancy separated.[5] She emigrated to Utah in 1852 and remained faithful to the Church the rest of her life. She died on July 13, 1902.

After the Nowell family left Nauvoo, Nancy's eldest son, William, lived for several years in St. Joseph, Missouri, where he married Rebecca Crites in 1860. Their two children—Josephine (Josie, Howard Hunter's grandmother) and Edward—were born in St. Joseph before the family moved to Salt Lake City in 1864 to be closer to William's mother. A prominent contractor and builder, he died in Salt Lake City in 1882. His wife, Rebecca, died in 1916.

Right after her 1878 marriage to John Hunter, Josie accompanied her new husband to Wyoming and, as he said in his history, "became the mistress of Hampton." John's partnership with Judge Carter seemed particularly promising that fall when a Mr. Hawkins from Oregon brought a herd of over 3,000 cattle to the stockyards at Hampton. Armed with information from John on how to sell the cattle, Mr. Hawkins made a successful trip to stockyards in Chicago and Iowa. On the way home, he stopped at Hampton and convinced John he should resign "all present positions and join hands with him" at the beginning of the year. After severing his association with Judge Carter, John was stunned when his new partner, Mr. Hawkins, died suddenly before their partnership was formalized.

Forced to find work, John and Josie moved to Salt Lake City, where he worked for a few weeks in a mine at Alta. Then he went into railroading, as an agent in Park City, Utah; Granger, Wyoming; and Pocatello, Idaho. In 1887 he and his family moved to Boise, where he became the first agent on the new Boise branch of the Oregon Short Line railroad. A year later he became involved in some gold mines in a wilderness area about 140 miles north of Boise. Later he had mining interests for a time near Pearl, thirty miles north of Boise, before returning to the railroad.

The eldest of John and Josie's seven children, John William (Will) Hunter, was born in Salt Lake City April 16, 1879. This was Howard W. Hunter's father.

At about age twenty-four, Will was working with his father in the mines near Pearl when some friends in Boise introduced him to Nellie Marie Rasmussen, a vivacious young woman six years younger, who had recently come to Boise to live with her aunt and uncle, Bertha Christina (Christie) Christensen and Wythuel Wood (Fred) Moore. Since Will was working and boarding out of town, much of their two-year courtship was conducted through letters, with occasional buggy rides when he visited his family in Boise.

The Rasmussens and Christensens

NELLIE MARIE RASMUSSEN descended from pioneers who helped settle Mount Pleasant, Utah, in the Sanpete Valley some 125 miles southeast of Salt Lake City. Her maternal grandfather, Morten Rasmussen, was born in 1834 in Braendekilde, Odense, Denmark, where his father's family had lived for several generations.

In 1851 missionaries of the Church came to Braendekilde. Morten responded to their message—the only member of his family to be converted to the Church—and was baptized in November 1851, five weeks after his eighteenth birthday. Less than three years later he immigrated to America to join the Saints in the Great Salt Lake Valley. Crossing the plains by ox train, he arrived in the valley October 5, 1854. About three years later he moved to Ephraim, a small town in the Sanpete Valley. There, on April 1, 1859, he married Karen Maria Christiansen, another Danish convert to the Church.

Karen was born in 1842 in Lunge Gelsted, Odense, Denmark, the daughter of Christian Nielsen Christiansen and Ane Margrethe Jensen. She and her parents joined the Church in Denmark in 1854, and three years later they immigrated to Utah. After a few years in Ephraim, Christian and Ane moved to Mount Pleasant.

About the time of his marriage, Morten Rasmussen was called by Brigham Young to help build a fort in Mount Pleasant and colonize the new community. The first of his and Karen's twelve children, a son named Martin (Howard W. Hunter's grandfather), was born in December 1859 in a cave on the bank of the creek that flowed through the fort. At the

Pedigree chart of Howard W. Hunter's Mother, Nellie Rasmussen

Martin RASMUSSEN

Born: 6 Dec 1859
  Mt Pleasant, UT
Marr: 27 May 1880
  Salt Lake City, UT
Died: 11 Mar 1924
  Salt Lake City, UT

Morten RASMUSSEN

Born: 27 Oct 1834
  Braendekilde, Denmark
Marr: 1 Apr 1859
  Ephraim, UT
Died: 28 Jun 1885
  Mt Pleasant, UT

Rasmus RASMUSSEN

Born: 19 Jun 1804
  Braendekilde, Denmark
Died: 26 May 1888
  Braendekilde, Denmark

Maren JENSEN

Born: 18 Dec 1808
  Tommerup, Denmark
Died: 1 Feb 1889
  Braendekilde, Denmark

Karen Maria or Marie CHRISTIANSEN

Born: 26 Jul 1842
  Lunge Gelsted, Denmark
Died: 19 Mar 1900
  Mt Pleasant, UT

Christian Nielson CHRISTIANSEN

Born: 1 Nov 1818
  Lunge Gelsted, Denmark
Died: 11 Dec 1880
  Mt Pleasant, UT

Ane Margrethe JENSEN

Born: 22 Jun 1805
  Seden, Denmark
Died: 16 Mar 1883
  Mt Pleasant, UT

Nellie Marie RASMUSSEN

Born: 30 May 1885
  Mt Pleasant, UT
Died: 11 Nov 1971
  Maywood, CA

Nicoline CHRISTENSEN

Born: 24 Oct 1861
  Mt Pleasant, UT
Died: 1 Dec 1887
  Mt Pleasant, UT

Anders CHRISTENSEN

Born: 18 Nov 1830
  Stillinge, Denmark
Marr: 1 Apr 1859
  Salt Lake City, UT
Died: 29 Nov 1917
  Mt Pleasant, UT

Christen ANDERSEN

Born: 18 Feb 1796
  Svendstrup, Denmark
Died: 21 Mar 1884
  Mt Pleasant, UT

Karen JENSEN

Born: 16 Sep 1809
  Sr. Hojrup, Denmark
Died: 9 Feb 1897
  Mt Pleasant, UT

Nilla PEDERSEN or TORGERSEN

Born: 22 Jan 1840
  Skedsmo, Norway
Died: 8 Jan 1876
  Mt Pleasant, UT

Peder TORGERSEN

Born: 13 Jun 1805
  Skedsmo, Norway
Died: 21 Nov 1862
  Norbyeie, Norway

Berthe NIELSEN

Born: 1 Jan 1804
  Lund U Nerdrum, Norway
Died: 26 Jun 1877
  Mt Pleasant, UT

time of his death twenty-five years later, Morten was a prominent farmer, businessman, and Church and community leader.

Martin Rasmussen, Morten's son, married a young
woman from Mount Pleasant, Nicoline Christensen, in the
Endowment House in Salt Lake City in May 1880.

Nicoline's parents, like Martin's, emigrated from Scandinavia. Her father, Anders Christensen (Howard Hunter's
great-grandfather), was born in Stillinge, Soro County, Denmark, in 1828, and was baptized into the Church in March
1853. His parents, Christen and Karen Jensen Andersen, his
half-sister Maren, and his younger brothers, Jens and Niels
Christian, were baptized soon thereafter. In January 1855 Jens
immigrated to America, and Anders and Niels Christian followed in 1860. Their parents immigrated in 1862, walking
most of the way between Florence, Nebraska, and Salt Lake
City, and settled in Mount Pleasant.

Anders was twenty-one when he walked across the plains
with the tenth handcart company, which left Florence July 6,
1860, and arrived in Salt Lake City September 24. This was the
last and, with 124 Saints, the smallest of the handcart groups
to journey to Utah between 1856 and 1860.[6] Another member
of this company was Nilla Pedersen, a twenty-year-old Nor-
wegian convert, whom he had met on the ship crossing the
Atlantic.

Nilla (Howard Hunter's great-grandmother) was born in
Skedsmo, Norway, a daughter of Berthe Nielsen and Peder
Torgersen,[7] in 1840 and was baptized in 1858. She was the first
of her family to immigrate to the Salt Lake Valley, traveling
alone with other European Saints. Her mother, two of her sisters, and her brother also joined the Church and later immigrated to Utah. Her father died in Norway two years after
Nilla left, and her youngest sister did not join the Church and
stayed in Norway.

Anders and Nilla apparently fell in love during their
handcart journey to Utah, for they were married two months
after they arrived. They went to Mount Pleasant, where they

first lived inside the fort, for protection against the Indians. Anders later built a dugout with a sod roof outside the fort, and it was there that his daughter, Nicoline, was born in October 1861.[8]

In the summer of 1865, when Nicoline was three, her father took a second wife, Kristen Nielsen, who was divorced from his brother and had three children. He moved his two families, as well as his parents and his sister, seventy-five miles south to Richfield, to help settle that community, but because of severe Indian troubles and raids of the settlement, they all returned to Mount Pleasant two years later. Two children were born of Anders's marriage to Kristen; a third child was stillborn, and Kristen died the same day.

Nilla cared for the children of her sister wife, along with six of her own (three others died in infancy) until her death January 8, 1876. As the oldest child, Nicoline at fourteen assumed responsibility for her five younger siblings and the two children of Kristen. Five months later Anders married Christina Jonsson, a widow with one son of her own. (In 1884 he took another wife, Christina Frantsson.) Anders died in November 1917.

Nellie Marie Rasmussen

AFTER THEIR MARRIAGE and sealing in the Endowment House, Martin Rasmussen and his eighteen-year-old bride, Nicoline, returned to Mount Pleasant, where he built a log house one block from the home of his father, Morten Rasmussen. Three children were born to the couple in their new home: Henry Arthur, on March 8, 1881; Lawrence Martin, December 17, 1882; and Nellie Marie, May 30, 1885.

In early December 1887, Martin was in Colorado working on a road project with his brother John when he received a message that Nicoline was desperately ill at home. He left for home immediately, riding all day, through the night, and all the next day, stopping only to rest his horses. When he arrived in Mount Pleasant, he learned that Nicoline had died three

Nicoline Christensen and Martin Rasmussen, maternal grandparents of Howard W. Hunter

days earlier, on December 1, and had been buried just a few hours before he arrived. She was twenty-six years old.

Before she died, Nicoline asked that her half-sister, Annie Cecelia, take her two-year-old baby daughter.[9] Cecelia was still in her teens at the time and living with her grandmother, Karen Jensen Andersen, a widow. Four years later Cecelia married William Burt Reynolds, and Nellie lived with them until 1895, when she was ten. The Reynoldses decided to move to Colorado, and Nellie was at the train station with them, waiting for their train, when her father arrived and refused to let her go.

Two and a half years after Nicoline's death, Martin married Emma Elizabeth Jeffs. By the time six-year-old Nellie went to live with her father and stepmother, Emma had given birth to two children, one of whom died in infancy. Within the next eleven years the couple had four more children. Nellie lived with them for about three years, staying home from school much of the time to help care for the younger children. Then one day her father felt that she had been punished unjustly by her stepmother, so he made arrangements for her to live with his mother, Karen Marie Christiansen Rasmussen. She remained there until her grandmother died in March 1900.

Nellie, by then nearly fifteen, next went to live with Andrew Christensen, her mother's brother, in Castle Dale, sixty miles from Mount Pleasant. John Rasmussen, Martin's brother, also lived in Castle Dale, and Nellie stayed alternately with her uncles' families for nearly two years. Then she was invited to live with her mother's sister and brother-in-law, Christie and Fred Moore, in Salt Lake City.

Nellie stayed with the Moores for about two years, attending school and working part-time for a family named Metras. When the Moores moved to Boise, she moved in with the Metras family. After Christie Moore lost a baby about two years later, Fred invited Nellie to come and live with them in Boise.

Nineteen-year-old Nellie had no trouble finding a job. She worked for a while as a waitress and a switchboard operator at the Idanha hotel and then went to work for the Mountain States Telephone Company. And soon after she arrived in Boise, she was introduced to Will Hunter.

Marriage and a Family

AFTER COURTING Nellie mostly through letters, Will decided to leave the mines and return to Boise. He worked for a short time for the Oregon Short Line Railroad before accepting a position with the Boise Valley Traction Company, an interurban railway that hauled mail and passengers on a loop from Boise to several communities west of the city. With a more secure job, sometime in the spring or early summer of 1906 he proposed to Nellie and then went to Fred Moore to get permission to marry her.

Uncertain about marrying a man who was not a member of the Church, Nellie decided she needed time and space to

Downtown Boise in the early 1900s

think things out. That summer she went to Sanford, Colorado, to visit her aunt Cecelia, and while there, she met a young man who wanted to marry her, but she declined his offer and went to Mount Pleasant to visit family members. Will, concerned about her long absence, followed her there and talked her into getting married.

On December 3, Will and Nellie took the morning train to Manti, got a marriage license at the county offices, and caught the train on its return trip to Mount Pleasant. While they were gone, several of her relatives made her a wedding dress, and in the early evening the couple were married at the home of her aunt Maria Sophia Rasmussen Madsen. Daniel Rasmussen, her father's brother, performed the ceremony. Many friends and relatives, including her father, attended the hurriedly planned wedding and congratulated them afterwards. The next day the newlyweds returned by train to Boise, where they would make their home.

After staying with Will's parents for a few days, Will and Nellie rented a small house at 1402 North 11th Street, on the northeast corner of 11th and Sherman streets. There, on November 14, 1907, their son, Howard William Hunter, was

*Nellie Rasmussen and
John William Hunter
in a photograph
taken at the time
of their wedding*

born. Dr. John Beck, the family's doctor for the next twenty years, attended the birth, and a practical nurse came to stay with the new mother for a few days.

When Howard was five months old, on April 5, 1908, Nellie took him to fast and testimony meeting at the Boise Branch of the Northwestern Mission, where the branch president, Heber Q. Hale, gave him a blessing.

At the time of Howard's birth, Idaho, like other states in the West, was experiencing rapid growth. Between 1900 and 1910, the state, which had been admitted to the Union in 1890, doubled in population, from 161,772 to 325,594. Boise, the state capital, was growing even faster, with 5,957 inhabitants in 1900 and 17,358 in 1910. Automobiles were still a rarity (Henry Ford didn't introduce his Model T until Howard was a year old), and the city streets hadn't yet been paved. But houses and businesses were going up everywhere, and the city limits were being pushed outward.

The LDS Church, which was strong in eastern Idaho just north of the Utah state line, had very little presence in west-

Howard W. Hunter at eight months, about one year, and two years of age

ern Idaho at the turn of the century. The first LDS meeting in Boise was held at a local boarding house on January 18, 1903, by eight men, some of them members of the Idaho legislature who were in Boise for the legislative session. After their meeting they contacted Church authorities in Salt Lake City, and the next week Church representatives arrived to investigate the situation and meet with the members. On their recommendation, a branch was organized February 8, 1903, as part of the Union Stake in eastern Oregon.[10] The next year the branch was assigned to the Northwestern States Mission. Heber Q. Hale served as branch president from 1905 till November 3, 1913, when the Boise Stake was organized and the branch became a ward.

Nellie was an active member of the branch and made certain that her children attended regularly and received religious instruction both at church and at home. Though Will was not a member of the Church, he did not stand in the way of his family's participation, and occasionally, when his work schedule allowed (he often had to work on Sundays), he would go to the Sunday evening sacrament meetings with them.

When Howard was nearly two, the family moved around the corner to another home their landlord owned, at 1012 Sherman Street. This home was a little larger than the other

Nellie Rasmussen on the porch of the Sherman Avenue home
where Howard's sister, Dorothy, was born

one, and it was there that Nellie gave birth on November 1, 1909, to her second child, a daughter whom she and Will named Dorothy Elaine.

Not long after Dorothy was born, Nellie sterilized some water by boiling it in a pan on the living-room stove that the family used for heat. She had taken it off the stove and, because it was too hot to hold, set it on the floor when Howard came running through the house. He fell headlong into the pan, throwing his left hand in front of himself, and it was badly scalded. In his history many years later he described what happened:

"A call was made to the doctor and he recommended that my arm be packed in mashed potatoes and bandaged. Some of the neighbor ladies came in to help. I can remember sitting on the drain board in the kitchen while boiled potatoes were mashed and packed around my arm and cloths were torn into strips to make a bandage. Fortunately the serious burn did not hinder the growth of my arm, but I have carried the scar all my life."[11]

2

A Happy Childhood in Boise

IN EARLY 1910, Will and Nellie Hunter bought a quarter-acre lot in a new subdivision just outside the west city limits of Boise. The lot was at the end of Vine Street, a dead-end lane going south from Valley Road (later renamed State Street). A quarter of a mile away, beyond the fields and pastureland at the end of the lane, was the Boise River.

To help build the three-room frame house, Will hired the brother-in-law of Nellie's aunt Christie Moore. He also purchased a small hammer for two-year-old Howard and let him pound nails into the living-room floor, an "apprenticeship" that foreshadowed Howard's lifelong interest in woodworking.

That fall the family moved from Sherman Street to their new home. The house, which faced east, had a long living room, a bedroom, and a kitchen. A coal stove in the living room and a coal range in the kitchen provided heat in winter. For the first few years the house was lighted by kerosene lamps. Outside, a lawn extended along the north side, a favorite playground for the children and their friends. On the west side of the house, some fifty paces from the back door, Howard recalled, "was a small, well-ventilated square building, placed over a hole in the ground, that was called the 'out house,' a term much too dignified for the structure."

Between the house and the outhouse was a brick-lined cellar where canned and fresh fruits and vegetables were stored.

*The Hunter home
on Vine Street, Boise.
At left is the porch
where Howard slept*

The vegetable garden and crab apple and plum trees were on the south side of the lot, while raspberry and gooseberry bushes lined the back fence. Later Will added a chicken coop and a detached garage.

With only one bedroom, the family soon needed additional sleeping space for Howard and Dorothy, so Will added a porch across the front of the house. The children slept on cots on the south half of the porch; the north end was a pleasant place where the family could sit and visit on warm evenings. The porch was enclosed with siding extending about three feet up and screening above the siding. Inside the screen, a canvas could be lowered from a roller with a crank; the canvas kept rain and snow out but not the winter cold or the summer heat.

Nellie cooked on the coal range, which had a warming oven above the cooking surface and a reservoir at one end to heat water. One of Howard's chores was to go over the stove with stove blacking and then polish the nickel letters that spelled out the brand name: Majestic. He also brought in coal from a shed attached to the house and chopped kindling wood.

To pump water into the sink, Will drove a pipe into the ground through a hole in the kitchen floor under one end of the sink and mounted a hand pump at the top of the pipe. For their Saturday night baths, the family pumped water into a galvanized tub and heated it on the stove.

"Most of the time we lived on Vine Street, we had chickens," Howard remembered. "I had the responsibility of scattering a can of grain for them each morning and evening and changing the water in their pens." Occasionally he also cleaned the coops and roosts.

Will took great pride in his garden and kept it meticulously tidy, even dragging a board across the ground so it would be level. About once a week the family flooded the garden and lawn with water diverted from a nearby irrigation ditch. Once Will asked Howard to weed the potato patch. When he checked his son's work that evening, he became livid. "You've pulled up the potato plants!" he exclaimed. Howard, who had helped his father plant the potatoes, replied defensively, "That is not where we planted them."

Because their home was outside the city limits, the Hunters' address was RFD 1 (many years later the house received a street number, 303 Vine Street). As soon as they were old enough, the children walked down the lane and across Valley Road to collect the mail from box 23. The postman, driving a horse-drawn buggy, delivered it at 10:15 each morning.

In the evening Howard and Dorothy walked to Anderson's Dairy, about half a mile away on the north side of Valley Road, for fresh milk. Frequently they brought back milk for widows in their neighborhood, carrying the heavy bottles in a canvas bag Nellie had made. A Mrs. Williams, who lived on the Hunters' property, would pay Howard for bringing her milk and cutting her lawn.

The Hunter family kept milk and other perishables in an icebox in the kitchen. When the iceman came to their area, the children followed him around, hoping to get slivers and small chunks of ice to suck. Dorothy sometimes skimmed the cream off the milk and then froze it on the ice so she could have "ice cream." This didn't please her father, who would complain pointedly, "Well, Dorothy's been freezing the cream again."

As a boy, Howard loved animals. For several years he had a pet dog, and, he said, "every stray cat could find a haven at our house, even against family objections." Once some neighborhood boys found a stray kitten and entertained themselves by putting the animal in a sack and throwing it into the canal. When the kitten crawled out, they threw it back in again. After they finally tired of this, Howard rescued the animal and took it home to warm it up and dry it out.

"It won't live," his mother said, but he wouldn't give up.

"Mother, we have to try," he told her.

She found a quilt, lined a box, and put the box under the range, where it was warm. The cat soon revived, and for many years it lived with the family.

Someone told Howard a cat would do tricks if a drop of turpentine were put on its tail. He experimented with a drop of turpentine on the tail of one of his cats, but nothing happened. He put a few more drops on the tail. Nothing happened. Finally he dipped the tail into the turpentine container.

"All was quiet," he recalled, "and then suddenly the cat arched its back, jumped into the air with a screech, cleared the fence with a leap, and took off through White's wheat field. I could see the ripple of the wheat heads as it raced through the stems of grain." He searched and searched, but with no success. "For several days I was deeply troubled," he said, "but this turned into joy when the cat forgave and came home."

Howard also had pet rabbits, which he kept in a hutch his father made, letting them run loose occasionally so they could

Howard and Dorothy and their dog liked to cool off in the irrigation ditch

eat grass on the lawn. Each of the rabbits had a name; two favorites were Bunny Boo and Mary Jane. In a diary begun shortly before his eleventh birthday, Howard described one time when he let Mary Jane run around the yard:

"I was tring [trying] to catch her. A little boy came over and thought he would help me. I wish he had stayed home because he pulled my bunnies tail right off, it made me sick. I went in the house cring [crying,] so mother came out and helped me catch her."[1] Even seventy-five years later he remembered that experience as "a tragedy in my young life."

With many children in the neighborhood, there were always friends for Howard and Dorothy to play with. They particularly enjoyed playing around the ditches, canals, and river. When they were younger, they waded in the irrigation ditch that carried water from Sand Creek. As they grew older, they swam in the Boise River and the Ridenbaugh Canal, which diverted water out of the river. To get to the river, they had to go through the barbed-wire fence enclosing a neighbor's property and hike to the far side of his alfalfa patch and pasture. Along the river they found inviting thickets, trees, and patches of cattails.

"There was a wooded area there that I loved to go to after school or on Saturdays," Howard recalled in an interview for the *Friend*. "My dog was my pal, and we went there together and sailed boats or made whistles out of willows. We watched the beavers make dams and the fish swim in the water. We watched the birds build nests and hatch their young."[2]

Howard collected birds' eggs—pheasants, meadowlarks, bluebirds, robins, wrens—and could identify each. According to Dorothy, he would never take an egg if there were only one or two in the nest. If there were more, he would take one or two, pierce each end with a pin, and blow out the egg. He kept his collection in partitioned cigar boxes lined with cotton.

In winter, the swimming holes froze over and became skating ponds. "Under the light of a stark winter moon shining down through the leafless trees, it was a great winter sport to skate for a few miles down the canal, build a fire on the ice, and roast weiners before skating back," he wrote in his history.

Winter snow also brought another favorite sport: hookybobbing. The children tied long ropes to the front ends of their sleds and waited beside the road for a buggy or wagon to come by on the hard-packed snow. Then, Howard explained, "we ran up behind, looped the rope over the rear axle, and climbed on the sled, holding the other end of the rope to steer by moving it to the right or left. Trotting horses took us for miles until a team going the other way would give us a chance to hookybob back."

In his childhood diary, he mentions going hookybobbing several times during the winter of 1918–19. On November 27, he wrote: "John Henry and I fixed a big sail on my pushmobile and took it out on the road. It took us both to town just a flying. We stop[p]ed to see his sister, and everybody from everywhere came to see our buzzmobile. Then we took the sail down and hookeyed on back a wagon and came home."

Though the World War I battlefields were thousands of

miles away, the Hunters and their fellow citizens in Boise followed developments from the war front with great interest, participating in war-bond drives and willingly giving up commodities that were needed for the war effort. Nellie learned how to make a cake that required neither sugar nor eggs—and was actually quite edible. Then Will's brother George returned from navy duty and described how flour, sugar, and other items on his ship were sometimes thrown overboard. "I can still see Howard's face when he heard this," Dorothy remembers. "He was livid!"

The Hunters celebrated with the rest of the world in November 1918 when they learned that an armistice had been signed in Europe. In his diary Howard described what happened in Boise when word came that hostilities in Europe had ceased:

"I was dreaming away when I heard a cannon go of[f] twice. I woke up and was so scared I couldn't move. Then Mr. Harvey holerd 'The wars over'. Then all us kids got up and celebrated. John Henry had four battery. We hooked my motor up to them and was runing it when Mrs. Harvey came over and said there was going to be a parade up town. John and I went up [to the center of town] on my wheel and watched the parade. Finaly we joined in. Their was t[w]o Chinaman in back of us that had about 100 boxes of fire crackers. Theyed shoot them of[f] under us. Then we went up to the Capatal and hear[d] some speaking. Then we came home. After dark we built a big fire and beat big tin cans and had a good time."

Family Togetherness

IN THE HUNTER FAMILY, the children did their share of chores. Howard mentioned in his 1919 diary several occasions when he and Dorothy helped their mother during the busy summer and fall canning season:

"Aug. 26 After lunch Mother and I went down to Mrs. Williams to pick beans. We had just started when we saw Aunt Ida and Carl coming down the road. . . . After supper

Mother Dad and I went down to pick the beans. I went for my milk."

"Aug. 27 Dady came home and brought 10 dozen ears of corn. Dady Sister and I cleaned it while Mother cut it of[f] the cobs to dry."

"Aug. 29 Took the wheel barrow and went out to the Valley Road to meet Mr. Starn. He was bringing us some tomatos and a couple big water mellons. Come home and had sum water mellon, then took Dads lunch out to him. At 12 o'clock went out to get a sack of corn that was sent down to the [street]car. Sister and I helped her [their mother] clean the corn as she was buisy can[n]ing the tomatoes and wanted to get the corn can[n]ed. Played a while in the afternoon. After supper sister and I took 2 dollers down to a lady for the tomatoes."

"Aug. 31 Got Mother some apples and cleaned the back yard."

"Sept. 12 Sister and I went down the orchard and got a lot of apples for Mother to kooke."

Nellie worked hard both at home and away from home. Will's pay didn't stretch far enough to pay all the bills, and she added to the family income by working at various outside jobs, including pressing suits at a dry-cleaning company and demonstrating White King soap. She also volunteered in such activities as scouting and selling war bonds.

Will was a motorman on passenger cars of the Boise Valley Traction Company, the interurban electric railroad that ran from downtown Boise to communities to the west—Eagle, Star, Middleton, Caldwell—then looped back through Nampa and Meridian.[3] There was a train station at the Old Soldiers Home, on Valley Road about a quarter of a mile west of the Hunters' home, and the children loved to board the train there and ride around the loop with their father.

Though Will didn't have much formal education, he was well read and had a keen curiosity about the world, which he passed on to his children. Their set of the *Wonder World Encyclopedia* was well used. In the evening, while Howard lay on

*Will Hunter was a motorman on the interurban electric railroad
connecting Boise with communities to the west*

his stomach on the living-room floor at his father's feet, Will
would ask, "Where shall we travel today?" Then, armed with
an atlas and the encyclopedias, they would "explore" exotic
places of the world. At a very early age Howard knew the cap-
itals of the United States and many other countries.

Both Nellie and Will read to their children, and Howard's
and Dorothy's cards from the downtown Carnegie Library
were well used. Dorothy devoured the Pollyanna series and
the works of James Fenimore Cooper and Louisa May Alcott,
while Howard read *Tom Sawyer, Huckleberry Finn*, and the Tom
Swift series.

Their house wasn't large, but the Hunters found room for
a piano so Howard and Dorothy could take lessons. Though
Howard studied for only about a year, he frequently sat down
at the piano and played by ear. Dorothy's ninth birthday in
November 1918 brought an exciting surprise. Howard wrote
in his diary:

"Nov. 1st To-day is sisters birthday. Mother and Dad give
her a thimbel a little doll and a pair of slippers. I gave her a
little cupie [doll]. John Henry moved in next door. All the kids
were over there watching them unload when a big dray came

in[;] all us kids went to see what it was. It was our player piano for Sisters birthday, but it was realy for both of us. They didn't send any roles [music rolls] with it. Wilda played a couple of peases [pieces]. After supper Mr. Castle brought some roles down and stayed until 12 o'clock."

The next morning, "We played the piano for awhile when the dray came in again, and brought us a Victrola. . . . Mother and Papa were undecided whether to get a straight piano and a phonagraph or a player piano, so had the house full of music."

Two weeks later, on November 14, Howard wrote: "To-day is my birthday. Mother gave me 50 cents and a spanking and Dad gave me 50 cents, sister gave me a pair of gloves. The girls has some kind of a fang dangle sowing [sewing] club, there were six of them, they chased me all over and finely got me down. I brased [braced] my foot up against the little heat-ing and pushed it half way off the zink [sink]. They must of each hit me 250 times. Then we went out in the road and played games. Then Mr. Smith took Mother and I to town. We came home at 7 o'clock and played the piano."

Decorating the Christmas tree on Christmas Eve was a family tradition. "We used real candles, which fit into holders that clipped onto the branches," Howard recalled. "Father kept two buckets filled with water, so that if the tree caught fire, he'd be able to put it out quickly. He always made sure the candles were out before he left home."

In his diary, Howard described Christmas in 1918:

"We woke up bright and early and found a lot of pretty things Santa Claus had left us. We got a nice sled and I got a Scout nife a mackenaw [a heavy woolen coat] and a battery to run my motor. Mother gave me a tie and Sister gave me a tie pin and clip. Sister and I went hookybobing. We met the post man and he gave us a package from Uncle Henry. Sister got some hankerchiefes and I got a gyroscope top. It worked on the same princible as the world[;] it would spin on a string on the top of a hat pin on your head or anything. Daddy had

Nellie, Dorothy, Will, and Howard, with the Hupmobile, at Starky Hot Springs

layed off and Auntie had sent us a great big turkey and we sure had some big dinner. We had everything good there was. Sister and I went sled riding after dinner. We sure had a fine day."

The family's mobility increased when Will brought home his first automobile, a Hupmobile. That summer they drove to Starky Hot Springs, a mountain resort near New Meadows, about 120 miles north of Boise. Their anticipation of an exciting vacation was almost dashed when, just as they reached the resort, one of the rear wheels broke through a wooden culvert and the tire dropped into a pool of boiling-hot water from some underground springs. Will quickly pulled a heavy pole from a nearby fence, put the end under the axle, and, using a log as a fulcrum, lifted the car out of the water before the tire could cook. With the tire and wheel repaired, they enjoyed a relaxing vacation, swimming in the warm-water pool and hiking in the hills.

Howard and Dorothy had a close relationship, though they were quite different in looks, temperament, and interests. She had darker skin, brown eyes, and blond hair, while he had fair skin, blue eyes, and dark hair. She describes herself as a reprobate, always getting into trouble, while she claims that he was sweet, refined, and a peacemaker.

Despite their differences, however, they were fiercely protective of each other. For a time some older boys, knowing that Howard wouldn't fight back, would grab his cap and put it on the railroad tracks that ran down Valley Road, waiting for it to be flattened when a train ran over it. After Nellie lost her temper and declared she was tired of buying caps for her son, Dorothy confronted the bullies and threatened them, "If you don't lay off, I'll beat you up."

Howard was admired by adults for his good manners, his sister remembers. He would tip his hat to people on the street and give up his seat on the streetcar if anyone was standing. "Oh, I wish my son were like that," women would comment. He treated Dorothy with the same respect as other girls—usually. Their mother used to tell how Dorothy came home in a rage one day. She had gone down to the river with Howard and one of his school friends, Beatrice, and he had held the barbed wire up longer for Beatrice than for Dorothy!

Visits with Grandparents

WHEN HOWARD WAS nearly four, his mother took him and Dorothy to Utah on the train. They went first to Price, about 120 miles southeast of Salt Lake City, for a short visit with relatives. From there they backtracked 50 miles to Thistle Junction, where they stayed in a hotel overnight, then took a morning train south to Mount Pleasant.

"This was the only time I saw my great-grandfather, Anders Christensen," Howard recalled. "Even though he was elderly and spent most of the time in a chair, he played with me and caught me with the crook of his cane each time I ran by him." Anders died five years later, on November 29, 1917, at eighty-seven.

While Nellie and her children were in Mount Pleasant, Howard became ill and had to stay in bed for a week at his aunt Sophia's home. Nellie received a letter from Will, who wrote that during their absence, Howard's friend Buster Grimm had been diagnosed with polio. When the family returned home, Nellie learned that Howard's symptoms were similar to Buster's, and that because of the disease, Buster would be crippled for life. The only lasting effect of the disease on Howard was a lifelong stiff back: he was never able to bend forward and touch the floor.

Grandfather and Grandmother Hunter lived on South 13th Street in Boise, near the Oregon Short Line Railroad tracks. Howard and Dorothy looked forward to visiting their grandparents. Their grandfather would give them each a penny or a nickel to spend at the small grocery store across the street, where they could select a favorite treat from the tempting display of jawbreakers, licorice, lollipops, and other sweets, or, on a hot summer's day, an icy Popsicle. The children also loved Grandfather Hunter's two fox terriers.

Grandfather Hunter followed news events with great interest and liked to discuss politics and government with his next-door neighbor, U.S. Senator William Borah. Dorothy and Howard remember seeing Senator Borah ride down the street in his horse-drawn buggy. Sometimes he would have his driver stop and let him out so he could join neighborhood boys in a softball game.

Howard was ten when his grandparents sold their home and moved to Salt Lake City. He missed them, of course, but he was thrilled to get custody of their dog Daisy. She quickly became his constant companion.

School and Work

IN JANUARY 1914, two months after his sixth birthday, Howard entered the first grade at Lowell School, about a mile from home. His mother took him the first day and enrolled him in the class of Barbara Anderson.

Two years later, when Dorothy turned six, she balked at going to school because, she said, Howard knew how to read and she didn't. "But," he recalled, "after gentle but firm persuasion, Mother took her to the same classroom where I had started two years before. From then on, we walked to school together."

Dorothy had one other obstacle to overcome. Whenever she entered a class Howard had previously attended, the teacher would say, "Oh, you're Howard Hunter's sister," and express the hope that she would be as good a student as her brother. Dorothy would mutter under her breath, "Well, she'll find out."

For the most part Howard did well in school. However, he claims he did have two handicaps: "I was not good in sports and I had a problem telling colors—not all colors, but shades of red, green, and brown."

He devised an ingenious way to solve his color-blindness problem. He would put his crayons at the top of his desk, and when the art teacher asked the students to pick up a crayon of a certain color, he would run his finger over the crayons on his desk and Beatrice Beach, who sat behind him, would touch him on the shoulder when he came to the right one. He was embarrassed to admit to the teacher that he couldn't distinguish the colors.

As for Howard's other "handicap," his lack of interest in sports, the closest he got to even attending an athletic contest was when he went to football games one year in high school and called in the scores to the local newspaper. He enjoyed reading, writing, and most other academic subjects, but he didn't always work hard to master them. He had many other interests as well, such as a succession of after-school and summer jobs.

Adults seemed to sense that Howard Hunter was conscientious and dependable. As a young boy he helped around the neighborhood, mowing, doing yard work, bringing milk from the dairy to the widows, picking fruit, or any other work. Sometimes he was paid for such work; other times he did it just because he liked helping others.

His first jobs away from his neighborhood came through relatives. His aunt Flora Hunter Grebe, who managed the Western Union Telegraph office, hired him to deliver telegrams, and his uncle Carl (Pete) Peterson, a pressman at the *Evening Capitol News*, helped him get a job selling newspapers on the street after school. Howard sold about twenty papers in an evening, at five cents each. Since the papers cost him two and a half cents, he pocketed fifty cents in profit.

For a time he was a "cash boy" at the Cash Bazaar, a Boise department store. When a clerk made a sale and rang a bell, Howard would run to pick up the goods and the money, take them to a cashier who wrapped the purchase and made change, then dash back to the clerk, who gave the package and change to the waiting customer. He was paid one dollar for working from nine to nine on Saturdays.

The money Howard earned at his after-school and summer jobs allowed him to begin saving for future needs and to pay for some of his personal interests, such as music and stamp and coin collecting.

A Rancher at Heart

WHEN HOWARD was five, Will and Nellie took a two-week vacation trip to Oregon and Washington, leaving Dorothy with Grandfather and Grandmother Hunter and Howard with Fred and Christie Moore, who had moved to a ranch at Barber, a sawmill town on the Boise River on the northeast outskirts of Boise.

The ranch was an exciting place for the young city boy. His cousins taught him to ride horses and to swim. They went berry picking and gathered eggs from the coops, then hitched a horse to the buggy and drove into Barber to sell their products door-to-door. Howard earned enough money to buy a pair of jeans, a cowboy hat, and a pocketknife.

This was the first time the children had been separated from their parents, and Howard had his first experience with homesickness. "So the boys wouldn't think I was a sissy," he

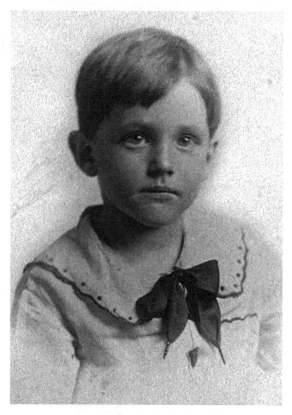

Howard at age five

said, "I went down the orchard into the grape vineyard where no one could see me cry."

A few years later Fred Moore received a homestead of some sagebrush land at Melba, about forty miles southwest of Boise, where he built a home and cleared the land. Howard loved visiting the new ranch. "There was always plenty of work to do—cattle to feed, cows to milk, chickens to care for, and work in the fields," he remembered. Once he helped dig a cistern for a neighbor on a nearby ranch. Another time he and his cousins worked on a potato farm, throwing the vines from the rows behind the digger. While it was hard work, he appreciated the pay: one dollar and eighty cents for a nine-hour day.

There was also time to play, swim, and ride horses. After a hard day of work or play, Howard and his cousins sometimes slept on the top of the haystack and watched the stars twinkling in the black sky.

In his diary, ten-year-old Howard described a week at the ranch in August 1918:

Aug. 8th Got up at 5 o'clock as Mother, Dorothy, Vera, and I were going to Melba. Started for the car at 5:30 while still dark, went to Nampa, and took the train for Melba. Woody [Howard's cousin] met us at the train with the buggy. Mother, Vera, and Sister rode in the buggy. Woody and I walked. When we got there Woody took me around the place then we went swiming. Woody could swim but I was just learning. . . . That night we sleep on a pile of hay.

Aug. 9th . . . Mother and Sister went home this morning. Mother wanted me to go too, but I wanted to stay. With a little coaxing, she was a good Ma and let me stay. . . . That evening Robert [Woody's older brother] and I went Jack Rabbit hunting.

Aug. 10th Got up about 9 o'clock. James and I walked along the bank looking for Rabits and saw about a 100. Robert and I took a hay rake [rack] home. Robert sat on the seat and I sat on the tongue of it. Robert drove the horses fast and I bounced up and down.

Aug. 11th Woody and I went walking one lovely summer day. We saw a little rabbit that quickly ran away. We went in swiming by a little falls. We had lots of fun. That afternoon we went to Sunday School. After wards we walked up to the rimrock. It was a mile up there. There was a falls that droped 100 feet so we went swiming and stayed in about an hour, got out and made a big fire in a hole in the side of the mountain. The water looked so pretty we went swiming again. . . .

Aug. 12th . . . I went to work with Woody this morning, and I drove derick while Woody went to town. Woody only had to work until noon, so we went home and went in swiming. After supper we went in swiming again. Played cow boy until dark then went to bed.

Aug. 13th . . . Woody and I went out in the field and chocked wheat until about noon. Then James and I went to town for some groseries, we went to the post office and got a

Will, Nellie, Howard, and Dorothy in about 1919

letter. When we got home Vera opened the letter. It was from Mother and inside was a letter for me. After dinner we went in swiming. After I got out Auntie ask me if I would go down to the pond and see if James and Eugine were all right. They were in swiming. I went down and went swiming again. After we got back Vera read us stories then Vera Auntie and I went swiming and had a lot of fun. Before supper Woody and I went swiming. [That day, Howard went swimming four times!]

Aug. 14th The next morning Vera and I got ready to go home. Auntie and Edna walked to the train with us. . . . When we got home the folkes were glad to see [me]. Daisy [Howard's dog] was glad to see me also.

Church Activities

THOUGH WILL HUNTER had been raised an Episcopalian and had served as an altar boy in his youth, by the time he married he affiliated with no church. But he had no objection to Nellie's or his children's participation in The Church of Jesus Christ of Latter-day Saints, though he sometimes commented that the members seemed to hold lots of meetings. He usually had to work Sundays and couldn't go with them to Sunday School, but occasionally he accompanied them to the Sunday evening sacrament meetings. One of Howard's warmest memories is of coming home on the streetcar in the arms of his father, while his mother carried Dorothy.

Eleven days before Howard's sixth birthday, on November 3, 1913, the Boise Stake was created at a special conference in Gooding, Idaho, and the branch became the Boise Ward, with George W. Lewis as bishop. The following year the Church purchased from the Boise Christian Church a clapboard building, affectionately known as "the little white church," on the southwest corner of Fourth and Jefferson streets. The building had one large meeting area, the chapel, with a platform at one end for the choir and pulpit and two small rooms behind the choir. Classrooms for Sunday School were formed by pulling curtains hung from wires strung across the ceiling. Deacons were responsible for pulling the curtains, an assignment to which Howard looked forward eagerly.

The Catholic church was the dominant church in Boise in those days, and there were only a few hundred Latter-day Saints. Howard and Dorothy were in the minority at school, and, he said, "it wasn't very popular to say that you're a Mormon."

But Howard had a testimony, one that had developed from earliest childhood. "I knew that God lived," he remembered. "My mother had taught me to pray and to thank Heavenly Father for all the things that I enjoyed. I often thanked Him for the beauty of the earth and for the wonderful times that I had at the ranch and by the river and with the Scouts. I also learned to ask Him for the things that I wanted or needed."[4]

Nellie Hunter taught a Sunday School class in the Boise Branch, and when the first Primary in the newly organized Boise Ward was begun in 1914, she became a Primary teacher. Later she served as a counselor in the Primary presidency and then as president. She also served as president of the Young Women's Mutual Improvement Association. The Hunter home was the setting for many branch parties and activities.

When Howard turned eight, he was not baptized because his father thought it would be better if he waited until he was old enough to decide for himself which church he wished to

*The Natatorium, an indoor swimming complex where Howard
and Dorothy were baptized on April 4, 1920*

belong to. Dorothy was not baptized at eight either; she too
was to wait until she could decide for herself. When Howard's
friends in the ward turned twelve, they were ordained deacons and allowed to pass the sacrament. When Howard
turned twelve, he could join the Boy Scout troop sponsored by
the Church, but he longed to be able to pass the sacrament
with the deacons, and he implored his father to change his
mind.

For a time Will continued to oppose his son's request, and
Nellie respected her husband's wishes, but finally he gave his
consent. On April 4, 1920, nearly five months after Howard's
twelfth birthday and Dorothy's tenth, they were both baptized
in the Natatorium, a large indoor swimming complex.

Eleven weeks later, on June 21, Howard was ordained a
deacon by Bishop Alfred Hogensen. At last he could pass the
sacrament with the other boys. "I remember the first time I
passed the sacrament," he said. "I was frightened, but thrilled
to have the privilege. After the meeting the bishop compli-
mented me on the way I had conducted myself."[5]

As a deacon, he could perform other services in the small
ward besides pull the curtains for Sunday School. "Occasion-

ally I had the assignment to pump the bellows for the organist by putting my weight to the pump handle at the end of the organ," he remembers.

"The job I didn't like was to cut kindling on cold mornings and light the fire in the stove in the room behind the choir loft."

Becoming an Eagle Scout

THE BOY SCOUTS of America had been in existence only ten years when Howard became a deacon, but the movement was spreading rapidly, and he was eager to become involved. Soon after his baptism, he began to learn the Boy Scout Oath and Scout Law, and in December 1920 he qualified as a Tenderfoot in the troop sponsored by the Boise Ward. By spring he had completed the requirements for Second Class Scout.

In July 1921 he went to Camp Tapawingo (an Indian word meaning place of joy), the Boise Council camp at Smith's Ferry on the North Fork of the Payette River. There he qualified to become a First Class Scout, and he received his First Class badge and his first merit badge at a court of honor after he returned home.

Over the next year he worked hard on merit badge requirements and looked forward to returning to camp. "By this time I had been in high school for one semester and was beyond the rookie stage of scouting," he explained. "At the encampment I was selected as the Patrol Leader of the Bear Patrol and was on the camp staff. Each day there were events to keep us busy from early morning when the bugler played reveille at six o'clock until the last notes of taps at 9:30 in the evening."

When Howard returned from camp that year, he had passed nine more merit badges. These badges, and one he had earned before camp, were awarded at a court of honor September 14, 1922, at a joint meeting of the Rotary Club and the Boise Council, with the mayor and other prominent men of the city present.

Howard in his
Boy Scout uniform

"By the time the court of honor was held," Howard said, "I had qualified for fifteen merit badges and for the Life Scout and Star Scout awards. Only six more were required for the rank of Eagle Scout. The scouting magazine had carried stories of boys who had gained the rank of Eagle, but we were told there had not yet been one in Idaho. The race was on between Edwin Phipps of Troop 6 and me."

When the next court of honor was held, both boys had earned twenty-one merit badges, the number necessary for Eagle rank, but Edwin had completed all the required ones, while Howard still lacked the required badges in athletics, civics, and cooking. Thus, Edwin received his Eagle in March 1923, two months before Howard received his.

An article in the *Idaho Statesman* on Saturday, May 12, 1923, under the headline "Eagle Scout Qualifies," reported:

"Howard Hunter of troop 22, Boise council, Boy Scouts of America, having qualified for merit badges in 32 subjects, was honored Friday at the city hall by the court of honor of the Boise council, with the degree of 'eagle scout.' Hunter was given awards for athletics, civics, first aid to animals, camping, poultry keeping, physical development, pathfinding, horsemanship, marksmanship, cooking and painting. The honor attained by Scout Hunter is the highest in scouting, and he is the second Boise scout to reach this rank. The first eagle badge was awarded to Edwin Phipps some months ago."[6]

Nellie proudly sewed the merit badges on a piece of cloth, meticulously outlining each badge with a buttonhole stitch. This cloth and photographs illustrating some of the things her son had done to earn the badges were displayed in the window of a local pharmacy.

On February 26, 1923, when Howard was fifteen, he was ordained a teacher in the Aaronic Priesthood at a ward priesthood meeting. The following Sunday, March 4, the Boise Ward was divided at stake conference, and the Hunters became members of the new Boise Second Ward. The First Ward remained in the old chapel, while the Second Ward began meeting in the Jewish Synagogue at the corner of Eleventh and State streets, which was offered at no charge to the Church.

Soon after this, the Saints in Boise met to discuss a proposal to build a tabernacle, which would serve as a center for both the stake and the new ward. When an appeal for pledges was made, Howard raised his hand and made the first one—twenty-five dollars, a substantial sum for that time, especially for a teenager. "I worked and saved until I was able to pay my commitment in full," he remembers.

The tabernacle was completed two years later and dedicated by President Heber J. Grant.

3

High School, Work, and a Cruise

IN JANUARY 1922 Howard graduated from the eighth grade and entered Boise High School. There he took such subjects as ancient, medieval, and American history, three years of English, botany, zoology, physics, chemistry, algebra, plane geometry, two years of French, and manual arts training.

He had a choice of enrolling in either gymnasium or the Reserve Officers Training Corps (ROTC). He selected ROTC and was issued an army uniform, which he was required to wear during all school hours. In his junior year he was made an officer, a second lieutenant for part of the year and then a first lieutenant. He commanded the platoon that escorted the first train into the new Boise station on April 6, 1925, when the railroad line was completed. The next year, promoted to captain, he was a company commander, and at the last formal dress parade he was commissioned a major, the highest ROTC rank at the high-school level. He won several awards and qualified on the gunnery range at Fort Boise for marksman and sharpshooter.

Because Howard worked after school and on Saturdays and was becoming increasingly involved in music, he had little time for extracurricular activities at school. He participated mainly in service-related programs, such as Pep Hounds, an organization to stimulate and promote school spirit; Hi-Y Club, sponsored by the YMCA to promote Christian standards at school and in the community; and the Radio Club, whose members learned about amateur broadcasting.

Howard also found little time for dating, though he certainly attracted the attention of girls. Dorothy, a vivacious girl, wasn't always sure if her friends were interested in her or in her handsome brother. Frequently girls would ask her, "Are you going to be around this afternoon?" When she assured them she was, they would come to her home—often with the hope that Howard would be there.

When name bands came to Boise, Dorothy's friends wished Howard would take them to the dances, but more often than not he would go alone to listen to the music.[1]

Three young women whom he dated in high school were Harriett Rinehart, the niece of Mary Roberts Rinehart, a popular novelist; Rosemary Brunger, whom he escorted when she was named "Miss Idaho" in 1925; and Eunice Hewitt, a favorite date in high school and for a year after graduation.

An Ambitious Worker

HOWARD ALMOST ALWAYS had an after-school or summer job. One of his earliest jobs was at the Idaho Country Club, on Valley Road about four miles west of his home, where he was a caddy while attending the Lowell School and for a while after entering high school. He rode his bicycle to the club, often going early to swim in the lake off the fourth tee and to dive for golf balls, for which he received ten cents for each one recovered.

Caddies earned thirty cents for nine holes, and on a full day Howard could caddy for thirty-six holes, earning $1.20. Sometimes he caddied for the golf pro, from whom he picked up some good pointers. One year he took first place in the annual caddies' tournament. He also met some of the area's prominent businessmen, making contacts that might later prove helpful.[2]

Howard's next job was at the Owyhee Pharmacy in downtown Boise, preparing syrups for ice cream sodas and sundaes and serving customers at the soda fountain. When the fountain wasn't busy, he helped the pharmacist fill simple prescriptions and delivered them on his bicycle. One day a salesman from the International Business School came into the drugstore and told Howard he could take the school's correspondence course in pharmacy if he convinced the drugstore owner to let the school put a display for the school in one of the windows. The owner agreed, and Howard, who at the time was leaning toward a career in medicine, began the course. "I took toxicology and some of the other courses," he recalled, "but I didn't quite finish the course. I always regretted that I didn't."

In the fall of 1923, the Hunter family took their first trip to Southern California to visit Will Hunter's uncle and aunt, Edward and Sarah Eliza (Lyde) Nowell, in the Los Angeles suburb of Huntington Park. Palm trees, the ocean, and the burgeoning metropolitan area, with its booming movie and oil industries, made lasting impressions on the family, and within five years they would all move to the West Coast.

When they returned to Boise, Howard stayed out of school for the rest of the school term and worked in the classified advertising department of the *Evening Capitol News*, answering telephones, writing advertising copy, and preparing billings.

The following January Howard returned to school and began a new job, at Boise's premier hotel, the Idanha. He ran the elevator and served as a bellboy for the first hour and relieved the switchboard operator the next hour. Then it was time to put on a porter's uniform and go on the hotel bus to the railroad station to meet arriving hotel guests and help them with their baggage. While they registered at the hotel, he changed back into his bellboy's uniform and then showed them to their rooms. For the last hour or so he wore work clothes and emptied wastebaskets, cleaned and polished cuspidors, and mopped the lobby floor.

"Sometimes the young people I knew came into the hotel

*The Idanha Hotel,
where Howard
worked while
in high school*

on their way to or from dances or parties," he said, "and I was always embarrassed to have them see me in my maintenance clothes."

One of Howard's favorite jobs was at an art store. He went before school each morning and cleaned the place. After school he returned to make picture frames and cut mats and glass. The owners, a couple named Faust, were both artists, and they taught him basic framing techniques, such as using silver rather than gold to frame watercolors. Because he was color blind, he learned to select the frame colors mechanically. On this job he picked up skills and an appreciation of art that would serve him well the rest of his life.

Hunter's Croonaders

DURING HOWARD'S second year in high school, he entered a sales contest sponsored by Sampson Music Company. Purchasers of merchandise in the store received one point for every dollar spent and could designate which contest entrant would receive the points. Howard encouraged all his friends and acquaintances to shop at Sampson's, and the points credited to him gave him the second-place prize, a marimba. He soon taught himself to play it well enough to perform at school, church, and other programs, and then as part of a dance orchestra.

"Most orchestras were not large enough to have a marimba player unless he doubled on other instruments," Howard explained, "so I commenced to play drums as well. As I played more and more on a professional basis, I started to play saxophone and clarinet and later added the trumpet." He also played the piano and the violin, which he had studied for about a year each while in elementary school.

In the fall of 1924, after playing with several orchestras, Howard organized his own group, which he named Hunter's Croonaders. That November and December the group played for six dances, and the next year they had fifty-three dance engagements at public halls and restaurants, private parties and wedding receptions, schools and churches, civic clubs and fraternities. Most of the work was in Boise and nearby towns, but occasionally the group played a little farther afield. During one such trip, Howard had a close brush with death.

The group was returning at dawn from a dance in Idaho City, a former mining town in the mountains about forty miles north of Boise. The open touring car in which Howard was a passenger was going up a steep hill on a narrow, winding road when the driver suddenly had to swerve to avoid colliding with an approaching car. The driver managed to jump out, but Howard did not. The car rolled over three times down the hillside, coming to rest in the creek bottom below, and Howard was thrown out on the last roll-over. The car crashed down on him and he was crushed into the sand, but because one corner of the vehicle rested on a large rock, he had no broken bones.

The other musicians, following in another car, raced down the hill and managed to raise the roadster so that Howard could crawl out. Dazed, he got to his feet, staggered about fifty feet into the bushes, and fell, unconscious, to the ground. The group carried him up the hill to the road and were relieved when he regained consciousness and was able to stand up. The only thing broken was his bass drum, which had been tied to the running board of the roadster; it was, he said, "smashed beyond recognition."

After a few days in bed, he was able to resume his normal activities, and one week after the accident, the orchestra played another dance.

Howard wasn't the only member of his family who had a near-disaster with an automobile. In his history he wrote:

"In 1926 the Hupmobile, our family car, was commencing to show its age and had received a few hard knocks. It was at its wheel [that] I had learned to drive, and Dorothy wanted to do the same thing. One day as we came home from Sunday School, Dorothy coaxed Mother to let her drive the car. She took over like an experienced driver and took us home. As she turned to go into the garage she shouted, 'How do you stop this thing?' By that time there was a crash and the closed doors of the garage were torn from their hinges at the front and lodged against the rear wall where we came to rest.

"Dad came running out of the house to see what had happened and, as I remember, he was not very well pleased at what he saw. The car was soon traded in on a new Overland Whippet Sedan. This was our pride and joy."

In his senior year, Howard cut back on his music activities, playing only twenty-three dances. His main goals were to complete high school and save money for college. He graduated from Boise High on June 3, 1926, and that summer he became assistant to the soda-fountain manager at Ballou-Latimer Drug Company.

A Cruise to the Orient

TOWARD THE END of 1926, Howard was offered a contract to provide a five-piece orchestra for a two-month cruise to the Orient on the passenger liner *S.S. President Jackson* of the Admiral Oriental Line. For a young man whose only travel

Howard (center, holding saxophone) and his band, Hunter's Croonaders

experiences so far had been visits to relatives in Utah and California, this would be an exciting opportunity to see an exotic part of world and at the same time be paid for doing what he enjoyed most—performing music. The group was hired to play classical music at dinner, background music for movies shown on board the ship, and music for dinner and ballroom dancing.

Howard selected four musicians to go with him: a piano player, a tenor saxophone and clarinet player, a trumpet player, and a violin and banjo player, each of whom could also play most of the other instruments. Howard played alto and soprano saxophone, clarinet, trumpet, and drums. He also pulled together a library of music, and they began rehearsing.

On Thursday, December 30, Will and Nellie Hunter took their nineteen-year-old son to the train station in Boise, where he met the other orchestra members for the overnight trip to Seattle. On New Year's Day they moved into their new "floating hotel," docked at Smith's Cove in Seattle.

Since the ship wouldn't sail until four days later, Howard went sightseeing. He also visited the University of Washington. That night he wrote in his journal: "It has long been my desire to go to this school. The campus and buildings are beautiful, and incidentally, I noticed that this is true of the girls also. I made arrangements for enrollment and to have a transcript of my grades sent from Boise High School."

At sailing time on January 5, he recorded, "thousands of rolls of serpentine [were] thrown by the passengers to the people on the pier and from the pier to the ship's deck. With a long blast of the whistle at eleven o'clock, the gang planks were pulled back and the ship moved quietly away amid the shouting and waving of good-byes."

The ship sailed smoothly through Puget Sound, docked for two hours at Victoria, British Columbia, and then headed through the Strait of Juan De Fuca and into the Pacific. As night fell, the musicians "stood on deck watching until the last lighthouse disappeared from view."

That was the last smooth sailing they would experience for some time. It was midwinter on the north Pacific, and that night a major storm struck. By morning the ship was tossing wildly amid high waves. "Nearly every person on board is seasick," Howard reported. "It was said that the captain is seasick for the first time in twenty-five years." When the ship crossed the international dateline six days later, losing one day on the calendar, he observed that "those who are sick wish we could lose a week."

At last the seas became calmer. On Thursday, January 13, the ship crossed the 180th meridian, entering the eastern hemisphere, and that evening Hunter's Croonaders played their first gala party, the Meridian Costume Ball and dinner, with passengers dressed in costumes representing mythical and real sea creatures. From then on, there was a full schedule of programs, parties, movies, and other activities.

On Sunday, January 16, when Howard went to the forward deck late in the evening, the sailor on watch pointed out a distant light and explained that they were nearing land. "For eleven days," Howard wrote, "we have seen nothing but water except two whales and the two seagulls, Pat and Mike, that have followed us from Seattle. They rest in the water and then catch up and live on the garbage from the ship."

Early the next morning the ship eased through Tokyo Harbor and docked at Yokohama. As soon as they were given shore leave, Howard, with two of his companions, headed for the railroad station and caught a train to Tokyo, about thirty miles away. There they had a unique experience, which he described in his journal:

"Tokyo is a beautiful city and the people seem friendly, but they are in mourning because of the recent death of Emperor Yoshihito. His body is lying in state at a large Buddhist Temple, near the Royal Palace. We went to the temple grounds, got in the long line of people who had come to view their leader, and were able to go through the temple and see the Emperor. . . . The Emperor's oldest son, Hirohito, who succeeds him, came to the temple while we were there. A long runner of red velvet was rolled out for the royal party to walk on from the automobile to the casket in the temple."

Wherever he went, Howard made friends. On board ship he became acquainted with Jack Carlton, who had been attending college in the United States and was returning with his parents to their home in Shanghai. Jack showed Howard and his friends around Tokyo, and that evening he and his parents took them to a suki-yaki restaurant in Yokohama, where they sat on grass mats in a room enclosed by screens and ate exotic food served by Japanese women in colorful kimonos.

After a tour of earthquake-ravaged Yokohama the next morning, Howard concluded, "People here dress differently, act differently, and are very curious about those of us who wear Western clothes and speak a different language."

Over the next few weeks he would see many people who dressed differently and who spoke different languages. He also would see sights unlike anything he had ever envisioned

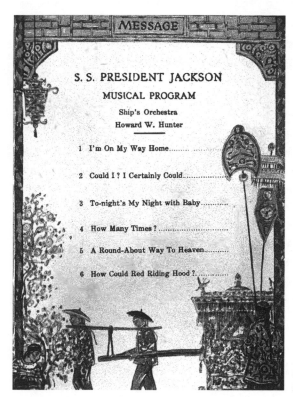

Program played on Orient cruise by Hunter's Croonaders

in the evening sessions with his father when they had "visited" exotic places through atlases and the encyclopedia.

At Kobe, Japan, he took a cable car to the top of Mount Maya, where he saw several hundred shrines and temples dedicated to Maya Fujin, the mother of Buddha, and observed pilgrims making their way to this sacred place. Sailing through the Inland Sea separating Japan's main islands, he saw brilliant green mountains and a sea swarming with sailboats, sampans, and junks—all a stark contrast to the barren hills and desert-like landscape around Boise.

On Saturday, January 22, the ship entered the mouth of the Hwangpu River and dropped anchor at the main dock area about six miles downstream from Shanghai, China's largest city and one of the largest ports in the world. The country was on the brink of revolution after an unstable period in which it had been organized by Chiang Kai-shek under a coalition of

Nationalists, Soviet advisors, and Communists. Shanghai itself was divided into two parts: a section under Chinese sovereignty and the International Settlement and French Concession. In his journal Howard wrote:

> There is a civil war going on and fighting between the two armies is in progress just outside of the city. The Nationalist troops, under the command of Generalissimo Chiang Kai-shek, are laying siege in Shanghai. Three United States Navy vessels are in the river to protect American interests, and we saw French, Japanese, Italian, and two British Navy vessels, all alerted for battle.
>
> Jack [Carlton] lives in the French Concession of the city and his family is very much concerned about the war. There seems to be a deep feeling against foreigners. I went into the city with Jack but returned to the ship early because we were uneasy. Tonight, two of the seamen on our ship came back badly beaten.
>
> Sunday, January 23, 1927 . . . Jack took us [Howard and George Jullion, his trumpet player] for a drive to the border between the Chinese city and the International Settlement. In many places the streets were barricaded by barbed-wire entanglements and the border was being patroled on both sides by soldiers. The Mountain Police and the French Reserves were called out today. Another United States warship came into the harbor, also a British aircraft carrier. It appears that the fighting may become very serious.

After lunch at Jack's home, the young men went to tea at the home of one of Jack's friends, and then with her and two of her friends to a roof-garden club for dancing. "We didn't stay long," Howard wrote, "because travel was being restricted and it was dangerous to stay out late."

The *S.S. President Jackson* sailed from Shanghai at midnight that Sunday. While the ship was at sea, Howard's orchestra was busy every day and evening, rehearsing, playing dinner music, providing background music for movies, and playing for dances in the ballroom or on deck.

When they were in port, they took advantage of sightseeing as much as they could, often until late at night. In Hong Kong they were fascinated by preparations for the Chinese New Year, to be celebrated the following week.

The South China Sea was placid and warm as the ship crossed to Manila in the Philippines. There Howard and George set out to see the sights, and once again they made friends with individuals who took an interest in them and showed them around the city. Pat Coyle, a former Philippines golf champion, took them to dinner, for a long ride around the city, and to a prize fight. In a music store they met a man from Boise, who took them to lunch and sightseeing. Howard began to see how small the world really is when he learned that their new friend was the man who had delivered the player piano on Dorothy's eighth birthday.

Their last morning in Manila, Howard and George ran into two friends from Boise who were stationed at a U.S. airbase in Manila. They also visited the radio station known as the Voice of Manila, on the roof of the Manila Hotel, where they played a few numbers and sent messages home by radio.[3]

When the ship set sail from Manila, Howard commented in his journal, "We are on our way home." That journey would take them back through the same ports they had visited on the outward-bound voyage.

The ship docked at Kowloon in Hong Kong harbor on February 3, the Chinese New Year's Day. "On the Fourth of July celebrations at home," Howard wrote in his journal, "we light one firecracker at a time, but here whole packages or large bundles are set off with a fuse to frighten away the evil spirits."

After dinner that night, Howard and George Jullion crossed the bay by ferry to Hong Kong. "As evening came," Howard wrote, "the tempo of the celebration increased. We walked so far we found ourselves away from the crowds and in a poorly lighted area. I became alarmed at a native Chinese whom I had pushed out of my way because he became insistent that I let him take me to see a girl. I noticed he was following us in the shadows and I became frightened. We walked in the middle of the street and increased our steps, trying to get to a place where there was more light. Suddenly we came to a policeman, a British 'bobby.' He spoke English and led us back to one of the lighted streets where we could find our way to the ferry and get to the ship in Kowloon. I will never forget Chinese New Year's Day in Hong Kong."

At Shanghai, Jack Carlton again hosted Howard for an activity-filled day and evening: sightseeing, lunch at his home, afternoon refreshments with two girl friends, and dinner and a movie with his parents. Late that evening Jack and Howard took the two young women to the Plaza, a French dinner club. "It was my first glimpse of Parisian night life coupled with a dash of Broadway," Howard wrote. "The dinner, music, chorus girl review and dancing, made a spectacular evening."[4]

The young men returned to Jack's home at 2:30 in the morning, and soon after they went to bed, Howard was awakened by artillery fire. "The war is now close to the city and I was uncomfortable," he wrote.

Early the next morning the two friends drove through the city and out into the countryside to see a portion of the Great Wall. Returning to the city, they stopped at Jack's father's egg-canning factory, where Howard was fascinated to see how eggs were candled, broken, and put in tins, then frozen and sent on refrigerator ships to Europe. When he returned to the ship that afternoon, he was "overjoyed to get several letters" from home, the first mail he had received since he left Seattle five weeks earlier.

At Kobe, the Croonaders played an engagement in the dining room of the Oriental Hotel,[5] and at Yokohama they played for a dinner dance at the Tent Hotel. In both cities, Howard went shopping for souvenirs and gifts to take home. "My money is nearly gone," he wrote, "because in each port we have gone sightseeing and traveled about to see as much as we could knowing there is little possibility of returning to

*In May 1983 Howard Hunter returned to Shanghai and found
the Jing Jiang Club, formerly the Plaza, which he had visited in 1927*

this part of the world again. The education has been worth what we have spent."

Finally, "with deep bass blasts from the ship's whistle at one o'clock, the shrill whistles from the tug boats, and the cheers of the crowd, the ship commenced to move away from the dock. . . . Yokohama gradually disappeared in the background. We are leaving behind the fascinating Orient and are on our way home. In eleven days we will be back in the United States."

The ship had taken on scores of new passengers in the Orient, mostly American missionaries from various Christian churches who were being evacuated from China because of the war. "Not many of them participate in the dancing and other activities," Howard wrote, "so there is a more subdued crowd on this return trip." The missionaries comprised nearly 70 percent of the passenger list. While they didn't participate in many of the social activities, they did guarantee a large attendance at the religious services. And when the orchestra played classical music at dinner, they stayed late and listened, and "were generous with their applause."

Unlike conditions during the westbound trip, relatively calm seas and warm weather marked the return voyage. Finally, after the last dance on Wednesday, February 22, Howard packed up his drums and other instruments. His contract with the steamship company had come to an end.

The next day, after stopping briefly at Victoria to let some of the passengers off, the ship reached Seattle in the early afternoon. Two friends from Boise who were living in Seattle were at the dock to welcome the musicians home and take them to dinner and sightseeing.

When the orchestra returned to the ship the next morning to claim their belongings, they received a shock. Howard described the experience in his journal:

"Police officers came aboard with warrants for our arrest. We were put in a police car and taken to the police station in Seattle without knowing why we were arrested. After we got there, officers interrogated each of us and we learned there had been a burglary in Boise and a number of musical instruments stolen. We were prime suspects until it was learned that we had left Boise before the burglary occurred. After an exchange of telegrams to verify this fact, they turned us loose. I tried to persuade the police to take us back to the ship, but they were tough and wouldn't do anything to help us, so we went in a taxi. Because we had been taken away and were not on board when the customs officials cleared the removal of baggage and possessions, ours had been gathered up and locked in a warehouse."

The next morning the young men recovered their bags from customs. They remained in the Seattle area for a few days, and even played an engagement at a hotel in Everett one evening. Then they bought a cheap used Oldsmobile and began to head back to Boise, enjoying sightseeing along the way and playing at a hotel in Portland, Oregon. Two days out of Portland the Oldsmobile gave out, and they stayed overnight at a farmhouse until the father of one of the musicians could come get them.

On Friday, March 11, ten weeks and one day after they had boarded the train in Boise, their journey ended. Howard wrote: "It was early in the morning when we got to Boise. I called Mother and Dad and they came to get me. Home never looked as good to me as it did when we got there. This is the first time I have been away for more than a few days and I was glad to be back after a trip nearly half way around the world."

A Time for Decisions

HOWARD WAS THRILLED when he returned home to learn that his father had been baptized in his absence, on Sunday, February 6. Allowing for differences in time zones and crossing the international dateline, he estimated that the baptism had taken place on the return voyage as his ship was moving up the Hwangpu River to Shanghai.

Though Will had occasionally attended church with his family, it wasn't easy for him to decide to be baptized. However, Bishop J. Emer Harris was persistent. He reportedly declared, "That man is a Mormon and doesn't know it. I'm going to baptize him before I'm released as bishop." Eventually Will agreed. A week after Howard returned from the Orient, he was proud to accompany his father to their first priesthood meeting together.[6]

The young man lost no time in finding jobs. Two days after he arrived home, his orchestra played on a radio broadcast on station KFAU, and the following week he played with another orchestra for dances in Weiser and Hagerman, Idaho, and Ontario, Oregon. He also rehearsed with an orchestra organized by his ward's Mutual Improvement Associations.

On March 30 he and a friend auditioned to provide dinner music at the YWCA cafeteria, a popular eating spot in downtown Boise. That evening they played classical and popular music during the dinner hour and were hired for the job.

Falk's department store in downtown Boise

Howard played saxophone and clarinet, accompanied by his friend on the piano.

He also landed a job selling women's and men's footwear in the shoe department of Falk's department store. At the end of his first day, he wrote in his journal: "I didn't know there were so many kinds of shoes in existence, but I am commencing to learn the details and how to satisfy customers' needs. The work is pleasant and I am sure I will like it."

Howard's busy schedule with orchestra rehearsals and engagements, selling shoes all day, and playing dinner music five evenings a week left him little free time. He did, however, find time for dates with Eunice Hewitt, who was now attending college in Caldwell, twenty miles west of Boise. They enjoyed taking walks together and going for rides in the Ford roadster he purchased soon after he arrived home—"not a very fancy car, but it will be good transportation." (He had car trouble the day after he bought it and spent the next two days making repairs.)

Balancing work with pleasure took effort, but as he wrote in his journal that spring, "All work and no play makes Jack a dull boy. I am not dull because I do both."

That summer Howard quit his job at the YWCA cafeteria, as he was working six days a week at the department store. In addition, his orchestra played at the Tree Top Pavilion in Boise on Tuesday and Friday evenings and at the Roseland Pavilion in Emmett on Wednesday and Saturday evenings, and often they played for parties and dances on Mondays and Thursdays. They drew big crowds wherever they performed, but the pace was tiring.

In his journal Howard described one Saturday: "This was a usual Saturday—at work before nine o'clock in the morning—left at six for Emmett—played until midnight—home at two-thirty in the morning." Another day he explained his secret for keeping up this hectic schedule: "I have to sleep fast to keep going."

When the dance pavilions closed in the fall, Howard and Glenn Scott, the display manager at Falk's, decided to lease the clubhouse at the Idaho Country Club, the golf course where Howard had caddied, and convert it for supper dancing. The dance hall, remodeled to resemble the manor house of a southern plantation, opened on Friday, October 7, to a "fair-sized crowd."

It was Howard who suggested the name and theme. "When our family was in Los Angeles three years ago," he wrote in his journal, "I was interested in the 'Plantation' on Washington Boulevard, a place where most of the big-name bands have played. They feature southern fried chicken dinners and good music in the plantation style. Glenn was agreeable to my suggestion that we name our supper club 'Plantation Roadhouse.' He will manage the operation and I will furnish the orchestra."

A few days later he noted: "We have heard many complimentary remarks and people seem to like it. The food and the music are excellent."

The Plantation was popular, but it soon became apparent that the business would not support Howard's large orchestra. Because he had offers for his group to play other engage-

Majestic Theatre, where Howard performed with the Fanchon Marco Review

ments, he decided to hire a three-piece ensemble for the Plantation, and soon afterwards he sold his interest in the club.

Howard's orchestra continued to play for dances in the area. He also found time to perform a novelty number with the orchestra of the Fanchon Marco Review, a touring show appearing at Boise's Majestic Theatre. Then he was offered a contract to provide an orchestra to replace the one that had been touring with the review. His orchestra's stage work ended, however, when the musician's union served notice that the group could not perform because the theater organist was nonunion.

Trying to juggle music with earning a more stable living, Howard transferred to Falk's music department, where he supervised outside sales. His responsibilities included demonstrating and repairing radios, which were quickly becoming a favorite source of family entertainment, and selling and servicing pianos and other instruments.

Still looking for ways to make money, Howard conceived the idea of publishing large display cards listing train, bus, streetcar, and postal schedules, with advertisements from merchants and other businesses in the outside margins. He planned to place the cards in hotels, rooming houses, and public places, hoping the advertising would pay the publishing and distribution costs and net a good profit.

In January 1928 he tried out the business scheme in Nampa, where it was moderately successful. The next month, on a three-week trip to Baker, La Grande, and Pendleton, Oregon, he again succeeded in signing up advertisers and distributing the cards to places catering to tourists and residents. He also found time in the evenings to socialize with friends living in those areas, go to some parties and dances (mainly to observe the techniques of the orchestras), and, occasionally, even get to bed early.

Returning to Boise, Howard worked at the store for a week, then decided to take his advertising idea to other Idaho cities. After a profitable week in Twin Falls, he moved on to Pocatello. There, despite persistence and hard work, he encountered his first failure. When three and a half days of pounding the pavement resulted in few sales, he decided it was time to move on.

This time he was going to take a detour—to the land of sunshine and opportunity, California.

4

California, Here I Come!

WHILE HOWARD may have decided quickly to go to Southern California after his disappointing experience in Pocatello, seeds for such a move had already been sown.

Bill Salisbury, who traveled with the Croonaders to the Orient and played piano with Howard at the YWCA cafeteria, had recently moved to California and invited him to come and visit. Howard had good memories of his family's California vacation four years earlier, and extended family members lived there, so he would have a place to stay. And, if things didn't work out, he could always return to Boise.

Thus, on Thursday, March 8, 1928, Howard checked out of his hotel in Pocatello and headed south. A man he met at the hotel offered him a ride to Ogden. There he caught the interurban Bamberger Railroad to Salt Lake City and checked into a hotel for the night. Early the next morning he took a streetcar to the southern end of the line on State Street and began to hitchhike.

Several motorists picked him up and took him various distances that day, with the last one dropping him off late in the evening in Meadow, a tiny town about 135 miles south of Salt Lake City.

"The only hotel was a house with two rooms for rent," he recalled, "but both of them were occupied. A school bus was parked in front of the school and it was unlocked. I lay down on the long seat, pulled the leather jacket of the driver over me, and spent the night." His sleep was cut short when the driver arrived early the next morning and angrily evicted him. The young hitchhiker stood by the roadside, thumb extended, for several hours before someone picked him up.

By the end of that day Howard reached Cedar City, where he registered at a hotel. "If there had been a train from Cedar City," he said, "I would have given up hitchhiking." But because there was no train, he hit the road again the next morning, riding with a succession of drivers for short distances each. He managed to hitch a ride from St. George to Las Vegas with "a man with a Dodge coupe and a kind heart." After another night in a hotel, he spent most of the next day trying to flag down a ride and getting a sunburn in the process. Finally, late that afternoon, a motorist heading for Los Angeles stopped, and the two of them drove through the night.

The sun was shining brightly when they reached San Bernardino, gateway to the Los Angeles area, on Tuesday, March 13. As they drove along Foothill Boulevard, Howard suddenly spotted a large sign announcing that they were entering Upland. "Until this time I had no idea where Upland was, except it was near Los Angeles," he remembers. "I told the man that this was the place where I was going, and he let me out." Upland was where Bill Salisbury and his family lived.

Finding a telephone, Howard called the Salisburys, and Bill's mother told him her son was working on a home construction job. Howard walked to the address she gave him and found his friend. "He was certainly surprised, because I had not told him I was coming," he said.

Howard stayed with the Salisburys for the next nine days, sightseeing with Bill and, when Bill had to work, enjoying the California sunshine. On the third day he spent five dollars for a second-hand Ford, "a two-seated car without a top—just the thing to take us around." He and Bill spent two days fixing it up, then drove into Los Angeles. There they visited with a saxophone player who had been on the cruise with them, slept on the beach at Venice, and went to see his father's uncle and aunt, Edward and Lyde Nowell, in Huntington Park. A few days later Howard took his bags to their home to stay with them.

"When I came to California I thought I would spend a week or ten days and then go back home," he wrote in his journal three weeks after he arrived, "but now that I am here, and have no particular obligations at home, I think I will stay for a few weeks."

Sightseeing, learning how to get around, and looking up friends occupied much of his time. "This is a lazy life I lead without anything to do," he confessed after spending a day at the beach with some of his cousins.

Compared with the hectic pace he had led in Boise, it must have seemed heavenly to relax, take stock of his life, and think about what to do next. One day he worked with Bill at the Sunkist packing house in Upland, unloading and stacking bundles of wood used to make crates. "By the time the day was over I could hardly stand up," he commented. "There must be a better way of making a living." He didn't return the next day.

"When I came to California," he wrote, "I thought I would stay a week with Bill and then go home, but since being here, I've decided there are advantages in California if I can find employment with opportunity—but not as a stevedore."

Returning to Huntington Park, he went to a shoe store on Saturday morning, April 7, for a new pair of shoes. While the owner, a Mr. Hunter, was fitting him, Howard mentioned that he had sold the same line of shoes in Boise—and by the time he paid for his new shoes, he had been hired to work in the store on Saturdays, starting immediately.

On Monday he returned to the Sunkist plant and loaded boxes of oranges into refrigerator cars. At the end of the day he figured he had loaded a little over forty-six tons. Another day, after loading fifty tons, he commented, "I didn't know there were this many oranges in the world."

One day he sorted lemons on a sorting belt, but he had "a terrible time." The lemons had to be sorted into various grades depending on the color at the tip, ranging from dark green to light yellow—but because of his color blindness, he couldn't differentiate between the shadings. "Before the day was over I thought I would have a nervous breakdown," he noted.

Howard stayed with Bill's family during the two weeks he worked in the packing plant, driving to Huntington Park on weekends to work at the shoe store. Finally he reached a decision: "As I have looked around Los Angeles and considered job opportunities, I have come to the conclusion that I would like to work in a bank."

On Monday morning, April 23, he went to the Bank of Italy and applied for a job, and was hired immediately. The next day he began working at the bank's main office in downtown Los Angeles, where he learned to operate adding and bookkeeping machines and to process deposits. That evening he enrolled in the adult education department at the Huntington Park High School, where he planned to take classes leading to a college degree, and arranged for continued board and room with the Nowells.

He also became a member of the Huntington Park Ward, within walking distance of his uncle's home. On Wednesday evenings he sometimes accompanied his aunt Lyde to testimony meetings at her church, the First Church of Christ Science—"not because I had an interest," he said, "but I knew it pleased her and I felt I owed her that courtesy."

Putting Down New Roots

HOWARD HUNTER was one of more than two million people who moved to California during the 1920s, a decade of unprecedented growth. More than 70 percent of the new arrivals settled in the Los Angeles area, where the population soared from just under one million in 1920 to over 2.2 million in 1930. Many were lured by the prospect of making their fortunes in the richest oil fields yet discovered in America, fertile farmlands that produced plentiful crops year-round, and the glamorous, thriving motion-picture industry. Homes and commercial structures were going up everywhere, and the opportunities for the good life never seemed better.

This great westward migration was also the first migration of the automobile age. One author described it thus:

"Like a swarm of invading locusts, migrants crept in over the roads. . . . For wings, they had rattletrap automobiles, their fenders tied with string, and curtains flapping in the breeze; loaded with babies, bedding, bundles, a tin tub tied on behind, a bicycle or a baby carriage balanced precariously on the top. Often they came with no prospects, apparently trusting that heaven would provide for them. . . . They camped on the outskirts of town, and their camps became new suburbs."[1]

The bank where Howard worked, the Bank of Italy, had been founded in 1904 in San Francisco by Amadeo Pietro Giannini, the son of an Italian immigrant, and by the 1920s it was the largest bank in California.

Eager to get ahead in his new career, Howard enrolled for a banking class after work on Tuesday and Thursday evenings at the American Institute of Banking, which meant he had to drop his adult-education classes in Huntington Park. At the bank he met Alma Nelson (Ned) Redding, a member of the Church who had recently returned from the North Central States Mission. Ned was taking the same banking class, and they soon became close friends.

Within a short time Howard was as busy as he had been in Boise. His parents shipped his musical instruments to him, and that summer, after weighing several offers, he signed on as drummer for a dance band that also had a contract to perform on radio. Occasionally he played with other groups as well.

Los Angeles, like other major metropolitan centers of business, culture, and education, attracted many talented young adults, and there was always a wide choice of activities, some sponsored by the Church and others organized by individuals who simply enjoyed being together. Nearly every night there were dances and programs to choose from. Howard and his new friends went swimming and picnicking at the beach, hiking in nearby hills and mountains, and to the movies to see the latest films, oftentimes participating in more than one activity in an evening or on a Saturday. Sometimes he took a date, but more often he went as part of the larger group.

On Sundays the young adults attended church, not infrequently two or even three wards in a day. One Sunday, Howard reported, he and Ned went to the Wilshire Ward in the morning, Huntington Park Ward in the afternoon, and Glendale Ward in the evening. The next Sunday they attended meetings at the Adams, Wilshire, and Matthews wards, followed by a get-together at a friend's home.

One of the most popular Church-sponsored groups was the Los Angeles Thrift Chorus, which took its name from a fund that members established for travel and other expenses. Singers came from wards and stakes all over Los Angeles to rehearse on Thursday evenings at the Adams Ward. For many it was both a social and a musical experience. The year before Howard moved to California, the chorus had sung at the Arizona Temple dedication in Mesa. He and Ned joined the group after their banking class ended in June and were soon preparing for the chorus's summer appearance at the Hollywood Bowl.

When business dropped off at the shoe store during the summer, Mr. Hunter had to let Howard go, but he indicated he wanted his young employee to return in the fall. However, by then Howard's schedule was full, and he did not go back. Since he worked at the bank until noon or later on Saturdays, he welcomed having the time for other interests.

Howard was popular with his California friends. He liked being with people, but he never monopolized the time or the occasion. He was a good listener, thoughtful, and considerate

of others. An avid reader, he was well-versed in many subjects. Even while on the road in Idaho and Oregon, he had
sought out the local library to read and study. During his first
few weeks in California, while Bill was working, he again
found the nearest library. In one journal entry he recorded that
he had "spent the evening at home reading Shakespeare and
some old French classics—[and] finally the Examiner funny
papers." Another evening he read about the lives of the
world's most noted philosophers.

The transplanted Idahoan enjoyed lighthearted fun. Once
at a YWMIA fashion show, he drew laughs when he came
onstage dressed in female clothing. On election day in
November 1928, he and two friends engaged in a mock political rally in busy downtown Los Angeles. Standing on boxes
at the intersection of Seventh Street and Broadway, Howard
Hunter as Al Smith, Ned Redding as Herbert Hoover, and
John Madsen as the Los Angeles mayor bantered through
political speeches that drew a large crowd, backing up traffic
for several blocks in every direction. "Finally the police
arrived and dispersed the crowd," he wrote in his journal,
concluding tersely, "We got away."

A Family Reunion

HOWARD HURRIED HOME from work on September 4, 1928,
to greet his parents and sister, Dorothy, who had just arrived
at his uncle's home. Will and Nellie had decided to move to
Los Angeles when Will's job at the Boise Valley Traction Company, where he had worked for more than twenty years,
ended because the interurban railroad cars were being
replaced by motor buses. They sold their home in August,
shipped their household goods and personal belongings to
Los Angeles, and drove by way of Portland and San Francisco
to visit relatives.

Howard lost no time in introducing Dorothy, who was not
quite nineteen, to the Church-centered social whirl that was so
much a part of his life. They had always been close, and he

Howard and Dorothy
in spring of 1931

enjoyed her lively, vivacious personality. Three days after she arrived, he danced with her all evening at a Los Angeles Stake dance, and over the next few weeks they went to several other parties.

Dorothy was soon integrated into the young adult groups. She was also adjusting to a new job. Having worked for the telephone company in Boise, she had no difficulty getting a position with the Southern California Telephone Company at a building just a block from Howard's office at the bank in downtown Los Angeles.

The family stayed with the Nowells for a few days, then moved to an apartment, and Howard moved with them. Over the next year they lived in several different apartments, and once they "house sat" for Ned's parents when the Reddings went to Florida. Finally Will and Nellie were asked to manage an apartment building in exchange for an apartment. Will also found work at an aircraft parts plant in Venice, a suburban beach community.

Though Howard worked five and a half days a week and his evenings were filled with classes, rehearsals, dance jobs, and social activities, he found time for an occasional quiet evening at home visiting with family and friends or reading a good book. He also found time to serve in his ward and to begin pursuing an in-depth study of the scriptures and other gospel-related books.

In the past he had attended church whenever he could, but because he worked long hours and got home late after dance engagements, he had not held many callings. And though his parents had a set of scriptures that they had been given as a wedding present, they had few other books on religion, so he had not studied the gospel consistently.

When Howard returned from his cruise, his bishop in Boise had asked him to think about serving a mission. Howard, knowing his father's income would not stretch far enough to support him on a mission, began saving with the thought that he would accept a call when he had enough money to pay all the costs. But the account grew slowly, since he paid his own living and personal expenses and did not earn big wages in either Boise or Los Angeles.

After Howard moved into the apartment with his parents, his church membership records were transferred from the Huntington Park Ward to the Adams Ward. There he became a home teacher, was assigned by the elders quorum president to visit sick members of the ward, served as counselor in the elders quorum presidency, and was scoutmaster of the Boy Scout troop. But it was in the young adult Sunday School class that he experienced a major turning point in his hunger for gospel knowledge. In his history he wrote:

"Although I had attended Church classes most of my life,

my first real awakening to the gospel came in a Sunday School class in Adams Ward taught by Brother Peter A. Clayton. He had a wealth of knowledge and the ability to inspire young people. I studied the lessons, read the outside assignments he gave us, and participated in speaking on assigned subjects. I suddenly became aware of the real meaning of some of the gospel principles, an understanding of the degrees of glory, and the requirements of celestial exaltation as Brother Clayton taught and instructed us. I think of this period of my life as the time the truths of the gospel commenced to unfold. I always had a testimony of the gospel, but suddenly I commenced to understand."

The subject of one of Brother Clayton's lessons in early March 1930 was patriarchal blessings. "I had never really understood patriarchal blessings, but now they had meaning," Howard wrote. "That day I went to see Brother George T. Wride, the stake patriarch, and he asked me to come to the office in the mission home behind the Adams Ward Chapel the next Sunday."

That March Sunday, after talking with Howard for a few minutes, Brother Wride laid his hands on the young man's head and gave him a patriarchal blessing.

The blessing stated that Howard was one "whom the Lord foreknew," and that he had shown "strong leadership among the hosts of heaven" and had been ordained "to perform an important work in mortality in bringing to pass [the Lord's] purposes with relation to His chosen people." He was promised that if he remained faithful, he would have showered upon him "intelligence from on high," he would be "a master of worldly skill and a teacher of worldly wisdom as well as a priest of the most high God," and he would use his talents in serving the Church, would sit in its councils, and would be known for his wisdom and righteous judgments.

A Memorable Meeting

ON JUNE 8, 1928, twelve weeks after he arrived in Los Angeles, Howard attended an M Men and Gleaner dance sponsored by the Mutual Improvement Associations at the
Wilshire Ward. Afterwards, some of the young adults decided
to go to the beach, and he was invited to come along. Among
the group were Ned Redding and his date, Clara May (Claire)
Jeffs. They all went wading in the surf near Santa Monica,
with the young women hitching up their long evening gowns.
Then the young men decided to go swimming. Howard
reported what happened:

"Because we had no swimming suits, the girls waited in
the cars. They thought it funny to turn the headlights of the
cars on us so we couldn't get out of the water. We had to swim
up the beach to get out, and when I got back, my tie was missing. Claire walked with me down the beach to find it, and we
got better acquainted. It was four o'clock when we got home.
The next time we went out, I took Claire, and Ned went with
someone else."

Claire's maternal ancestors, like Howard's, joined the
Church in Europe, where they suffered severe persecution for
their beliefs. Her great-grandparents, Karl Gottlieb Reckzeh
and Anna Rosina Lothe, raised their seven children on a farm
in Brandenburg, a province of West Prussia (then part of Germany). The fifth child was Claire's grandmother, Maria Emilie, who was born January 21, 1860. She left home in her late
teens and went to the village of Droskau, and a few years later
she returned to the farm with her two daughters, Martha
Emma, five, and Ida Anna, two. Maria Emilie and the girls'
father, Paul Lehmann, had not married.

The girls dearly loved their grandparents and their new
life on the farm. The Reckzehs, devout Lutherans, went to
church on Sundays, and every evening Karl had the family
read a chapter out of the Bible.

On September 30, 1893, about six years after Maria Emilie
returned to the farm, one of her friends invited her to a meet-

ing conducted by missionaries of The Church of Jesus Christ of Latter-day Saints. "It all had to be under cover," her daughter Martha remembered, "as the elders were not allowed in the country at that time, and many times the elders had to leave the town at night. Two left on a hayrack with the hay piled over them. Mother went to the meeting and said she believed every word of what she heard, and applied for baptism in two weeks. She was baptized in the winter in a pond" at the village of Grabig.[2]

When Karl learned of her conversion, he became extremely angry and turned her and her daughters out. No member of her family ever spoke to her again. Maria Emilie and her daughters moved to an apartment in Sorau, where they lived for about two years. But when the girls were taunted and abused by their classmates, Maria Emilie decided they should go to America. She applied at the magistrate's office for a permit to leave the country, and he told her she could go, but she could not take her children. According to Martha, Maria Emilie retorted that no one had helped her raise her children so far, but if the magistrate could take care of them, he could keep them. "I asked her later if she would have left us," Martha said, "and she said she knew the Lord would answer her prayers."

The magistrate granted permission, and Maria Emilie and her two daughters began their journey that night. Some friends walked with them fifteen miles to another town, where they all knelt down in a forest and prayed for a safe journey. Then the friends left them, and the young family walked several more miles to catch a train to Hamburg. From there they traveled by ship to Liverpool, England, and sailed on another ship to New York. The family completed their long journey to Salt Lake City by train. After staying a week with the family of one of the missionaries who had converted her, Maria Emilie found her own lodgings and hired out to do housework in order to support her small family.[3]

In 1900, Martha, nearly nineteen, was married to Jacob

Clara May (Claire) Jeffs as a baby and as a teenager

Ellsworth Jeffs, who was in the construction business in Salt Lake City. Jacob's family was not LDS. His father, Abraham Jeffs, had emigrated from England to the midwestern United States, where he met and married Julia Anderson Phillips, who was born in Missouri. After their marriage, Abraham and Julia lived for a time in Kansas, where their son Jacob was born July 28, 1882. The family subsequently moved to Salt Lake City, where Abraham died in 1901 and Julia, in 1913.

Martha and Jacob's first child, Clara May (Claire), was born February 18, 1902. She was followed by three other children: Thelma, Ellsworth, and Leona, who died of whooping cough at six weeks. Claire attended Salt Lake City's Riverside Elementary School and West High School, and began working at the Mountain States Telephone Company while in high school.

In 1926 Jacob and Martha, accompanied by Claire, moved to Los Angeles, where Jacob went into the construction business and built a spacious home. A year later Thelma, recently

The Jeffs family in 1921: Martha and Jacob, seated; Thelma, Ellsworth, and Claire

divorced, joined them with her baby daughter, Leatrice (Lee). Ellsworth also moved to Southern California.

In Los Angeles, Claire began modeling at Blackstone's, an exclusive department store frequented by society and entertainment personalities, and within a short time she became assistant manager of the personnel department. That was her position when she met Howard Hunter.

A Three-Year Courtship

THOUGH THEY SAW each other at church socials and were both members of the Thrift Chorus, Howard and Claire dated only a few times during 1928. Usually they were together as part of a larger group. One evening Howard and Ned went to an outing at Long Beach with the GB's (Gloom Busters), a club of young women from several of the Los Angeles wards. "It wasn't a date affair," he wrote, "but I spent most of the day with Claire Jeffs. There was a full moon tonight and we went swimming before coming home." In October, Claire invited him to a dance for Blackstone employees. They wore old, tattered clothes, in keeping with the theme, "Hard Times."

In January 1929 Howard was promoted twice—to manager of the central clearing department and then to working on individual ledgers. His new assignments meant working long hours, sometimes until nine or ten at night, and half a day on Saturday.

Because he was also still taking banking classes and playing for dances two or three times a week, Howard had little time to date—and he was still playing the field. Though he and Claire went to the theater and to dinner with four other couples on New Year's Day, less than two weeks later he took another young woman to the stake Gold and Green Ball. On February 14, he wrote that he had received a valentine in the mail from Claire, but "until then I hadn't known that this was Valentine's Day."

That spring Howard was away from the main office for several weeks, working as a relief bookkeeper and teller at other locations. One week he was assigned to the Redondo Beach branch, where he ate his lunch in the sun on the pier each day. Another week he worked in the Hollywood main office, where, by the end of the first day, he was "familiar with the accounts of most of the well known stars of the movie colony."

His new assignments were less pressured than the old and gave him more free time, though the times and settings for some of his dates were sometimes unconventional. Many evenings Claire accompanied him when he played for a dance. One Saturday he picked her up after a dance job and took her to a midnight movie, then to dinner. He got home at five o'clock in the morning and managed to catch a little sleep before going to Sunday School.

Soon after that, he began playing with an orchestra once a week at Oakwilde Lodge, in the canyon of the Arroyo Seco above Devil's Gate Reservoir in Pasadena. "To get there," he wrote, "we drive as far as possible, park the car and hike the last distance on the trail to the lodge." After the second week, he noted, "I thought I was lucky to be playing saxophone instead of drums because of the hike, but all of us have to help the drummer get his trappings up the trail to the lodge."

One evening the orchestra played late at the lodge, then stopped to eat on the way back, and Howard didn't get home until three in the morning. He didn't go to bed, because at four o'clock Claire and three other couples came to pick him up to go to Arrowhead Lake for a day of hiking, picnicking, swimming, and boating.

As Howard and Claire became more serious about each other, they decided it was time for their parents to meet. Jake and Martha Jeffs invited the Hunters to their home. Dorothy, who was with them, has a vivid memory of the occasion. Martha Jeffs greeted them at the door, and Howard began to make the introductions, saying, "This is Claire's mother." Suddenly, just as Nellie reached to shake Martha's hand, Jake appeared in the doorway and exclaimed, in a booming voice, "Hell, it's Nell!"

That summer Howard and Claire made plans to take their vacations at the same time, the last two weeks in July. They swam at the beach, played tennis, drove to Santa Barbara, and swam and danced at Balboa, a peninsula off Newport Beach. For three days they went on a cruise to Ensenada, Mexico. "Neither of our families liked the idea," Howard wrote, "but we convinced them that it was all right." They danced until late before going to their cabins, "which," he explained, "are on different decks."

In October 1929 the stock market collapsed, thrusting the national economy into a nosedive. Many people, particularly

Howard in 1930

those who had speculated in stocks during the bullish trend of the preceding four years, panicked under staggering losses. Banks and other financial institutions began to close, and factories shut down.

Though Howard read with interest what was happening, he didn't feel the effects immediately. The bank he worked for seemed strong enough to survive, and crowds still flocked to the dances he played for, as people sought escape from the cares and uncertainties of the world around them.

The Hunter family had worries of a different kind in early 1930. One January evening while working at the telephone company, Dorothy, who had not been feeling well, had a lung hemorrhage. She stayed home and rested for two months, then was admitted to the Los Angeles County General Hospital for extensive tests. The diagnosis: tuberculosis. After a month in the hospital, she was transferred to a sanitorium in the San Fernando Valley, where she would remain for the next twenty-eight months. Howard visited her frequently with his parents and often with Claire.

In November of 1930, a year in which many banks closed their doors, the Bank of Italy merged with the Bank of America of California, which was renamed the Bank of America National Trust and Savings Association. Howard worked on the bookkeeping for the merger and helped to set up the books for the new institution, which had a combined net worth of nearly $1.25 billion.

Soon after the merger was completed, a vice president of the bank told him that the president of the First Exchange State Bank in Inglewood was looking for a junior officer with bank training. Would Howard be interested? The offer sounded promising, and Howard agreed to meet with the First Exchange officers. They offered him a position as assistant cashier at their Hawthorne branch. Because First Exchange Bank, with just four branches, was considerably smaller than Bank of America, he felt that he would have better opportunities to learn all phases of banking, so he accepted.

Some Major Decisions

BY EARLY SPRING in 1931, Claire and Howard were talking seriously about marriage. In his history he wrote: "I had not given up the hope of going on a mission and I had saved some money with that in mind. Claire offered to help support me and wait for me until I returned. Even though I appreciated the offer, I could not accept the proposal of having her work and support me. We finally decided that it would be better for us to get married and at a later time, as soon as conditions might permit, we would go on a mission together.

"One beautiful spring evening, we drove to Palos Verdes and parked on the cliffs where we could watch the waves roll in from the Pacific and break over the rocks in the light of a

Courting time:
Howard and Claire

full moon. We talked about our plans and I put a diamond ring on her finger. We made many decisions that night and some strong resolutions regarding our lives. The moon was setting in the west and dawn was just commencing to break when we got home."

The couple decided to be married in the Salt Lake Temple in June. Howard went to his bishop, told him of his plans, and asked for a temple recommend. He was stunned when Bishop Brigham J. Peacock said he couldn't understand how Howard could support a wife on his small income.

"When I told him how much I was making," Howard wrote, "he said the reason for his doubt as to my ability to support a wife was based on the amount of tithing I had paid. Suddenly I became conscious of the seriousness of not being a full tithe payer.

"Because my father had not been a member of the Church during my years at home, tithing had never been discussed in our family and I had never considered its importance. As we talked, I realized that the bishop did not intend to give me a temple recommendation. In his kindly way he taught me the importance of the law and when I told him I would henceforth be a full tithe payer, he continued the interview and relieved my anxiety by filling out and signing a recommendation form."

Howard related his experience to Claire, who had always been a full tithe payer. As a result, he said, "we resolved that we would live this law throughout our marriage and tithing would come first."

As his wedding day approached, Howard made another major decision. For several years he had played with orchestras at dances and parties, in public ballrooms, and on radio and the stage. "It was glamorous in some respects," he reflected, "and I made good money, but the association with many of the musicians was not enjoyable because of their drinking and moral standards." Such associations were not compatible with the lifestyle he envisioned with a wife and family, so he decided to give up professional music.

On June 6, 1931, four days before their wedding, Howard played his last engagement at the Virginia Ballroom in Huntington Park. After he got home that night, he packed up his saxophones and clarinets and his music and put them away. He had already sold his drums and marimba and packed up his trumpet and violin.

"Since that night," he said, "I have never touched my musical instruments except on a few occasions, when the children were home, [and] we sang Christmas carols and I accompanied on the clarinet. Although this left a void of something I had enjoyed, the decision has never been regretted."[4]

Howard was still driving the Model A Ford Coupe he had bought when he arrived in California three years earlier, and Claire was willing to drive to Utah in it—"a test of true love," he commented. But he had other plans. He went out and ordered a black 1931 Chevrolet Sport Coupe "with red wheels, a rumble seat and a number of fancy extras." The price was

$766.50 less a trade-in allowance of $75.00 for the Ford (which he had purchased for $5.00), and he was able to pay cash.

Marvin Rasmussen, a cousin from Mount Pleasant, Utah, was in Los Angeles on business and planned to return home with Howard and Claire. Howard asked him to pick up the new car a few days before they left for Utah and to drive it around slowly to break it in. On the departure day, Howard met Marvin, turned in his old car to the car dealer, and drove the new one to Claire's house. "She could hardly believe her eyes," he said. "After loading her things, we were soon on our way in grand style—the bride, the groom, and the chaperon."

Marvin had notified his family they were coming, and a large crowd was on hand to greet them in Mount Pleasant. "I hadn't realized there were so many relatives!" Howard remembered. After visiting and hearing some of the family stories, he and Claire continued on to Salt Lake City, where they stayed with her grandmother, Maria Emilie Reckzeh.

That afternoon the couple went to the county clerk's office for a marriage license and to the Church offices to ask Elder Richard R. Lyman of the Quorum of the Twelve Apostles if he would perform their marriage and sealing the next day. He agreed and gave them some wise counsel that they never forgot. "Stay out of debt," he said. "Live within your means. Do not spend more than you make. Don't hesitate to walk or ride the streetcar if you can't afford a car. Don't buy anything unless you can pay for it. Save your money until you can pay cash."[5]

The next morning, Wednesday, June 10, 1931, Howard William Hunter and Claire Jeffs, accompanied by her grandmother, went to the Salt Lake Temple. There they received their endowments and were married and sealed for time and eternity.

5

Husband, Father, Lawyer, Bishop

HOWARD AND CLAIRE began married life in a furnished apartment overlooking the ocean at Hermosa Beach. Each morning, he recalled, "we were up early. I put on my swimming trunks, ran across the beach, and dived into the breakers. After a vigorous swim and a warm shower, breakfast was ready. It took only fifteen minutes to drive to the bank in Hawthorne and I was ready for the day's work. We often went swimming together in the evening after I got home, and we usually walked down the beach under the stars before we went to bed. Even though the days were warm, the sea breeze made the evenings cool and comfortable, and the pounding surf was a lullaby."

When they rented the apartment, he said, they knew they couldn't afford to live there long—"but we wanted the luxury of a nice place to start our marriage."

Soon afterwards they moved to a three-room unfurnished house within walking distance of the bank at Hawthorne. Claire had a bedroom suite and they bought a few other furniture and household items, but they were determined to follow Elder Lyman's advice not to go into debt. "For this reason we didn't have all the things we wanted, but we had what we needed to make us comfortable," Howard said.

They became active in the Inglewood Ward, where Claire was called to serve as Gleaner leader in the YWMIA and Howard became a counselor in the YMMIA superintendency.

By late 1931, two years into the Great Depression, business conditions in the United States had continued to deteriorate, with soaring unemployment and the threat of financial disaster. Many banks across the country were forced to close— among them, the First Exchange State Bank. In January 1932 the four branches were seized by the state and, after audit, placed in receivership for liquidation. Howard had gone to work at the bank because of the opportunities it offered, but suddenly his employment came to a halt.

Because he and Claire had no outstanding debts, they were perhaps better off than many Americans during the depression years. Still, with no regular paycheck coming in, they tightened their belts and learned to buy only necessities. They used public transportation whenever possible, and Claire washed their clothes by hand, using a scrubbing board, because they were determined not to go into debt for a washing machine.

For the next two years Howard worked at a succession of odd jobs. When he left the bank, he arranged with the receiver to purchase coin wrappers, adding machines, and other supplies and equipment, which he then sold to other banks at bargain prices, repaying the receiver as the money came in.

He and Claire's father produced souvenir statues and bookends to be sold in connection with the 1932 International Summer Olympic Games held in Los Angeles. A sculptor in Hawthorne designed the model for the mold, and Howard and his father-in-law cast and bronzed the statues in Howard's garage. But though the items were beautiful pieces of art, few people could afford to purchase them.

Another time Howard purchased from a soap manufacturer one-ton lots of granulated soap, which he repackaged in ten-pound bags for home use and sold door-to-door. He also purchased and repackaged liquid bleach to sell with bags of soap to hand laundries. "It was hard work making the deliveries of soap and bleach to the laundries and ringing doorbells to sell soap," he recalled, "but I was able to make enough to pay the rent and buy groceries."

For a time he worked for the state banking department's receiver who was liquidating the First Exchange State Bank, but he was forced to give up this job because he was named in a suit against stockholders of the bank (he had earlier purchased a few shares when he thought he had a future in the organization). "The receiver was paying me a salary and at the same time was suing me for a stockholder's liability," he explained. "I later settled my portion of the suit for a small percentage, but again I was left without a job."

Next Howard was employed on a Works Progress Administration project to construct a storm drain, putting in seven hours a day, seven days a week, for thirty cents an hour.

"By talking with the engineers and keeping my eyes open, I was able to do a good job by the end of seven days, when I got my check for $14.70," he noted. "Again we were saved from starvation."

Howard and Claire had been determined to be independent as long as possible, but in January 1933 they finally accepted an invitation from Jacob and Martha Jeffs to live with them in their spacious four-bedroom home on West 84th Street in Los Angeles. Claire's sister, Thelma, and Thelma's daughter, Lee, were also living there at the time.

That summer Howard and his brother-in-law, Ellsworth, worked for Jacob, who had a contract to paint the structural steel on four new bridges under construction over a new highway. With no place to stay nearby, they camped out. Claire went along to cook for them. Not long afterward, the family was stunned when Jacob died suddenly while on a business trip to Utah. Martha and Ellsworth drove to Utah and arranged to bring him back to California for burial.

A Year of Hope and Sorrow

IN JANUARY 1934, as a result of his experience at the First Exchange State Bank, Howard was offered a job in the title

*Claire camped out with Howard and his brother-in-law, Ellsworth,
when they painted highway bridges*

department of the Los Angeles County Flood Control District,
where he would work with land titles and real estate con-
veyances. Two months later, on March 20, he and Claire
became the parents of their first child, a son, whom they
named Howard William Hunter Jr.

Howard's work with the County Flood Control District
involved many legal matters—examining titles, writing legal
opinions concerning the documents, and preparing eminent-
domain actions leading to condemnation of property for
flood-control purposes. He also helped attorneys prepare
cases involving these actions and on occasion attended the
ensuing trials.

These experiences fueled his desire to obtain a law degree.
After surveying the programs offered by colleges in Los Angeles, he decided to enroll at Southwestern University, California's largest law school, which offered an evening program.
But because he did not have an undergraduate degree, he first
had to take the required classes for entrance into the program.

It had been eight years since Howard graduated from high school, and though he had taken some night classes in those years, "it was difficult to form study habits again," he said. "It was particularly hard to keep up with the younger students who had been engaged in undergraduate college studies."

He enrolled for ten credit hours, a heavy load for someone who worked full-time. His weekday schedule consisted of studying on the bus and streetcar on the way to the office; working from eight to five, with more studying at noon while eating a sack lunch brought from home; munching an apple and memorizing as he walked several blocks to the university; attending classes from six to nine; studying on the ride home; eating dinner with Claire after ten; then studying again until midnight or later. On evenings when he was too tired to stay up and study, he would set the alarm clock to wake him up earlier in the morning. He followed this schedule for the next five years.

That summer, as Howard was settling into his work-and-school routine, he and Claire noticed that their baby son, Billy, seemed lethargic. The doctor diagnosed the problem as anemia. Howard gave blood for a transfusion, and Billy recovered briefly, then suffered a relapse. In early September he was admitted to a hospital for additional tests, and Howard gave blood for another transfusion.

When there was still no improvement, the worried parents took him to Children's Hospital, where tests finally revealed that an intestinal diverticulum had ulcerated, causing loss of blood. The doctors recommended surgery.

"We were assured that the surgeons selected were outstanding in this field, so we gave our consent," Howard wrote. "At the time of surgery, I was taken into the room on a table beside him and gave blood during the operation. At the conclusion, the doctors were not encouraging.

"We stayed with him constantly for the next seventy-two hours, which the doctors said would be the critical period. On the evening of the third day they told us it would be better for

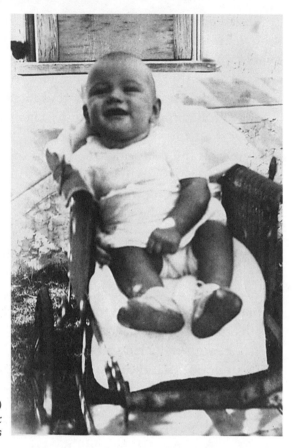

*Howard William (Billy)
Hunter Jr. at six
months*

us to go home and get some rest. We had not been home long when a call came asking us to return to the hospital because there had been a turn for the worse. Later that night, October 11, 1934, he slipped quietly away as we sat by his bed. We were grief-stricken and numb as we left the hospital into the night."

Two days later, after a "lovely, comforting service," the earthly body of little Howard William Hunter Jr. was interred in a grave beside that of his grandfather, Jacob Ellsworth Jeffs.

That fall was a difficult time for the sorrowing parents, especially Claire. While Howard had to keep his mind on work and studies, she suddenly found herself without the responsibilities of caring for their baby. To keep her mind off her heartbreak, she finally decided to go back to work. Bullock's Department Store, which had taken over Blackstone's, was happy to have her return to her former position as assistant personnel manager.

"This was the only time during our marriage that Claire was employed," Howard noted.

Struggles and Blessings

WHEN THEY MOVED IN with Claire's parents, Howard and Claire thought it would be for a short stay, so they decided to keep their Church membership records in the Inglewood Ward of the Hollywood Stake rather than have them transferred to the Vermont Ward, which Claire's mother attended. In early 1935 Howard was called to direct the scouting program for the stake. In this position he represented the stake on the Los Angeles Metropolitan Area Scout Council and was appointed assistant district commissioner. Both he and Claire continued to serve in the ward MIA. It was through these callings that they were given another assignment.

"One evening we had a dinner for the M-Men and Gleaners," Howard explained. "While we were talking at the table, someone asked why the ward couldn't have its own building instead of meeting in the rented hall of the Woman's Club. We decided to talk with the bishopric. They told us they were waiting for the members to develop a sufficient desire to be willing to make contributions, and as a result, they appointed us as the finance committee with me as chairman."

Soon the fund-raising program was under way and a site for a new chapel was selected. Howard negotiated with the Los Angeles Investment Company for two lots and a house adjacent to Centinela Park at a price of two thousand dollars.

On July 26 and 27 the ward sponsored a Mormon Pioneer Days celebration. The first evening, the Salt Lake Tabernacle Choir sang at the Inglewood Bowl.[1] The next day, a Saturday, there were athletic events, musical performances, and exhibitions in the park, with a program at which the mayors of

Inglewood and Los Angeles and the governor of California spoke. That evening members of the stake presented a pageant, "The Call of the Mormon Battalion."[2]

"The events were successful and helped swell the building fund," Howard reported. When he entered law school that fall, he had to be released from the finance committee, but he was pleased three years later to be invited back to the dedicatory services for the new chapel.[3]

Howard entered law school in September 1935, and he soon found that law classes required more study time than had undergraduate work. He extended his study time to one or two o'clock in the morning. When Claire, who had been awaiting the birth of their second child, announced one Sunday evening that it was time to go to the hospital, he grabbed one of his textbooks, *Blackstone's Commentary on the Law,* and rushed her to Methodist Hospital of Southern California. She was put to bed immediately, and he remained with her until the medication she had been given took effect and she fell asleep. Then he went back to his studies.

"The night wore on," he wrote, "and midnight passed. By this time I had finished my lesson assignment. It was not unusual for me to study far into the night, but not all through the night. After a few short walks and reading several weeks ahead in the textbook, the sky was commencing to turn red in the east and the mocking birds were chattering in the trees outside the window.

"The nurse came in a few minutes after five o'clock, while I was still reading Blackstone, to tell me we were parents of a baby boy. This was May 4, 1936. Claire got along well, and in a few days I took her home with a baby to take the place of the little one that had been called home."

At fast and testimony meeting in August, Howard blessed his new son and gave him the name John Jacob Hunter—John in honor of Howard's father, grandfather, and great-grandfather Hunter, and Jacob for Claire's father.

Howard and Claire had appreciated being able to live in

her parents' home for three years, but with the security of Howard's position with the Los Angeles County Flood Control District, they began to look for a house of their own. They found a five-room house in Alhambra at a price and with terms they could afford. It was also near the electric railway line, so Howard could commute to work and school easily. The seller accepted their offer of $3,600, with a $500 down payment and the mortgage for the rest to be paid off three years later. During that period they would pay only the interest—$15 a month. "Nothing could have been better," Howard commented.

In their new ward, the Alhambra Ward of the Pasadena Stake, their bishop recommended that Howard complete his schooling before he received a church calling, but he also counseled them to attend their meetings as much as possible. "To work all day and go to school at night, and, in addition, to find the time to study was not an easy task," Howard wrote in his history. "Our social life was almost nil other than visits to our families."

Family ties were important to both Howard and Claire. The Pasadena area, where the couple would live for the next twenty-two years, was less than an hour's drive from their parents' homes and from Thelma and her daughter, Lee. While courting Claire, Howard had become very fond of Lee and occasionally took her along on their dates. When they all lived at his in-laws' home, he taught her how to skate and to ride her first two-wheel bike, and once he made stilts and helped her learn how to balance on them.

For Lee, who had never known her birth father, Howard became a much-loved father figure. Her mother remarried when Lee was eight, and her stepfather, Eddie Waldman, legally adopted her, but Lee also remained close to the Hunters and to her grandmother Jeffs. Her mother was not active in the Church, and Howard and Claire took her to church with them and encouraged her in church activity.

Howard's sister, Dorothy, also eventually settled in the Los

Angeles area. In December 1935 she was married in the Salt
Lake Temple to Marvin Rasmussen, the man who was
Howard and Claire's "chaperon" when they drove to Utah to
be married three and a half years earlier. Dorothy and Marvin
lived for a year in Mount Pleasant, Utah, then moved to Los
Angeles, where they became the parents of three daughters.

Howard and Claire's immediate family circle was completed on June 29, 1938, when their third baby was born. The
summer term at law school had just begun, and this time,
when the doctor came from the delivery room and told him he
had another son, Howard was reading a book on wills and
testaments. Claire's labor, however, was much shorter than
before. They arrived at the hospital in the early afternoon, and
the baby was born shortly before seven o'clock that evening.

At fast and testimony meeting in the Alhambra Ward in
November, Howard blessed his baby son and gave him the
name Richard Allen Hunter.

A Lawyer at Last!

"WITH A CRESCENDO that ended in final examinations, law
school came to an abrupt end in the first week of June 1939,"
Howard wrote in his history. When the grades were in, he and
two other students were tied for top honors, so officials had to
go back and compute the grades in decimals to determine the
exact ranking. Howard's score was two-tenths of one percent
behind the highest score and one-tenth of one percent behind
the second highest. At commencement exercises in the Hollywood Memorial Auditorium on June 8, 1939, he was graduated third in his class and received the cum laude degree.[4]

The week after graduation, he began to take a bar-review
course given by one of his professors, in preparation for the
California bar examination. At the last session, Howard said,
the professor told his students that when they sat down to
write the examination, they should "take a good look at the
man on the right and the man on the left, and realize that out
of the three, only one would receive a passing grade."

Howard took the examination, "one of the most grueling experiences of my life," October 23, 24, and 25. "After the third day I was completely exhausted. I had done my best but there was the anxiety of not knowing whether or not that was good enough."

The wait seemed interminable, for "several years of intense work was all focused on the results of one single event." He knew that if he received a thin letter, it meant he had not passed the examination. A thick letter would include not only a letter with the happy news that he had passed, but also several application forms for admission to the bar and the courts.

"It was on the morning of December 12 that Claire called me at the office and said the postman had just brought a letter from the Committee of Bar Examiners," he recalled. "'Is it a thick or a thin letter?' I asked. 'A fat one,' she replied. I felt a surge of blood to my head and I closed my eyes and waited for her to open and read the letter. The hard work and the sacrifices we had made were at a successful conclusion." And his professor was right: Of 718 who took the examination that session, 254, or 35.4 percent, passed. Nearly two-thirds failed.

In ceremonies at a session of the California Supreme Court in Los Angeles on January 19, 1940, Howard W. Hunter took the oath of office and was sworn in and admitted to practice law before that court and the other courts of the state. On February 5, he was admitted to the bar of the U.S. District Court for Southern California, and on April 8 he was admitted to the bar of the U.S. Circuit Court of Appeals for the Ninth Circuit.

That winter he rented space in the downtown Los Angeles office suite of attorney James P. Bradley, and on April 1 he began to practice law. "I had a number of legal matters pending, awaiting my admission to the bar," he said, "so I became immediately involved in practice." He continued to work part-time for the Los Angeles County Flood Control District, gradually cutting back his hours as his legal practice grew, until March 1945.

With law school behind them, Howard and Claire would now have time for other interests. That summer they left the children with grandparents and drove to San Francisco to visit the World's Fair, the Golden Gate Exposition. Howard's grandmother and grandfather Hunter had moved to San Francisco in 1933, and his grandmother had died a year later. Howard enjoyed visiting with his grandfather, now ninety, and his aunt Flora, who managed a Western Union Telegraph Company office in the city.[5]

And for the first time in three years as members of the Alhambra Ward, Howard and Claire received callings, he as instructor of the junior genealogy class[6] and she as a teacher in the Junior Sunday School.

A Surprise Calling

ON AUGUST 27, 1940, Bertrum M. Jones, president of the Pasadena Stake, telephoned and asked Howard to meet with him and his counselors that evening after MIA. At the meeting he explained that the Alhambra Ward was going to be divided, and the Hunters would be members of the new El Sereno Ward. Then he called Howard to serve as bishop of that ward.

Howard was stunned. "I had always thought of a bishop as being an older man," he recalled, "and I asked how I could be the father of the ward at the young age of thirty-two. They said I would be the youngest bishop that had been called in Southern California to that time, but they knew I could be equal to the assignment. I expressed my appreciation for their confidence and told them I would do my best."

Still shocked, he went home and shared the news with Claire. "We recalled the decision we made to get married instead of going on a mission, and that someday we would fill a mission together," he said. "Perhaps this was that mission in a different form than what we had expected."

On Sunday morning, September 1, at a special meeting in a rented hall, the El Sereno Ward was created. Howard Hunter was sustained as bishop, with Frank Brundage and Richard M. Bleak as his counselors.[7] One week later, after the Pasadena Stake quarterly conference, Howard was ordained a high priest and a bishop and set apart to preside over the new ward by Elder Joseph F. Merrill of the Quorum of the Twelve Apostles.

On the day he was sustained as bishop, Howard asked members of the stake presidency what his responsibilities were. They replied that he needed to find a place for the ward to meet, organize and staff the ward, "and get going." "This was all new to me, not having served in a bishopric," he commented, "but I followed directions."

That afternoon he and his counselors "got going." They began negotiations with the local Masonic lodge to sublet some meeting rooms that the lodge leased in the Florence Building in El Sereno. (For Sunday School classes, curtains were drawn in the large room—a reminder of Howard's experience as a youth in Boise.) They also began to staff the ward. Among the first persons called was Claire, who was asked to serve as supervisor of the Junior Sunday School.

Howard and Claire had been looking for a larger house, and just a few months later, they found one that fit their needs, at 3419 Winchester Avenue, on the boundary line between El Sereno and Alhambra. The house had three bedrooms, an unfinished top floor, and a basement. They converted one of the bedrooms into an office and library, which, Howard said, "made a nice room for interviews and other work as bishop." Because the ward had no chapel of its own, the home became the center of the ward's social life.

Wartime Challenges

AT THE CLOSE of fast and testimony meeting in the El Sereno Ward on Sunday, December 7, 1941, the Sunday School superintendent ran into the chapel and up to the podium with the shocking news that Japanese planes had bombed Pearl Harbor in the Hawaiian Islands. The United States declared war

Howard and Claire's home at 3419 Winchester Avenue in El Sereno

on Japan the next day, and on Germany and Italy on Thursday, December 11.

Two years earlier, Howard had wrestled over whether or not to enter the U.S. Army Reserves. With his high school ROTC service and rank as a cadet officer, he was eligible to enter the reserves as an officer if he filed an application before his thirty-second birthday on November 14, 1939. He talked with some commanding officers of the Judge Advocate's Department, the army's legal entity, and obtained the necessary application papers and manuals. In his history he described his dilemma:

"On September 1, 1939, while I was taking the bar review course, Germany invaded Poland, France declared war, and Russia came into the conflict. All Europe burst into flame in what became known as World War II. My application form for an officer's commission had been filled in and signed but not yet filed. After taking the bar examination, there were still two weeks to make the filing. Claire and I talked it over.

"We knew there was a possibility that the United States would be drawn into the conflict. In such an event the reserves would be the first to be called up. On the other hand all men might be called and there would be an advantage in having a commission. As the time approached we were more inclined to forfeit the commission, and my thirty-second birthday came and passed without the application being filed—so did my privilege of becoming a reserve officer."

With the country officially at war in December 1941, the lives of all Americans changed. "There were black-out restrictions, economic changes, shortages, rationing, and other emergency measures," Howard wrote. "All men over the age of eighteen were required to register for the draft. Because of my calling as a bishop, I was given a 4D classification as a minister with a deferment from the draft until the conclusion of the war. If I had taken out the commission as a reserve officer, which I almost did, I would have been called into service immediately."

One of the El Sereno Ward bishopric's first goals was to find property and begin raising funds for a new building. In May 1942 the Presiding Bishopric notified wards and stakes that no buildings were to be built for the duration of the war, but this did not curtail their efforts to start raising money for the future. Though the ward had only 265 members, California was still the nation's fastest-growing state, and the bishopric knew that the time would come when membership growth would require more adequate space for a full worship and activity program.

Ward members, led by their charismatic and dynamic bishop, plunged into a series of fund-raising projects. "We were known throughout the Pasadena Stake as the ward with the 'onion project,' where members of the ward go each week, on day shifts and evening shifts, to a nearby pickle factory and trim onions as a ward project," a ward historian wrote.[8] Howard commented, "It was easy to tell in sacrament meeting if a person had been snipping onions."

Another time the ward contracted with a sauerkraut plant to shred cabbage, which was then emptied in a big vat, sprinkled with salt, and stamped down by men in rubber boots. At the end of the war, the ward purchased a carload of Kix cereal, a surplus food item no longer needed by the government, and repackaged and sold it to ward members and their friends, with the profits earmarked for the building fund.

"These were happy days when we worked together, people of all classes and ability supporting the bishopric in raising funds to build a chapel," Bishop Hunter remembered. He loved his fellow ward members and they loved him in return. "Our ward was like a big, happy family, and we had many outings and parties in addition to the regular meetings of the Church."

Howard's son Richard recalls that "the ward had a particularly close spirit. I can remember a thermometer at the entrance of the second-floor quarters that measured how well we were doing in the fund-raising project to build a building. There was a bakery downstairs, and our meetings were often interrupted by wonderful smells from below. I can remember the plays the ward put on, and particularly the Christmas parties. As a young boy growing up in Primary, it was a wonderful experience."

As the war effort accelerated, the ward found itself with too few men available to fill leadership positions. "We had a group of fine young men who could not be neglected, so I assumed the responsibility of serving as scoutmaster," Howard recalled. "I trained them in qualifying for their ranks and helped them with their merit badges. They became quite proficient in camping, signaling, and all of the qualifications of scoutcraft. We frequently went on overnight campouts and did the things scouts like to do. I worked with the boys for nearly two years and they made excellent progress."

Howard taught the youth with love, but when necessary, he wasn't afraid to take firm—sometimes even unorthodox—steps.

Next door to the building where the ward met was a drugstore with a soda fountain that was open on Sundays. Mem-

The El Sereno Ward met in rented quarters upstairs in the Florence Building

bers of the Aaronic Priesthood began sneaking away after they had passed the sacrament at sacrament meeting and going next door for malted milk drinks. Their ward leaders, including their bishop, told them they shouldn't do this, but to no avail.

One day, after the boys had made their usual departure from sacrament meeting, Howard, who was conducting, fumed for a few moments, then left the stand and marched out the door and over to the drugstore. "Brethren," he announced, "when you have finished your malts, we will continue the meeting."

Those boys who had already been served hurriedly gulped down their malts, while the others, still waiting to be served, plunked down their money and followed their bishop back next door. Without saying a word about the incident, he proceeded to announce the rest of the sacrament meeting. And from that day forward, ward members report, the Aaronic Priesthood boys never again left sacrament meeting after they had completed their assignments.

Many years later, when Richard Hunter was a bishop, he

asked his father what he might do to get to priesthood meeting young men who were sleeping in on Sunday morning. "Dad told me of the day when some of the young men in the Aaronic Priesthood of his ward were absent, and he took the entire priests quorum to the home of one of them," he said. "The young man was still in bed, and so they held priesthood meeting in his bedroom. Dad said the boy didn't ever sleep in after that experience."

Howard's interest in youth extended to young adults attending college. In 1945 Claire's niece, Lee, was attending Woodbury College, and a group of the LDS students there wanted to organize a Deseret Club, the Church's organization for students at colleges and universities where there weren't enough members for an institute of religion. The college would not let them organize unless they could find an outside sponsor. Howard agreed to be their sponsor, and for the next year he went to the college at noon on Wednesdays and led the students in their study of *Jesus the Christ* by James E. Talmage.

Lee stayed with the Hunters frequently, helping to tend the boys when they were younger and enjoying being part of the family. During one of her visits, Howard arranged for a young man in his ward to take her to a church-sponsored Sweetheart Ball. He told her that though her date was short, homely, and awkward, he would really appreciate it if she would go to the dance and be nice to him.

Lee agreed—and was pleasantly surprised when her date, Richard Harrison Child, turned out to be tall, handsome, and articulate. Howard and Claire went with the couple to the dance, and three years later Howard performed their marriage, since there was not yet a temple in Southern California. The next day, accompanied by Claire, they went to the Arizona Temple to be sealed for time and eternity.

On November 10, 1946, Howard was released after six and a half years as bishop. "I will always be thankful for this privilege and the education of those years," he said. "They were difficult in many ways, and particularly hard on Claire, but she never once complained, and we were grateful for the values it brought to our family."

Joseph A. West, who had been Howard's bishop in the late 1920s in the Adams Ward and then a patriarch to the Pasadena Stake, gave Howard and Claire each a special blessing soon after Howard became a bishop. Howard's blessing stated: "You shall be known as an honest, just and honorable bishop among the members of [your] ward—and in future years, these members will come to you with tears in their eyes and thank you for your blessings, and your guiding hand, and the administration of the work you are now called upon to do."

Even decades later, many who had been members of the El Sereno Ward would indeed come to Howard, with tears in their eyes, or would write or call, and testify that he had truly blessed and guided them as their bishop.

A former member of the ward, Charles C. Pulsipher, shared some of his memories in a *Church News* article in 1981:

"As a bishop, he brought our small membership together in a united effort and taught us to accomplish goals that seemed beyond our reach. We worked together as a ward, we prayed together, played together, and worshipped together. . . . Elder Hunter had us all plant family gardens. We also planted a ward garden of beans. People in the neighborhood were amazed at the harvest we gathered. We also had many building fund projects. No great amount of money was realized, but the working together was far more beneficial than any monetary gains."[9]

New Assignments and Callings

THE DAY HOWARD was released as bishop, he was called to lead the high priests quorum of the Pasadena Stake, an assignment that was "much less time-consuming than the one of the last six years as bishop." But as with all callings in the Church, this one was no less important. One assignment of the quorum members was to visit Latter-day Saints hospitalized in Los

Angeles County General Hospital, one of the largest health-care facilities in the country. Every Thursday evening high priests from the stake would visit the hospitalized Saints to give them blessings and help them any way they could.

In 1948 Howard and Claire sold their house in Alhambra and purchased a newly constructed ranch-style house at 940 Paloma Drive in Arcadia. The house had a living room, dining room, library, kitchen, master bedroom suite for Howard and Claire, and bedrooms for each of the boys. A breezeway separated the garage from the house, and to the rear of the garage, a guest room opened onto a patio.

With this move, the Hunters became members of the Las Flores Ward, which met in the Temple City Women's Club. A few weeks after they began attending their new ward, the Women's Club notified ward leaders that their lease was going to be terminated. As no other suitable space was available, the bishopric decided to begin building the classroom wing of a chapel on a lot the ward had already purchased. It was decided that partitions between the classrooms would not be constructed at first, so that the large open area could be used for a chapel, with curtains drawn to divide it into classrooms.

At a meeting held as soon as the wing was completed, the bishop announced that that part of the building would be closed until the wardhouse was paid for in full, and members would continue to meet in rented quarters. Over the next few years the building was constructed piecemeal—the cultural hall, partitions between classrooms, the chapel, foyers, offices, and other rooms, with members providing much of the labor. Howard and his sons spent many evenings and Saturdays working at the site. They helped put chicken wire on a wall of the chapel for plastering, and installed many of the acoustic tiles on the ceiling of the cultural hall. When the tiles for the roof were passed up a ladder by a brigade, Howard said, "Richard was the top man on the ladder and handled every tile that went up." Finally the building was completed, paid for, and dedicated.

Howard was also pleased when a building for the El Sereno Ward was constructed. In 1944, while he was serving as bishop, a lot had been purchased for $2,000. Two years later, after Church officials informed Howard's successor, Bishop George W. Rands, that a church could not be built on that property, it was sold to the City of Los Angeles for $7,700. Another lot was purchased in 1947, but it was condemned and became a public playground.

In the meantime, the Congregational Church in South Pasadena was constructing a larger building and put its old one up for sale. The Church arranged in 1949 to purchase the old building, and it was extensively remodeled to serve the ward's needs. Howard Hunter, as a former bishop, was present on February 15, 1950, for the first sacrament meeting held there. Three months later, as stake president, he would preside over the sacrament meeting at which the name of the ward was changed from El Sereno Ward to South Pasadena Ward.

6

Family Life and Law Practice

IN THE EARLY 1940s, Howard and Claire were deeply concerned—as were all Americans—about the rapidly escalating
crises engulfing the world as the war spread in Europe and the
Pacific. But they also felt secure, after years of struggle during
the depression, with their own home, two healthy and active
sons, a growing law practice, and supportive and loving associations in their ward.

These peaceful feelings were shattered in May 1942 when
six-year-old John, who was just completing kindergarten,
became very ill. His family doctor and doctors from the city
and county health departments confirmed the diagnosis:
poliomyelitis. By then he was approaching the critical period
of the disease when paralysis might set in.

The medical profession at the time was experimenting
with a treatment for polio developed by an Australian nurse
and physiotherapist, Elizabeth Kenny. Under the doctor's
direction, Claire began to apply the treatment, which entailed
soaking a blanket in hot water in the washing machine, running it through the wringer, wrapping it around John, and
covering it with a dry blanket. As soon as the damp blanket
began to cool, it was replaced with another hot one.

"The doctors decided that because he was in the critical
stage of the disease and the fact that he was receiving better
treatment than could be given at the hospital, they would
quarantine the house and let him stay until the crisis has

*Richard and
John Hunter*

passed," Howard wrote. "We took Richard to Mother's house
and continued the treatments with John night and day for the
next three days, the doctor stopping in occasionally to check
the progress and watch for signs of paralysis."

At the end of that time, John began to improve, so the doctor decided against taking him to the hospital. "Our prayers
were answered," Howard reported, "and although he was in
bed for more than six weeks, he recovered without any permanent disability."

While John was the center of attention in this crisis at
home, his four-year-old brother, Richard, was the center of
attention—and of another family crisis—at his grandparents'
home. At the apartment house Will and Nellie Hunter were
managing at the time, one of the units was rented by the
mother of Margaret O'Brien, a popular child actress who was
a few months older than Richard. The two children became
friends and played together often.

At that time the Metro-Goldwyn-Mayer studio was casting parts for a movie starring Margaret O'Brien. The director had tested several boys for a role as one of her playmates but had not yet found one who suited him. One day when the children were playing together, Margaret's mother taught Richard some lines from the script and had him act out the part. She liked what she saw and called the director, who agreed to test him.

Nellie took Richard to the studio, where he worked for two days with the cast and crew. When MGM agents told Nellie they wanted to talk with Richard's parents about a possible movie contract, she contacted Howard and Claire. After discussing the matter at length, they decided they did not want their son to be in the movies.

"Margaret's mother was upset and my mother thought we were not very appreciative after all the work and effort," Howard remembered, adding, "I had been around enough people of the motion picture industry to cause me to dislike the environment, so Richard's movie life was short lived."

Family Life

THE HUNTER BOYS grew up in a home where loving parents taught them values, gave them responsibilities commensurate with their age and abilities, helped them develop their talents and interests, and provided a sense of security and well-being.

Claire kept an immaculate home, and her sons learned early to make their beds and straighten their rooms before they began their day's activities. Howard and Claire took time to talk with their sons and to listen to them. They set standards and expectations, not through overt preaching or coercion, but through example, gentle persuasion, and love.

"We always felt that there was a level of performance expected of us," Richard remembers, "and that we shouldn't do things any other way. In school, we were expected to get good grades, though I'm not aware of how that came about. We learned to become internally motivated, and much of that came from our father." Just as their father had found ways to earn money as a child, so did they. They sold lemonade at a stand on the front lawn on hot days, tended neighborhood children, delivered an early-morning newspaper, and sold hot dogs at Pasadena's Rose Parade. Because Howard went to work early and didn't return until evening, it was Claire who most often prodded and helped them in these activities.

John and Richard were taught to pray when they were very small, and they remember one or the other of their parents sitting beside them as they knelt in prayer before going to bed. At the dinner table and at bedtime, Howard told his sons about their ancestors and about his own boyhood in Boise.

They especially liked to hear about his cruise to the Orient. "Hey, dad, tell us about when you were on that trip," they would say, and he would regale them with descriptions of the exotic places he visited. His experiences seemed like tales from *The Arabian Nights*, except that these stories were better because they really happened.

One of Richard's favorite stories concerned a monkey Howard had purchased on his cruise. "Dad thought it would be a great pet," Richard recalled, "but when it was confined to the stateroom where he slept, he soon found that it was noisy and smelly. One day he returned to the stateroom and found that the monkey had gotten into his suitcase and had thrown clothes all over the place. The monkey soon disappeared, and Dad was always reluctant to tell us of its actual fate."

Long before the Church formally adopted Monday for family home evening, the Hunters reserved that night for their family. The boys were given assignments for the lessons, and minutes were kept. Sometimes the family played games or went someplace special. They did things together other times as well. On special occasions they went to Knott's Berry Farm for chicken dinner. Sunday evenings they liked to pop corn and gather around the radio to listen to their favorite programs.

Both John and Richard laugh about the times their father

Though he was no longer a professional musician, Howard sometimes played the piano at home and at parties

made root beer in a big tub and then bottled and stored it in their basement—and especially the times when the bottles exploded. They remember family gatherings each Thanksgiving at the home of Grandmother Jeffs. On Christmas Eve they stayed home and sang carols, with Howard accompanying them on the piano or his clarinet. Then he would open the Bible and read the second chapter of Luke. Christmas Day they went to Grandmother and Grandfather Hunter's home for turkey dinner and to exchange gifts with Dorothy's family. On New Year's Eve, Howard and Claire usually went to parties at church or friends' homes. And on New Year's Day the family went to the Rose Parade in downtown Pasadena, hauling two stepladders and a board to put across them so they could sit above the crowd.

When the boys were young, air travel was just beginning to be an accepted way of travel, and Howard would take them to the airport to watch aircraft take off and land. Later the three of them became interested in building model trains from kits. They nearly filled the guest room with tracks attached to large sheets of plywood mounted on tables.

"One of our favorite pastimes," Howard said, "was to go to the railroad yards on Mission Road near the Alhambra station of the Southern Pacific Railroad to get ideas for our switchyards and equipment." When they couldn't figure out how to install the air pump under the model cars, they went to the railroad yard and looked under the trains.

This hobby ended when Howard became president of the Pasadena Stake and the guest room was needed for visiting General Authorities. "It was a rather sad day for us when we had to dismantle our railroad," he commented. Howard put the engines and cars in storage, which he and then John kept for many years. In 1968 John and Richard, who by then had sons of their own, divided up the train pieces so each would have part of the railroad system they had helped build as children.

In the summer of 1951 John and Richard took diving lessons at Pasadena City College from Colleen Hutchins, a member of their stake who was crowned Miss America 1952 that fall. The next year the Hunters had a swimming pool installed in the backyard, replacing a badminton court, and the boys helped their father design and complete a four-room deck house with two dressing rooms, a room for the pumping and heating equipment, and a shop for Howard's power tools and woodworking equipment.

The patio between the house and the pool, with its built-in barbecue pit, provided a pleasant outdoor-living area where the boys could entertain friends, and the new rooms in the deck house could be used as a private guest suite.

The Hunter family's ranch-style home in Arcadia

Remembering how important music was in his own childhood, Howard saw that his sons took piano lessons as soon as they were old enough. When they practiced, he would help them with the notes, timing, and beats, and he even gave them some lessons. But eventually, he said, "the effort to get them to practice was more than I could cope with, and music lessons finally came to an end about two years after they started." The boys learned to play other instruments in school. For a time John played the cello until it was badly damaged when his bicycle crashed while he was hauling the bulky instrument between school and home.

Sometimes Howard would sit down at the piano and play popular songs from his dance-band days. And occasionally, at gatherings at friends' homes, someone would bring out a clarinet and say, "Here, try this." According to Richard, "He'd crank up the clarinet and do very well. He was good—he was very, very good."

Howard liked to listen to classical music, and he amassed an impressive collection of recordings. He and Claire, often accompanied by their sons, went to many concerts in the Los Angeles area. Once after a Hollywood Bowl concert featuring renowned pianist Arthur Rubinstein, the Hunter family went backstage to meet the artist.

Vacations and Travels

IN THE SUMMERS Howard and Claire usually rented a house on Balboa Island, off the coast at Newport Beach. Once one of Howard's clients let them stay for two weeks on a yacht berthed at the Balboa Bay Club. But though Howard had gone to the beach many times when he was courting Claire, he didn't particularly enjoy vacationing there. While his family swam and sunned on the beach, he commuted on week days to his office in downtown Los Angeles.

In July 1947 the family drove to Utah to participate in the celebration commemorating the one-hundredth anniversary of the first pioneers in the Salt Lake Valley. In 1949 they drove up the Pacific coast to Victoria and Vancouver, British Columbia, stopping along the way in San Francisco and Portland. Some nights they stayed in motels; other nights they slept out under the stars, which, according to Richard, Claire "tolerated in good humor." One night they camped near a swamp and Richard woke up covered with mosquito bites. Another time, John remembers, they heard strange noises during the night and discovered in the morning that their campsite was nearly surrounded by moose.

Three years later the family vacationed again en route to and in Canada. This time they drove north through Nevada and stopped in Boise. Howard had been there only once—a brief visit in 1930—since he moved to Southern California. He showed his wife and sons the places he remembered from his childhood: the homes where he was born and grew up, the old swimming holes in the Boise River, the country club where he caddied, the schools he attended and places he worked, and his uncle's ranch at Melba. "This was as interesting to me as it was to them," he wrote. During this trip the family visited the Cardston, Idaho Falls, and Logan temples, where the parents went through sessions while the boys performed baptisms.

Howard and Claire,
John and Richard

Until the Los Angeles Temple was completed and dedicated in 1956, the stakes in Southern California were in the Arizona Temple district. Howard and Claire went on many ward and stake excursions to Mesa to do temple work. "Usually we left on Friday evening, drove through the night, and attended two sessions of the temple on Saturday," he wrote. "We came home either on Saturday evening or we stayed overnight, attended church in the morning, and came home Sunday night." They also attended sessions at the St. George Temple on occasion, sometimes accompanied by the boys, who did baptisms for the dead.

When John and Richard became active in scouting, their parents helped them with their merit badges. To qualify for a badge in camping, John had to sleep in the open for fifty nights. "He had slept out on scout trips and father-and-son outings," Howard reported, "but he needed many more nights to complete the fifty." That year the father and his sons camped out often. A favorite camping area was the Los Angeles Arboretum, just down the block from their home in Arcadia. It had a lake surrounded by dense jungle-like foliage that had provided the set for Tarzan movies.

One unforgettable night they drove to the Mojave desert, arriving after dark, and were soon fast asleep in their sleeping bags. "In the middle of the night," Howard wrote, "a blast of a streamliner woke us with a start and the headlight was shining directly on us. We were terrified as the train rushed down on us, but suddenly it swerved to the left and screeched by us." They had made camp near a curve of the main line of the Santa Fe railroad! In his history Howard concluded: "Although we had many enjoyable nights together, I was glad when the fifty were completed."

In 1951 John's Explorer post floated on rubber rafts on a nine-day, ninety-mile trip down Oregon's Rogue River. This was the first time the treacherous white-water rapids had been negotiated by rubber rafts.

Three years later the scouts decided to float the Rogue River again, this time in kayaks. Howard, John, and Richard built a kayak in their backyard, cutting out the various parts in Howard's shop in the deck house. The kayaks were collapsible so they could be transported easily. On Saturdays the scouts and their leaders practiced steering them on the estuary of the Los Angeles River at Long Beach.

The two-week float trip in Oregon went well until the group came to a large waterfall and decided to go through it rather than portage around it. Howard and Richard, in the lead craft, positioned themselves to go through the rapids. Suddenly the boat picked up speed, and Richard's hat went flying off. He reached out to grab it, letting go of his paddle, and the boat went over the waterfall backwards.

They came through that harrowing adventure unscathed, but later, as they went through another chute, the kayak tipped over. Howard managed to get to shore safely, but Richard became trapped under the boat. Finally someone managed to throw him a rope from the riverbank, and he pulled himself to safety. "It was really a life-threatening adventure," he recalled.

Because they lost most of their supplies, their trip had to be cut short. They packed up their craft and remaining supplies and began hiking out of the wilderness. That night as they rested on a sandbar, Howard recounted the story of Job.[1]

Both John and Richard received their Eagle awards, and both achieved honors in school as well. John played varsity basketball in high school; represented his school at California Boys' State, where he received awards in athletics and was elected to the office of state assemblyman; and served as president of the Scholarship Club. Richard received honors in high school forensics, competing in state as well as local competitions, and participated in track and basketball.

After high school graduation, both boys attended Brigham Young University, where they excelled in scholastics and participated in class and student body government. And each of them was called to serve in the South Australian Mission after two years at BYU, with John leaving in 1956 and Richard in 1958.

Wife, Mother, Homemaker

CLAIRE TOOK her role as a wife and mother seriously. According to a daughter-in-law, she had three centers of focus: Howard, her children, and the Church. Though she was sometimes quiet and reserved around others, she was very much involved in caring for her family.

She helped her sons with their homework and in preparing their talks for church. When they were in high school, they attended different schools, and she picked them up after practices and other extracurricular activities. She cheered them in athletic competitions and speech and debate meets, and encouraged them to bring their friends home, making sure the barbecue grill on the patio was ready to use and the freezer was stocked with ice cream.

Claire with Duchess,
the family's pet collie

"My greatest ambition," she declared in an *Improvement Era* interview, "has been to be a good wife, to be a good homemaker, and to be a really good mother. I have always thought that if I could do this, I would fulfill my mission here on earth. We have worked hard to keep our boys close to the Church; the boys and I have had wonderful times together. I've gone through their scouting with them, because, well, Daddy just didn't have the time."[2]

As her sons grew up and became more independent, Claire found time to pursue personal interests, often with LDS friends in her neighborhood. After Loraine Major's family installed a swimming pool in their backyard, she, Claire, and Leda Duncomb hired a YWCA instructor to teach them how to swim. Once when Loraine started to sink and yelled for help, Claire calmly replied, "Just keep stroking," a phrase that might describe her own life.

Claire sewed some of her own clothes, perfecting her tailoring skills at an adult-education sewing class she took with Leda and Loraine. She was tall and elegant and preferred clothes that were both classic and stylish. Once she made a beautiful black velvet dress for her daughter-in-law Nan, and Nan's daughter Kathleen wore it in the 1990s.

Interior decorating was another of Claire's interests. She planned her home decor carefully and would search for just the right piece of furniture or accessory for her home. She and her friend Alicebeth Ashby frequently rummaged through items at antique stores and estate auctions, looking for additions to their collections of cut-glass dishes. But though Claire looked for quality in her purchases, she was frugal. Richard remembers coming home from college once and finding his mother clipping coupons at the kitchen table in order to save on groceries and household supplies. And when she and Howard were preparing to move to Utah, she did most of their packing herself in order to save on the movers' fees and so she could purchase a watch she wanted.

Claire read widely and had great curiosity about the world. One summer she and a friend took a two-month BYU-sponsored tour to Italy, the Riviera, Switzerland, France, Belgium, the Netherlands, and England. While she was away, Howard, John, and Richard plotted her itinerary on a map every evening to see what she was doing and where she was. For three semesters she took classes at Pasadena City College, receiving straight-A grades.

A student of the gospel, Claire studied the scriptures and other Church books and became knowledgeable on gospel principles. From the time she received her first Church calling at age sixteen, she was never without a calling. She served as the Gleaner leader in the Young Women's MIA and as an officer and a teacher in the Primary and Relief Society. She enjoyed working on her own and her husband's family research and kept scrapbooks on her sons' activities.

Howard's Law and Business Interests

AFTER HE GRADUATED from law school and passed the bar examination, Howard determined to specialize in corporate and business law and probate matters. He handled the legal work for many corporations as well as individuals, and soon began receiving appointments to boards of companies he represented. Within the next few years he would be elected to the boards of more than two dozen companies, including Thriftway, Inc.; Carts Incorporated; Aircraft and Marine Incorporated; J. N. Stevens, Inc.; Devey Manufacturing Company; Vetric, Inc.; Metal Specialties Company; Ensign Industries; Hollywood Trophy Company; the Presidential Company; Dominguez Water Company; Task Corporation; Silliman Memorial Hospital; and Los Angeles Trust Deed and Mortgage Exchange.

One of his most interesting appointments—and certainly the longest-lasting—came in July 1944. When California was still under Mexican rule, the Mexican government granted to a man named Manuel Dominguez property known as the Rancho San Pedro, which included what are now the cities of San Pedro and Wilmington, parts of Torrance and Compton, and Signal Hill in Long Beach, where rich deposits of oil were later found. Under terms of the Dominguez will, the ranch was divided after his death into five parts, one for each of his daughters, and companies were organized to operate and hold title to each part.

James P. Bradley, from whom Howard leased space for his office, had married a descendant of Dominguez and was a director of one of these companies, the Watson Land Company. Howard handled legal work for the company, whose holdings included refineries, large industrial buildings, and other major properties. On July 14, 1944, he was elected to the board. Two members of the Watson family, in a letter recommending his election, wrote, "Mr. Hunter is . . . capable and, we believe, fair-minded."

Until he liquidated his practice after he was called to serve in the Quorum of the Twelve Apostles, he did legal work for the company, and he was still on the board in 1994.[3] In February 1958 he was named to the board of Beneficial Life Insurance Company in Salt Lake City, an association that would continue when he became a member of the Twelve. In 1968 he became chairman of the executive committee, and in 1984 he was elected chairman of the board.

One of his clients was Gilles DeFlon, who specialized in buying and selling properties, often at tax sales. Howard did legal work for Mr. DeFlon in clearing the titles, and they soon became business partners, with Howard handling the legal matters and Mr. DeFlon managing the business end. The two men developed great trust in each other, and some of their business agreements were first reached with verbal commitments. Among the companies they organized were Sisar Oil Corporation, which had several small oil-producing wells, and Rancho Brea Corporation, a mobile home development. They also bought and sold cattle, and, according to Richard Hunter, his father "became quite expert in buying, feeding, and marketing cattle."[4] One of their biggest investments was a large cattle ranch near Promontory, Utah. After Mr. DeFlon's death, his son James became Howard's partner in overseeing the ranch, which was still flourishing into the 1990s.

Howard believed in the innate goodness of people, and he trusted them in their dealings. But sometimes he was disappointed. Once he sold some desert land he owned to a longtime acquaintance, but before the sale was completed, the client said he had secured a buyer for both that land and some adjoining property. Because Howard had known the client for many years, he entered into an oral agreement to sell the property to him with the understanding that he would be paid out of the proceeds of the subsequent sale. After the man received payment for the properties, he refused to pay Howard, claiming that his indebtedness had been paid in full. Because there was no written agreement, Howard had nothing to prove that the man still owed him for the property.

With genuine regret Howard filed an action, and when the case went to trial, the jury brought back a verdict in his favor. "Out of this experience I learned a great lesson not to rely on an oral agreement or to trust a fellow man," he said. But, he was quick to add, "Regardless of this lesson, I have chosen not to follow it."

John S. Welch, a prominent LDS lawyer in Los Angeles, in 1990 described this aspect of Howard's legal work:

"All the time in which he was in active practice of law, he also was serving as a spiritual leader and counselor. He never saw any need to draw a bright line between those two fields of service. As a result, he spent a lot of his time giving legal service on a pro-bono basis without ever needing to identify it by the use of that term, and often because he just did not have the heart to send a bill, sometimes even for the costs he had advanced.

"Old timers in Pasadena still recall how clearly he was perceived as a friend, guide, counselor, and a professional who was much more concerned about seeing that people got the help they needed than that he got compensated for it. He handled many adoptions, but mostly for people who were yearning for children but who could not afford a lawyer. His pay was bringing joy to such would-be parents and finding proper homes for babies who might otherwise never have a decent chance."[5]

Members of the legal profession respected Howard for his keen mind, his ability to cut through to the essence of a legal problem, and his ability to communicate to judge and jury in a clear, concise, and persuasive manner. "In one case," his son Richard reported, "he represented a plaintiff in an action to recover damages to a tomato crop caused by the drifting spray of a crop duster on an adjoining ranch. After his excellent opening presentation before the court, on the second day of trial arguments the twelve defense attorneys offered a substantial settlement, which his client accepted."

In 1989 Elder Cree-L Kofford of the Seventy, a lawyer and

former president of the Pasadena Stake, observed, "It would be accurate to say that he was a successful business and corporate attorney. . . . Yet there are those who would argue that he was first and foremost a 'people lawyer,' for he always seemed to have time and the interest to help people with their problems."[6]

From the earliest days of his career, Howard was concerned about the importance of integrity in every aspect of his life. In January 1945 he and four other businessmen held a weekend retreat at Twentynine Palms, a desert community east of Los Angeles, to brainstorm the subject of success and how individuals considered to be great achieved their success. "This was a very productive weekend," Howard wrote in his history, "and commenced a course of thinking and action for which I have always been grateful." Over the next three years the "Master Minds," as the group called themselves, met regularly to study the success philosophy in *Think and Grow Rich*, a best-selling book by Napoleon Hill.

One of the author's recommendations was that a successful person must have an objective in life that can be reduced to a concise written statement. Members of the group determined to each write such a statement. "I hadn't realized how hard this was to do until I made the attempt," Howard recalled. "After writing and tearing up several statements that were long and complicated, I was finally able to put my thoughts in writing and formulated this statement:

"'IT IS MY AIM to find pleasure and enjoyment in life by seeking after those things which are good and worth while, that I may gain knowledge and wisdom with each passing year; to carefully plan my allotted time so that none of it will be wasted; to give my family the benefits of education, recreation, and travel; to conduct my life in obedience to the Gospel of Jesus Christ; to so manage my business affairs that I will have an income adequate to provide my family with their wants and the advantages of some of the finer things in life;

and to set aside a portion for investments to provide an income for retirement.'"

On Washington's Birthday in 1946, the group went to Mount Wilson to study and to share with one another their statements. "Since that time I have made a conscientious effort to purposely bring these things into focus in my life and to constantly strive to obtain that goal," Howard concluded.

Later, as a General Authority, he sometimes quoted a statement of Napoleon Hill that summarized his own philosophy on the things that are truly important in life: "Riches cannot always be measured in money. To some, riches can be evaluated only in terms of lasting friendships, happy family relationships, understanding between business associates, or peace of mind measurable only in spiritual values."

Howard's status as a competent and fair lawyer was recognized in 1948 when an attorney friend wanted to recommend him to the governor of California to fill a vacancy on the bench in one of the state courts. Howard declined the opportunity. "My law practice was treating me well," he said, "and I wanted the freedom to work in the Church and carry on my own interests."

7

President of the Pasadena Stake

FOR HOWARD HUNTER and his family, Southern California was an exciting and challenging place to be during the 1940s and 1950s. Millions of people moved into the cities and suburbs, attracted by employment opportunities in education, industry, entertainment, medicine, construction, science, and government.

The first freeway, the Arroyo Seco Parkway (later renamed the Pasadena Freeway), constructed along an old riverbed between Los Angeles and Pasadena, was completed in 1940. Ten years later freeways were crisscrossing and connecting nearly every community in Southern California, and city and town boundaries became blurred as homes, business and government buildings, warehouses, shopping malls, and golf courses sprang up everywhere.

One author observed, "New cities and housing tracts as big as cities rose. One consisted of 3,000 acres and would accommodate 70,000 people. When construction crews set to work, a foundation was dug every fifteen minutes, 100 houses were begun in a day and, on one day in the late 1950s, 105 homes were sold. By 1960, this tract had blended into its nearest neighbors and, from ground level, was an indistinguishable part of the urban landscape."[1]

The population of the city of Los Angeles increased from 1.9 million in 1950 to 2.4 million in 1960, while the population of greater Los Angeles County soared from 2.7 million to over

6 million in that same decade. Many Latter-day Saints were among those who contributed to this growth.

The first stake in California, Los Angeles Stake, was organized in 1923; by 1950 there were ten stakes in metropolitan Los Angeles. One of the fastest-growing areas was around Pasadena, where a stake was organized in 1936 through a division of the Hollywood Stake.[2] Three years later Pasadena Stake was realigned, with some of the wards forming the new San Fernando Stake and several wards and branches added to Pasadena Stake from the South Los Angeles and San Bernardino stakes. By 1950 the Pasadena Stake membership was over nine thousand.

At a stake conference on Saturday and Sunday, February 25 and 26, 1950, Elders Stephen L Richards and Harold B. Lee of the Quorum of the Twelve Apostles were assigned to divide the stake again. It was nearly midnight Saturday, after many interviews and a stake priesthood meeting, when the two General Authorities sent for Howard W. Hunter and Fauntleroy L. Hunsaker, who had been serving as first counselor in the stake presidency, and called them to serve as president of the Pasadena Stake and the new East Los Angeles Stake, respectively. Then, Howard reported, "we were told to go home, get a good night's sleep, and call them in the morning by six o'clock and let them know our recommendation for counselors. I went home that night, but I didn't sleep. The calling was overwhelming. Claire and I talked for a long time."

Early Sunday morning he called the General Authorities and recommended that Daken K. Broadhead and A. Kay Berry serve as his counselors.[3] A few hours later the stake was divided and the new stake presidencies were sustained at the morning session of conference, held in the Monrovia High School auditorium.

The newly reorganized Pasadena Stake had six wards and 4,482 members and extended from Pasadena east to the San Bernardino County line, a distance of more than twenty miles.

William A. Pettit, who preceded Howard as stake president, wrote in a stake history:

"President Hunter assumed responsibility for Pasadena Stake early in the electronic age and at the beginning of a population explosion. Extensive housing subdivisions were rapidly bringing many new members into all of the wards, and new industries were bringing many trained executives and leaders. As a result, ward and stake facilities became overcrowded. Stake meetings could not be accommodated in any of the ward chapels. The Monrovia High School did not provide adequate facilities for stake conferences. Many wards soon required division."[4]

As he had done when he became a bishop ten years earlier, Howard immediately began the task of evaluating and reorganizing. Two of the six wards were divided and many new leaders were called and set apart. By May, when the next stake conference was held, he reported that Pasadena Stake "was well organized and settled down."

Elder Marion G. Romney, Assistant to the Quorum of the Twelve, was assigned to that conference and was invited to stay with the Hunters.

"I was nervous and fearful about conducting my first stake conference," Howard confessed. "Claire, too, was nervous. We had never before had a General Authority in our home, and she was anxious to have everything just right. Brother Romney came by train, and I went to East Los Angeles Station to meet him. As soon as we were in the car and commenced to talk, he made me feel at ease with his kindly manner. . . . I felt I had found a friend with understanding."

The two men found that they had much in common, for President Romney also had been a bishop and stake president and had struggled to get through law school and establish a practice while raising a family. The friendship they began that day would grow and strengthen through the years, particularly as they later served together for twenty-nine years in the Twelve. Over his nine and a half years as stake president,

Howard hosted and became well-acquainted with most of the General Authorities serving during that period.

Soon after he was sustained as stake president, Howard met with his counselors and members of the high council to discuss ways to increase spirituality in the stake. One of the decisions they made was to emphasize family home evening. "I was anxious to see a family home evening program developed which would be on the same evening in every home in the stake," he explained.

After considerable discussion and study, the stake leaders recommended that Monday evening be set aside as the time when, as Howard said, "no other events were held which would conflict with that sacred evening." Fifteen years later, in 1965, Monday evening was formally designated as family home evening churchwide.[5]

Creative Ways to Raise Funds

WITH CHURCH MEMBERSHIP in Southern California growing rapidly, members were frequently asked to contribute to ward and stake building programs—and some regional ones as well. The first such request during Howard Hunter's administration came on Saturday, June 10, 1950, less than four months after he became a stake president. Presidents of the ten Southern California stakes were invited by telegram to meet with Elder Henry D. Moyle of the Quorum of the Twelve at a special meeting in Los Angeles.

"We wondered what could cause such an emergency," Howard recalled, "but when we got to the meeting, he explained that the Church had purchased the 503-acre horse ranch of Louis B. Mayer at Perris, California, from the estate of Ellsworth Statler for the sum of $450,000." Elder Moyle said that the Church would sell the ranch to the stakes at cost if they could raise $100,000 as a down payment and pay the remainder over the next five years.

The stake presidents discussed the proposal during a brief recess, then reported that they could raise the down payment in six months. That did not satisfy Elder Moyle. "In his opinion, if we could not raise it in a month, it was a lost cause," Howard said. "We talked it over again and decided to show him we could do it."

What happened next set the pattern for an even greater financial commitment to come. The stake presidents decided they would each write a check for what they considered to be their own individual fair share of the money to be raised. Then each of them called his counselors and high council members that night and asked them to do the same. At six o'clock the next morning the stake presidents met with bishops, who responded with their fair share, and the bishops in turn met with their own counselors, ward leaders, and priesthood members. By mid-afternoon that Sunday, representatives of the ten stakes had collected the money and wired the $100,000 to Elder Moyle. It arrived in Salt Lake City before he did.

Sixteen months later, at the October 1951 general conference, the First Presidency met in Salt Lake City with the stake presidents from Southern California (by then there were fourteen) and announced that membership growth in their area justified the building of a temple. The stake leaders were delighted—though they did perhaps gulp when they learned that the members would be asked to contribute one million dollars toward construction costs.

"We had been working hard on fund raising for the welfare project and for the construction of stake and ward buildings throughout the area," Howard said. "The growth had been large and the costs were great; nevertheless we pledged our best efforts in carrying out the wishes of the Presidency."

At a meeting with President David O. McKay in Los Angeles in early February 1952, the stake presidents reported that they were already well under way with their plans to raise the million dollars in the next two years. After allocations were given to the individual stakes, each president once again pledged his own fair share, then met in turn with the counselors, high council members, stake clerks, and bishoprics in his stake. Howard explained, "Then we said, 'Go out into the wards and sell this program, and give the people the opportunity of receiving great blessings by contributing generously to the temple.' And they did."

At general conference that April, just six months after the stakes had been asked to contribute $1 million, William Noble Weight, president of the South Los Angeles Stake and chairman of the fund-raising committee, reported in general priesthood meeting that the members in Southern California had pledged $1.6 million.

During this same period, Howard Hunter and his counselors were embarking on an ambitious budget plan for the Pasadena Stake. On Sunday, February 17, 1952, they met with the bishops for five hours to discuss "the affairs of the stake, the operation of the wards, and the plan for the year by which we might accomplish the objectives we developed for the spiritual growth of our people."

One of these objectives was to solve an ongoing problem of raising funds to meet ward and stake needs. One bishop pointed out that the Saints were being asked to store a year's supply of food and other necessary items, so why couldn't bishops have a similar supply of funds? As a result, the leaders decided they would ask the members to increase their contributions by one-third each year, so that by the end of three years the wards would have a "year's supply" in reserve. At that point the members could go back to paying one hundred percent of their annual contributions.

"This was effectively carried out," Howard reported. "After the third year the funds for a whole year for budget, maintenance, welfare, and other funds were paid during the first week of the year and they were comfortable in not having any indebtedness."

Building a Stake Center

W HILE THE "year's supply" reserve helped solve the problem of meeting ward operating budgets, an even greater prob-

*Howard wields shovel
at Pasadena Stake
Center groundbreaking*

lem in Southern California during this period of unprecedented growth was the desperate need for new chapels and
stake centers. Pasadena Stake had outgrown the capacity of
existing auditoriums in the area for stake conferences, and
several units were meeting in rented halls or older buildings
with inadequate facilities for a full worship and activity program.

When two and a half acres became available on a
Pasadena hillside overlooking the San Gabriel Valley, the
Church purchased it for $50,000 and began preparing plans for
a building to be used jointly by the East Pasadena Ward and
the stake.[6] Ground was broken on Saturday, October 11, 1952.
"This was the commencement of a huge undertaking with

many problems and time-consuming supervision that only bishops and stake presidents can understand," Howard remembered.

Members of the ward and the stake were asked to help finance the building, which would cost over $400,000, a substantial sum for that time. In addition, the members would provide thousands of hours of labor.

At one point during the construction, according to Howard, "the work was proceeding so rapidly we came to the point where the pledges were not coming in fast enough to meet the material billings and the payroll for labor." The presidency called a meeting at the framed-in but not enclosed structure for priesthood members of all the wards. "We laid planks on nail kegs for benches," he recalled. After explaining the problem to those assembled, "we sat down and waited for their response."

A long period of silence ensued before, one by one, individuals stood up and pledged their support. The presidency then passed out souvenir checks printed with a picture of the stake center, and the priesthood members filled the "checks" in with pledges totaling more than $23,000.

"Everyone went away pleased and happy," President Hunter reported, "and from that time on the pledges came in so promptly, we did not have further financial problems."

Even young children contributed. Three months before the building was dedicated, a group of Primary children presented to Howard a check for $600 and a scroll with the names of the contributors. The scroll, placed in a metal box, was sealed in the floor at the entrance to the building, with a plaque to mark the spot.

In addition to giving overall direction to the construction, Howard did his share of manual labor, spending many Saturdays and evenings in his old clothes, wielding a shovel, hammer, broom, or paintbrush. But he did not insist on overseeing every detail. He told Richard S. Summerhays, bishop of the ward that would share the building with the stake, "Somebody has to see that the work gets done. There are only two of us available—and it's not going to be me."

Members of the stake still remember what they called "the day of the great pour." From eight in the morning till six in the evening, nearly one hundred men pushed wheelbarrows filled with sand and gravel to cement mixers, then pushed the concrete-filled wheelbarrows to forms for the electrical equipment room and two retaining walls. They poured the last load under floodlights after dark and just as rain began to fall. On another day, according to an article in the Los Angeles *Times*, "entire families joined in a block-long chain to pass 430 squares of French-style Comaco shake tile from the ground to the roof."

Howard made sure that materials of the finest quality were used, and he fought for only the best. While the Church Building Department at that time was recommending that electric organs be installed in chapels, the Pasadena Stake Center installed a Wurlitzer pipe organ purchased from a movie theater in the Los Angeles area.

When the landscaping was under way, Howard purchased for $350 each some olive trees that usually sold for $400. Then he called the building department in Salt Lake City and asked how much was allowed for the purchase of trees. "Thirty dollars each," he was told. The olive trees he purchased are still providing shade on the stake-center property, and long-time members sometimes refer to them as "the Howard Hunter trees."

President Stephen L Richards, first counselor in the First Presidency, dedicated the 25,000-square-foot building on Sunday, June 4, 1954. Proud stake members packed the 375-seat chapel and the adjacent cultural hall, which had a full-size basketball court with bleachers and could seat 1,500 people at stake conferences. Those who couldn't get into those halls sat in classrooms and listened to the proceedings over a public-address system. "It was a thrilling event for those of us who had worked so hard for this accomplishment," Howard said.

For many, it was an accomplishment that would be repeated again and again, as Church membership in Southern California continued to grow and wards and stakes continued to be divided. Not quite two years after the stake center was dedicated, Pasadena Stake was once again divided. Many who had contributed to ward and stake building projects were now members of the new Covina Stake and would again face extensive building programs.

Regional Council Chairman

ADDED TO Howard's responsibilities as president of a large and rapidly growing stake was a call in 1952 to serve as chairman of the regional council of stake presidents. The region extended from San Luis Obispo on the north to the Mexican border on the south, encompassing twelve stakes with 120 wards and approximately 65,000 members. Howard was responsible for coordinating and giving direction for numerous projects and activities, ranging from extensive welfare holdings and the building of the second largest temple in the Church to music and dance festivals and leadership conferences.

Even before he received this assignment, he was involved in helping to pioneer some far-reaching programs. In April 1950, at the first general conference held after he was called as stake president, he and the other presidents of Southern California stakes were invited to meet with President Stephen L Richards and representatives of the seminary program for high-school students. According to Howard, President Richards "explained that they would like to try an experiment with early-morning seminary classes in an area where the law did not provide for released time for religious education."

Howard was appointed chairman of a committee to survey the number of LDS high-school students in the Los Angeles area. On the committee's recommendation, early-morning seminary was introduced for the three high schools with the largest enrollment of Latter-day Saints. It met with enthusiastic response from the young people, and the following semester, the number of seminaries was increased. This was the beginning of early-morning seminaries in the Church.[7]

On May 15, 1955, at the first seminary graduation exercises held in Pasadena Stake, Howard's son Richard received a graduation certificate and was the student speaker.

As chairman of the region, Howard oversaw numerous Church welfare properties dotting the Southern California landscape, from lemon and orange groves to canneries and poultry farms. Often he pitched in and worked along with the Saints in the region on these welfare projects. In an article published in the *Relief Society Magazine* in April 1962 he wrote: "I have never been on a gloomy welfare project. I have climbed trees and picked lemons, peeled fruit, tended boiler, carried boxes, unloaded trucks, cleaned the cannery, and a thousand and one other things, but the things I remember most are the laughing and the singing and the good fellowship of people engaged in the service of the Lord. It is like the little boy who was carrying another little boy on his back. 'Isn't he heavy?' someone asked. The little fellow answered, 'No, he's my brother.' "[8]

One of the welfare properties was a large warehouse complex, southeast of downtown Los Angeles, that the Church purchased at auction in 1947 and dedicated in 1951. The property, according to William A. Pettit, "consisted of 107,000 square feet of land with a railroad spur into the plant, an air-conditioned building of 10,000 square feet with two walk-in safes, and 80,000 square feet of covered storage buildings in good repair."[9]

After major remodeling, the complex housed the regional bishops storehouse, Deseret Industries facilities, and offices and facilities for the Southern California region. President J. Reuben Clark Jr. of the First Presidency, Elders Harold B. Lee and Henry D. Moyle of the Quorum of the Twelve, and Marion G. Romney, Assistant to the Twelve, participated in the dedication of the welfare ranch in Riverside County June 8, 1951, and the Welfare Center the next day.

Howard served as chairman of the Southern California region until 1956, when the region was divided into the San Fernando, Southern California, and Los Angeles regions and he was assigned to be chairman of the latter. In 1958, the regional council decided to construct a cannery on the welfare square to replace three smaller canneries. The new plant would become the largest cannery operated by the Church, processing orange juice, turkey, stews, chili, beans, tomatoes, and many other commodities grown on welfare farms in the three regions.

Another first for Southern California came in August 1954, when leaders and young people from sixteen stakes participated in the first Mutual Improvement Association conference held outside Salt Lake City. It was patterned after the annual all-Church MIA June Conferences.

Many general board members came to Los Angeles to conduct departmental sessions for the leaders, and thousands of young people performed in cultural events. These included a music festival at the Hollywood Bowl featuring a 1,452-voice choir and a 75-piece symphony orchestra, with over 17,000 persons in the audience; a dance festival in the stadium of the East Los Angeles Junior College; and a closing Sunday morning session that filled the Hollywood Bowl for an address by President David O. McKay. As chairman of the regional council of stake presidents, Howard was the priesthood leader for these events.

Similar programs were held June 24 to 26, 1955, with President Stephen L Richards as the presiding authority, and June 29 to July 1, 1956, with President J. Reuben Clark Jr. in attendance.

President Clark stayed with the Hunter family during his visit and went with the family to the East Pasadena Ward sacrament meeting on Sunday evening. Early the next morning, while staying in the guest room near the swimming pool, he fell, striking his head and breaking the glass on the shower door. Howard called a doctor, who found that President Clark had broken a rib and cut his forehead. "We were terribly upset to think that the delightful weekend ended with such a tragedy," Howard said.

Apparently all was forgiven, because three months later, when Howard and Claire went to Salt Lake City for general conference, President Clark insisted that they come to dinner and stay overnight at his home. They spent the evening in President Clark's library, a two-story room with a balcony around all four sides and bookshelves lining the walls on each level from floor to ceiling. He showed them his extensive collection of books; a leather-bound portfolio of papers addressed to him and signed by seven presidents of the United States during his public career as an international lawyer, diplomat, and ambassador to Mexico; and other documents and photographs relating to his professional and church activities.

One of the most memorable events of the 1950s was the dedication of the Los Angeles Temple. Two dedication services were held each day from Sunday, March 11, through Wednesday, March 14, 1956. Howard and Claire were invited to the first session on Sunday morning. "The General Authorities and stake presidents were seated in the stands at the east end of the [temple] auditorium," he explained, "and the Mormon Choir of Southern California occupied the west end."

Claire had attended the Mesa Temple dedication in 1927 as a member of the Los Angeles Thrift Chorus. Now, nearly thirty years later, a similar choir, organized in 1953 and supervised by her husband as regional chairman, had the privilege of singing at a temple dedication in their own area.

On Saturday, March 24, Howard and five other stake presidents were invited to help perform baptismal ordinances in the new temple, with their own children as proxies, preparatory to the beginning of endowment work. John Hunter was attending Brigham Young University at the time, but Richard was able to participate in the baptisms. Three weeks later, on April 14, President McKay and Elders Richard L. Evans and Delbert L. Stapley of the Twelve, with their wives, and the stake presidents from the temple area and their wives participated in the first endowment session.

With a temple now close to home, Latter-day Saints in Southern California could participate more fully and often in the blessings of ordinance work. Previously they had had to travel either to Arizona or to Utah for endowments, sealings, and other ordinances.

In his history Howard described one never-to-be forgotten temple excursion that had taken place two years before the Los Angeles Temple was dedicated. On his forty-sixth birthday, November 14, 1953, he and Claire participated in a Pasadena Stake excursion to the Arizona Temple at Mesa. After the participants had changed into white clothing, they assembled in the chapel for a brief worship service. Arwell L. Pierce, president of the temple, called upon Howard Hunter to speak.

"While I was speaking to the congregation," Howard wrote, "my father and mother came into the chapel dressed in white. I had no idea my father was prepared for his temple blessings, although Mother had been anxious about it for some time. I was so overcome with emotion that I was unable to continue to speak. President Pierce came to my side and explained the reason for the interruption. When my father and mother came to the temple that morning they asked the president not to mention to me that they were there because they wanted it to be a birthday surprise. This was a birthday I have never forgotten because on that day they were endowed and I had the privilege of witnessing their sealing, following which I was sealed to them."

On April 30, 1956, six weeks after the Los Angeles Temple was dedicated, Howard's sister, Dorothy Hunter Rasmussen, was sealed to their parents. "This completed the eternal bonds of our family," he concluded.

Leading in Love

As A STAKE PRESIDENT, Howard Hunter was concerned
about all members of his stake, those who were less active as
well as those who participated fully in the Church's programs,
and he motivated bishops and other leaders to seek out those
who needed special encouragement and help. At a priesthood
leadership meeting held April 4, 1986, in connection with general conference, he shared this personal experience:

> While I was serving as a stake president in the Los Angeles
> area, my counselors and I asked our bishops to carefully
> select four or five couples who wanted to further their prog-
> ress in the Church. Some were less active, others new con-
> verts but they were motivated to spiritually progress. We got
> them together in a stake class and taught them the gospel.
> Rather than emphasizing the temple, we stressed a better
> relationship with our Heavenly Father and his Son, Jesus
> Christ. Our careful selection process assured success, and the
> majority of these couples did become active and go to the
> temple.
>
> Let me share an experience or two. We had a brother in
> one of the wards who didn't attend any meetings. His wife
> was not a member. She was somewhat hostile, so we could
> not send home teachers to the home.
>
> The bishop approached this brother by telling him that the
> brother had a relationship with the Savior he needed to
> expand and enlarge. The brother explained to the bishop the
> problem with his nonmember wife, so the bishop talked to
> her, emphasizing the same approach—a relationship with the
> Lord that needed to be expanded. She was still not receptive
> but was happy to learn that Latter-day Saints believed in
> Christ, and consequently dropped some of her defenses.
>
> Success did not come immediately, but those who visited
> the home kept stressing the couple's relationship with the
> Lord. In time she became friendly, and finally consented to
> come with her husband to the stake class taught by members
> of the high council. We stressed the covenant one makes at
> baptism and other covenants. Eventually she became a mem-

ber of the Church and he became a productive priesthood leader. Today all of their family is active in the Church.[10]

Howard practiced in his stake leadership the same kinds of people skills that made him a successful attorney and businessman, resulting in intense loyalty among his associates. "You felt appreciated and wanted and needed," observes Alicebeth Ashby, who served as president of the Pasadena Stake Young Women's Mutual Improvement Association. "He made people responsible when they received a calling, but if they needed his opinion or counsel, he was always there. We knew that we had his complete support and interest."

Sometimes after the formal business of stake presidency and high council meetings had been covered, Howard would take an opportunity to counsel his associates on Church policies and procedures. Elder Cree-L Kofford of the Seventy, who presided over the Pasadena Stake several years later, described a typical scene: "Sounds of gentle laughter as the clock strikes midnight, the meeting long since concluded, and President Hunter, mellowing with each passing moment, removes his coat and, while bishoprics and high councilors refuse to leave, talks into the night about matters of the spirit."

Ernie Reed, who served as assistant stake clerk, recalls several of these lessons. Once Howard informed the group, "There are no page numbers in the hymnal. There are hymn numbers, not page numbers. Now please refer to them as hymn number so-and-so." On another occasion he told them, "We don't thank people for jobs they do in the Church. They're not jobs. They're callings, and they're wonderful. We're glad to have callings—we appreciate them. And we don't say 'a job well done.' We say that a calling is well served." To both stake and ward officers, he counseled, "You have to be on the stand at the beginning of the meeting—you can't come in late. You need to be there, sitting quietly and reverently, to set the example."

"He had a list of little things like that," Brother Reed con-

Howard W. Hunter and his counselors in the Pasadena Stake presidency, with
their wives: Richard and Miriam Summerhays, A. K. and Beth Berry, Howard
and Claire Hunter, Daken and Olene Broadhead, Vera Jean and Talmage Jones

cluded, "homely little things that were important to him. And our meetings really toned up."

Though the meetings of the stake presidency and high council often went until late in the evening, no one wanted to leave. They could feel the love and concern of their stake president for them and for all members of the stake. "I've been acquainted with many stake presidents," one of them commented when Howard was called to the Twelve, "but I don't know of any other who knows the order of the Church, the order of the priesthood, and how things should be done in wards and stakes better than President Hunter."[11]

Daken K. Broadhead, who served twice as a counselor to Howard in the Pasadena Stake, characterized him as a good executive: "He delegated and he also followed through. He was very good with details. He was slow to take action or make a decision because he wanted to make sure the decision was right. He liked to take time to look at all angles."

Howard's standards of excellence in his own life were reflected in the activities and accomplishments of his stake. The stake sponsored dances or other social activities nearly every week, Sister Ashby remembers. "The hall would be beautifully decorated, and there would be lace cloths and fresh flowers on the tables. Young and old alike participated and danced with each other. Howard and Claire often stayed late to help do the dishes and clean up the hall."

Richard S. Summerhays, who served in the stake presidency and later succeeded Howard as stake president, summarized the feelings of many: "He praised people for their accomplishments and let them rise to high expectations. We were proud of the stake because he was proud of us."

These sentiments were expressed by Betty C. McEwan, who wrote about Howard Hunter, her "most influential teacher," for the *Church News:*

"I have always observed that this man loved others by putting them in high priority, by listening to understand, and by sharing his experiences with others, which was one of his great enjoyments. He has taught me to understand the importance of these virtues and to feel the joy in practicing them to a great measure.

"I vividly remember sitting in his living room one Saturday morning. I remember my anticipation to realize my stake president was going to interview me for a temple recommend. The Los Angeles Temple was to be dedicated and ready for work to be done, and I was excited to be involved. This great leader taught me how rewarding, strengthening, and comfortable an interview can be. . . . I have been blessed knowing this man of purpose, of dedication, of discipline."[12]

Donna Dain, who was Howard's legal secretary from 1952 to 1960 and a member of his stake, remembers times when they read the scriptures together during their lunch hour. He also played matchmaker when he introduced her to Karl Snow, a friend of his son John. Donna and Karl's marriage in the Salt Lake Temple in January 1960 was the first one Howard performed in the Salt Lake Temple as a member of the Quorum of the Twelve Apostles, and they named their youngest son Howard Hunter Snow.

Looking Forward to More Leisure Time

IN EARLY 1958 Howard took in his first law partner. Gordon L. Lund, a graduate of Stanford University Law School and former employee of Union Oil Company, lived in Arcadia Ward and shared an office with another lawyer. When the man died, Gordon decided he did not like working alone, so he called his stake president, Howard Hunter, and asked if he knew of an attorney who might want to join him. Howard replied that he was in somewhat the same situation—he had been thinking of tapering off in his own practice and was considering taking in an associate. "Well, let me be the first to apply right now, on the phone," Gordon said.

They met and agreed to create a firm under the name Hunter and Lund. They merged their client list and were together long enough that when Howard left the firm a few years later, the transition went smoothly and no clients were lost.

Now that he had a law partner, Howard began to look forward to traveling and spending more time with his family. In the summer of 1958, Richard received his mission call to the South Australia Mission and was scheduled to arrive in the field the same day John was released. Howard obtained permission from the Church Missionary Committee for him and Claire to accompany Richard to Australia and then pick up John and take him on a tour around the world. After completing a week's training at the missionary home in Salt Lake City, Richard returned to Los Angeles to join his parents for their journey. They flew on July 2 to Honolulu, where they visited for a few days before flying on to Fiji, New Zealand, and Australia, where they were reunited with John.

After saying farewell to Richard, the threesome—Howard, Claire, and John—traveled over the next two months to many exotic and exciting places, often arriving in a new city or country late at night and beginning their sightseeing early the next morning. By the time they returned home in mid-September, they had visited more than twenty countries, including the

Howard, Claire, and John at the Taj Mahal in India

Philippines, Hong Kong, Thailand, Cambodia, Burma, India, Pakistan, Egypt, Turkey, Greece, Italy, Switzerland, France, Belgium, and the British Isles, where they attended the dedication of the London Temple.

Howard had had an almost insatiable curiosity about the world since childhood, when he had taken imaginary travels with his father in their living room in Boise. His band tour of the Orient had only served to whet his appetite for adventure. Though he and Claire were tired but invigorated when they returned home, they had discovered how much they enjoyed traveling, and they looked forward to exploring more of the world together.

8

Called to the Quorum of the Twelve

WHEN HE RETURNED from his mission in September 1958, John Hunter resumed his pre-law studies at Brigham Young University. He also resumed his courtship of Louine Berry, daughter of A. Kay Berry, Howard's close friend and former counselor in the stake presidency. "December 27, two days after Christmas, was an important date in our family—the marriage of our oldest son," Howard recorded in his history. "On that morning, John, Louine, her parents, and Claire and I, with a few close friends and relatives, went to the Los Angeles Temple. All of us went through the temple session and Louine received her endowments. At the conclusion they were sealed in a lovely ceremony."

Five days later, on New Year's Day, the newlyweds returned to school in Provo. "After the rush of the holidays," Howard wrote, "1959 commenced as to what appeared to be a quiet year."

This prediction seemed to be coming true, as Howard found little during the first nine months of 1959 to record in his history. After a break following their return from their world tour, Claire resumed her college studies that February, enrolling in a biology class at Pasadena City College.[1] Howard's law practice with his new partner, Gordon Lund, seemed to be going smoothly, and he continued to diversify and expand his business investments with Gilles DeFlon.

Having traveled so extensively the year before, Howard

Claire, Howard, Louine, and John, with the Hunters'
first grandchild, Robert Mark

and Claire now enjoyed staying closer to home. In August they were in Provo for Louine's graduation from BYU, and less than a month later, on September 17, Howard wrote: "This was a red letter day in the Hunter family. The first grandchild, Robert Mark, was born at Provo."

General conference was scheduled for October 9, 10, and 11 that fall, and Claire left for Utah a week early so she could get acquainted with the new arrival. Howard and Bishop Eric J. Smith of the East Pasadena Ward took an early-morning flight from Los Angeles on Friday, October 9, arriving in Salt Lake City at 10:45. They went directly to the Salt Lake Tabernacle, where the first session of the 129th semi-annual general conference of the Church was half over. Howard wrote in his journal:

"After the conclusion of the first session, I talked with a number of people around the tabernacle grounds and then walked across the street to the Hotel Utah. Daken K. Broadhead, my counselor in the Pasadena Stake presidency, was waiting for me in front of the hotel. He told me that Sister Clare Middlemiss, secretary to President McKay, had been looking for me . . . and had asked him to have me come to the office of President McKay as soon as possible. He [Daken] said to me, 'You know there is a vacancy in the Council of the Twelve.' I said, 'I know you are joking with me. The First Presidency has asked me to secure some information for them, and I presume they want a report.'"

Howard walked quickly next door to the Church Administration Building, where Sister Middlemiss ushered him into President McKay's office. His account continues:

"President McKay greeted me with a pleasant smile and a warm handshake and then said to me, 'Sit down, President Hunter, I want to talk with you. The Lord has spoken. You are called to be one of his special witnesses, and tomorrow you will be sustained as a member of the Council of the Twelve.'

"I cannot attempt to explain the feeling that came over me. Tears came to my eyes and I could not speak. I have never felt so completely humbled as when I sat in the presence of this great, sweet, kindly man—the prophet of the Lord. He told me what a great joy this would bring into my life, the wonderful association with the brethren, and that hereafter my life and time would be devoted as a servant of the Lord and that I would hereafter belong to the Church and the whole world. He said other things to me but I was so overcome I can't remember the details, but I do remember he put his arms around me and assured me that the Lord would love me and I would have the sustaining confidence of the First Presidency and the Council of the Twelve.

"The interview lasted only a few minutes, and as I left I told him I loved the Church, that I sustained him and the other members of the First Presidency and the Council of the Twelve, and I would gladly give my time, my life, and all that I possessed to this service. He told me I could call Sister Hunter and tell her. . . . I went back to the Hotel Utah and called Claire in Provo, but when she answered the phone I could hardly talk."

Finally he managed to tell Claire what had happened, and she said she would come to Salt Lake City with John and Louine later that afternoon.

Howard returned to the afternoon session of conference with Daken Broadhead—"but I soon became so nervous," he said, "that I left the tabernacle and went for a walk up the hill to the state capitol building and got back just before the conclusion of the session."

That evening Howard and John went, as previously planned, to the annual football game between the University of Utah and Brigham Young University while Claire and Louine stayed at the hotel with the baby. "I don't know very much what happened at the football game because I couldn't concentrate on it," Howard wrote. John remembers that though it was an exciting game, his father stared at the fifty-yard line the entire time. (The University of Utah won, 20 to 8.) That night Howard and Claire talked for a long time before retiring.

At the Saturday morning session of conference, President J. Reuben Clark Jr. read the names of the authorities of the Church for the sustaining vote. "My heart commenced to pound as I wondered what the reaction would be when my name was read," Howard said. "I have never had such a feeling of panic. One by one the names of the Council of the Twelve were read and my name was the twelfth."

After completing the business portion of the meeting and addressing the congregation, President Clark invited Howard to take his place with the Twelve on the stand.

"I have never seen so many news photographers, and flashbulbs were going off like fireworks," Howard recalled. "My heart increased its pounding as I climbed the steps. Elder Hugh B. Brown moved over to make room for me and I took my place as the twelfth member of the Quorum. I felt the eyes of everyone fastened upon me as well as the weight of the

Howard W. Hunter,
sustained to the
Quorum of the
Twelve Apostles
October 10, 1959

world on my shoulders. As the conference proceeded I was most uncomfortable and wondered if I could ever feel that this was my proper place."

When they arrived at the Tabernacle for the Sunday morning session of conference, Howard and Claire for the first time had assigned seats: he on the stand with the other General Authorities, and she in the nearby section reserved for General Authorities' wives. That afternoon President McKay called on Howard as the concluding speaker, an experience that to the new apostle was both frightening and humbling. After briefly reviewing his life and bearing his testimony, he concluded:

"I do not apologize for the tears that come to my eyes on this occasion because I believe that I face friends, my brethren and sisters in the Church, whose hearts beat the same as mine today in the thrill of the gospel and in service to others. President McKay, I want you to know, and all of the membership of the Church to know, that I accept, without reservation, the call which you have made of me, and I am willing to devote my life and all that I have in this service. Sister Hunter joins me in this pledge."

On Tuesday Howard met with President Moyle and then President McKay to learn what was expected of him. Both suggested that for the time being he should come to Salt Lake City each week to attend the Thursday temple meeting of the First Presidency and the Twelve, but that he should continue to live in Southern California until he could wind up his business affairs and law practice and fulfill any pending obligations and commitments.

That afternoon Elder Spencer W. Kimball took him to the temple to show him the council rooms and explain the procedures of the meetings. "I appreciated this orientation because I feel so strange," Howard wrote.

For Howard W. Hunter, Thursday, October 15, was a day he would never forget. That morning, at the weekly temple meeting of the First Presidency and the Twelve, President McKay delivered the traditional apostolic charge to the newest apostle, a fourfold charge to bear testimony to the world as a special witness of Jesus Christ; to be one in purpose with his brethren; to subordinate all other responsibilities and duties to those he would have as an apostle; and to hold in strictest confidence all matters discussed by the council.

In his response to this charge, Howard declared, "This calling shall take precedence above all other things, and I am willing to set aside all other things for anything that is asked of me in the spirit of devotion and humility to this call."

The Brethren present then placed their hands on his head, and President McKay was voice in ordaining him an apostle, which office, Brigham Young explained in 1861, "puts him in possession of every key, every power, every authority, communication, benefit, blessing, glory, and Kingdom that was ever revealed to man."[2] President McKay then set him apart as a member of the Quorum of the Twelve.

Elders Harold B. Lee and Marion G. Romney, who were on official assignments overseas, sent cablegrams expressing their support. Elder Romney, in Austria, also sent a letter to Howard in which he said, "In a conversation Sunday evening Ida asked me who I thought would be appointed to fill the vacancy in the quorum. I told her, of course, that I did not know but that I had a feeling it would be someone from California and that Howard Hunter was in my judgment the man. You will therefore know that my whole soul responded with joy to the good news. I congratulate you and welcome you into full fellowship."

A Time of Transition and Change

HOWARD WILLIAM HUNTER became the seventy-fourth man in this dispensation to be ordained an apostle. The vacancy in the Twelve had resulted when Elder Henry D. Moyle was called to serve in the First Presidency in June 1959 after the death of President Stephen L Richards, first counselor in the Presidency. President J. Reuben Clark Jr., who had been second counselor, became first counselor to President McKay, and Elder Moyle was called as second counselor.

At fifty-one, Elder Hunter was only the third apostle born in the twentieth century, and the youngest member of the Twelve at the time of his call. Next youngest was Richard L. Evans, fifty-three, who sat three seats from him in the council room in the Salt Lake Temple. Between them were eighty-five-year-old George Q. Morris and seventy-five-year-old Hugh B. Brown. Eighty-three-year-old Joseph Fielding Smith, an apostle since 1910, was president of the Twelve.

The average age of the twelve men in the quorum at that time was sixty-seven, with nine of them still in their fifties and sixties. Over the next decade the decisions and leadership of these men would have significant and far-reaching impact on the Church.[3]

Members of the Quorum of the Twelve Apostles from October 1963 to January 1970: (seated) Ezra Taft Benson, Mark E. Petersen (on arm of chair), President Joseph Fielding Smith, LeGrand Richards; (back) Gordon B. Hinckley, Delbert L. Stapley, Thomas S. Monson, Spencer W. Kimball, Harold B. Lee, Marion G. Romney, Richard L. Evans, Howard W. Hunter

According to authors James B. Allen and Glen M. Leonard, the 1950s had been an "important time of transition for the Church" when

> new directions in missionary work, youth programs, temple activity, and educational programs as well as a renewed emphasis on building up the Church outside America laid the foundation for the two most dramatic developments of the next three decades: genuine internationalism and major administrative innovations that would help the Church accommodate both internationalism and growth. . . .
>
> As the Church entered the 1960s with over 1,600,000 members around the world, it had long outgrown the simple administrative structure established in the days of Joseph Smith. Three kinds of Church organizations actively served the needs of the Saints. One was the regular ecclesiastical system, with its well-defined chain of priesthood authority. Another consisted of the auxiliaries . . . each of which had its

own general board and officers, published its own manuals, held its own conferences, determined its own courses of study, and published its own magazine. A third type of organization included a multitude of professional services necessary to carry out the normal functions of the Church—and these would continue to burgeon.[4]

At the time of Elder Hunter's call in 1959, there were approximately 1.6 million Latter-day Saints in 290 stakes and 50 missions. By far the largest membership was in the western United States, and there were only three stakes outside the U.S.: two in Canada and one in Auckland, New Zealand. Within the next twelve years the number of members, of stakes, and of missions would all double, with much of that growth coming in Latin America and other areas far from Church headquarters.

The inauguration of jet airplane service just ten months before his ordination and the development of satellite transmission of television and other communications media heralded a new age. General officers could more easily visit, communicate with, and provide training and support to the members, the majority of whom, particularly outside the western United States, would be converts.

Howard W. Hunter, the newest apostle, would be in the forefront of those involved in these dramatic developments.

Preparing to Move to Utah

WHEN HOWARD and Claire returned to Los Angeles by airplane Thursday evening after his ordination, they were greeted at the airport by his proud parents, Will and Nellie Hunter; his sister, Dorothy Rasmussen, and her daughters Susan and Kathy; and J. Talmage Jones, his good friend and former counselor in the stake presidency.

After a joyful reunion, the weary couple returned home, where, Howard wrote in his journal, "we commenced to realize the change that has come about in our lives and in our plans by the happenings of this week. We have enjoyed our home in California and our family life with our sons. The thought of changing our residence and leaving our many friends had never occurred to us. We are now faced with the reality of getting our affairs in order so that we can respond to the call that has come to us."

At the office early the next morning, Howard found a large stack of mail, phone messages, and telegrams from well-wishers. His call to the Twelve had been reported in the major Los Angeles newspapers, some with front-page stories. One longtime client who called to congratulate him commented that "the Church must have made a very attractive offer" to entice him to leave his successful law practice and become a full-time church official.

"Most people do not understand why persons of our religious faith respond to calls made to serve or the commitment we make to give our all," Howard wrote in his journal. "I have thoroughly enjoyed the practice of law, but this call that has come to me will far overshadow the pursuit of the profession or monetary gain."

The next week he began a regimen that would last for many months: boarding a train in Los Angeles on Wednesday after a day at the office, traveling overnight to Salt Lake City, attending the weekly temple meeting of the First Presidency and the Twelve, taking care of business matters accumulating on his desk at the Church Administration Building, then taking an overnight train back to Los Angeles and going directly to his law office for another full day's work. Sometimes he varied the routine by leaving California on Tuesday evening, and occasionally he took a late-night flight rather than the train one or both ways.

It wasn't long before he was also assigned to visit stake conferences on weekends, and he continued to serve as stake president until the Pasadena Stake conference the last weekend in November, when President Joseph Fielding Smith came to reorganize the stake presidency.[5] After the conference

Howard wrote in his journal: "This has been the most enjoyable experience of my life. I have loved the work and the people I have worked with. I was called to serve as stake president on February 26, 1950, and this is the 40th quarterly conference I have conducted. . . . People were very kind to me afterward, and as I went to my office to get my hat, I had a big lump in my throat."

Assignments continued to come his way, including a 1959 Christmas address on the NBC "Faith in Action" radio program, two addresses for a special youth fireside series sponsored by the Church beginning in January 1960, and the setting apart of many stake presidencies and bishoprics in Southern California.

On Monday, January 2, he wrote: "All of the Church problems in Southern California come to my desk. I went to the office but got very little done because the phone rang continuously. It is easier for people down here to reach me by telephone than to communicate with the General Authorities in Salt Lake City."

On February 29 he wrote: "This is a day that comes only every four years and it might have been omitted this year for all that I got accomplished. I went to the office but was interrupted by so many details that I got very little done."

Howard's activities during and immediately after general conference in April 1960 illustrate his hectic schedule and the boundless energy required to keep up with the demands on him. Conference sessions were held on Sunday, April 3, and Tuesday and Wednesday, April 5 and 6.[6] Instead of speaking in a general session, he was assigned to speak on the nationwide "Church of the Air" broadcast preceding the Tabernacle Choir broadcast and Sunday morning session of conference. That evening he also addressed the semiannual Sunday School conference.

On Wednesday evening, April 6, he spoke at a ward dinner, and on Thursday he went to meetings, then worked until late in his Salt Lake City office. He boarded a plane for Los

Angeles at three o'clock Friday morning and went directly to his law office from the airport. Early Saturday morning he flew to Oregon for a stake conference, returning late Sunday evening.

He worked at his office until nearly midnight on Monday and until nine o'clock Tuesday evening, when he went to the airport for the late-night flight to Salt Lake City. After two full days of meetings Wednesday and Thursday, he took the overnight train back to Los Angeles and went directly to the office Friday morning.

Saturday, after doing some yard work and cleaning the swimming pool at home, he visited a sick friend, worked in his office for two hours, and attended quarterly conference meetings of the Los Angeles Stake. On Sunday he had an early breakfast with his parents, attended a preconference meeting and the two general sessions of the stake conference, and went to Dorothy's home for a birthday party for his father.

All this time Claire was in Salt Lake City looking for a home.

On Saturday, July 2, Howard's history records: "Today I finished most of my work at the office. Nearly all of the pending matters are completed. I was alone in the office today with the realization that my practice of law was now at an end. I made notes on a number of files and left them on the desk for Gordon [Lund]. I had a sick feeling as I left the office. I have enjoyed the practice of law and it has been my life for the last number of years, but in spite of this I am pleased and happy to respond to the great call which has come to me in the Church."[7]

Though Howard indicates that he had completed his work at the office, he went there to take care of business matters nearly every day he was in California until he and Claire moved to Salt Lake City in April 1961. The law firm of Hunter and Lund, under Gordon Lund's direction, continued to handle the legal work of its clients for several years thereafter, and Howard often visited the office when he was in Los

Angeles on a church assignment or to attend meetings of the
Watson Land Company board of directors. And while he
would not actively practice law in Utah, he was qualified: on
January 29, 1963, he was admitted to the Utah State Bar.

Travels and Assignments

IN THE SUMMER OF 1960 Richard Hunter was to be released
from his mission in Australia. Howard and Claire had long
been making plans to meet him and take him on a world tour
similar to the one they had taken with John after his mission
ended in 1958.

Now, with his call to the Twelve, Howard was reluctant to
be away for two months, but President McKay intervened and
insisted that he go ahead with his plans. And so, on July 4,
1960, the Hunters began their second world tour, which combined sightseeing with official and unofficial visits with
the Saints nearly everywhere they went. After five days in
Hawaii, they went on to Japan for a district conference, to Tai-
wan, and to Hong Kong for another district conference. They
were joined by Richard, who had flown there after he was
released from his mission.

From Hong Kong, the threesome flew to Saigon, capital of
South Vietnam, where they met with LDS servicemen and
other Latter-day Saints who were working there. At a sacrament meeting with these members, Howard organized a
group and set apart the leaders, after which the members par-
took of the sacrament and held a testimony meeting. That year
Communist-led guerrillas, known as the Vietcong, began
intensifying their fighting against the South Vietnamese, and
within months after the Hunters were there, the country was
wracked by full-scale war and devastation.

The travelers' next destination was Phnom Penh, capital of
Cambodia (which would also soon become embroiled in war
with the Vietcong), where Claire had taken pictures two years
earlier of two little girls at a temple. They managed to find the

schoolteacher of one of the girls and asked him to give the pictures to the children.

Continuing their whirlwind journey, the three tireless travelers flew to Bangkok, Rangoon, Calcutta (where Claire broke her wrist in a fall), New Delhi, Bombay, Cairo, Jerusalem, Beirut, Istanbul, Athens, Rome, Venice, Vienna, Zurich, Bern, Geneva, Paris, Amsterdam, London, and New York, arriving home late in the evening on Monday, September 5.

True to form, Howard did not take time to recover from jet lag. He worked all day on Tuesday and Wednesday, then flew to Salt Lake City Wednesday evening. Because of engine trouble, his plane was delayed in Las Vegas, and he didn't reach his destination until 4:30 Thursday morning. "The night was so far gone by that time that I went to the office without going to bed," he reported. After the temple meeting on Thursday, he flew to Great Falls, Montana, to meet Elder Delbert L. Stapley, and they drove to Lethbridge, Alberta, where they held meetings for two days to divide Lethbridge Stake and organize the new Taber Stake. After the stake conference sessions Sunday, Howard flew back to Great Falls, arriving just before midnight. Early the next morning he flew to Salt Lake City, spent a few hours in his office, and then returned to Los Angeles. And two days later he was on a late evening flight again, heading back to Salt Lake City.

In addition to stake assignments, Howard was quickly absorbed in general committee and board assignments, such as the Church personnel committee,[8] the general welfare committee, the general priesthood committee, the missionary committee,[9] the BYU board of trustees, the Church board of education, and several *ad hoc* groups, as well as adviser to the Sunday School and the Primary organizations. His assignments would change from time to time, with others added and some taken away. But one thing was certain: the load never lessened.

One of the most sensitive and time-consuming assignments came on November 17, 1960, when President Moyle called him to his office and handed him a letter appointing him to review for the First Presidency divorce clearances— petitions from individuals who had been divorced and who were seeking clearance to receive a temple recommend. President Clark had previously handled this assignment, but because of ill health he had had to be relieved of the responsibility. President Moyle told Howard the assignment was being given to him because of his knowledge and experience in handling the legal aspects of these matters.

Many times in the coming weeks, months, and then years, Howard noted in his journal long hours spent reviewing the applications. A year after he received this assignment, he reported to the First Presidency that he had reviewed approximately 2,600 cases. About that time a ruling was made that divorces that occurred before baptism would no longer need to be cleared, and Howard now recommended "that bishops and stake presidents be allowed to determine worthiness of divorced persons to go to the temple and that the First Presidency clear only those divorces which involved a temple sealing." The recommendation was unanimously approved. "This will reduce the number of applications and will make the work much lighter," he commented.

That didn't necessarily follow, however. The workload increased in June 1962 when, in addition to the divorce clearances, he was assigned to review requests for cancellations of sealings. "The endless chain of these cases continues day after day," he wrote a few months later. He had this assignment until February 1970.

"Glad to Be in Our Own Home"

DURING HIS FIRST eighteen months as a General Authority, because of his many trips to Salt Lake City and to stake conferences and his two-month world tour, Howard was away from home as much as he was there. When he traveled between Los Angeles and Salt Lake City by train, he often did paperwork in his roomette until late before retiring for a few hours' sleep, and he usually went straight to the office upon arrival. If he was in Salt Lake City overnight or longer, he stayed with relatives or at the Hotel Utah.

He and Claire began looking at homes and building lots soon after he was called to the Twelve, and she accompanied him to Utah several times to do some exploring on her own while he attended meetings.

Before they could make a commitment, however, they had to sell their home in California. Howard, always handy with tools, began making repairs to the house and sprucing up the yard so the property would attract prospective buyers. In February 1961 they finally accepted an offer. By then they had decided to build a new home in Salt Lake City, so they were grateful when President Bryan Bunker of the California Mission offered to temporarily rent them his home on the city's east bench.

The movers came and loaded the van on April 17, and by early evening, after saying goodbye to their neighbors and to John and Louine, Howard and Claire were on their way to Utah. He wrote, "We drove through the night and just before daybreak a police officer stopped us and gave me a citation for exceeding the speed limit. This was our welcome to Utah."

The couple soon settled into their rented home and began getting acquainted with their neighborhood, ward, and community. A few months later they selected a building lot in the new Oak Hills subdivision high in the foothills east of the city, only a ten-minute drive from the office. Howard's responsibilities continued to expand, and, after years of commuting in the rapidly growing Los Angeles area, it was wonderful to be able to live close to work.

One thing that did take getting used to was the climate, with four definable seasons and occasional extremes in the weather. In October 1961 Howard wrote, "After dinner tonight I drained the radiators of both of our automobiles and filled them with antifreeze. This is something I have never done before. It seems strange to live in a cold country."

That fall they were delighted when Richard and Nan Greene, whom he had been dating for about five years, decided to get married. On December 8 Howard officiated at their marriage and sealing in the Salt Lake Temple, and that evening Nan's parents, Sullivan and Florence Greene, hosted a dinner for friends and family at a restaurant near their home.

"We are so grateful that both of our sons have been married in the temple and have such fine companions," Howard wrote. "It doesn't seem long since they were little boys, and now they are on their way with their own families. No greater blessing could come to parents than to see their children grow in the faith and have strong testimonies. We feel greatly blessed."

For the Hunters, July 13, 1962, was a Friday the Thirteenth they would never forget. "During the early morning hours there was a terrific thunder and lightning storm," Howard wrote. "The paper said that the amount of rainfall during the one hour exceeded any other one-hour period in the history of Salt Lake City. I had no sooner reached the office when Claire called and said the basement was flooded."

He dashed home and found that a torrent had rushed down the street, over the curb, and through a window well into the basement, bringing with it mud and debris. About eight inches of mud and water covered the basement floor, where their furniture and household goods were stored. "We worked all day long carrying things out of the house and bailing water," he said. "It seemed as though I carried thousands of pails of water." By midnight, with most of the water and mud cleared out, they finally fell into bed, exhausted.

At six the next morning they began opening boxes to assess the damage. Richard and Nan had stored many wedding gifts and other items in the basement, and Howard called them in Provo, where Richard was completing his undergraduate courses prior to entering law school in the fall. They came quickly, and by afternoon "the driveway was covered with wet paper cartons and packing cases which we had emptied.

The new home Howard and Claire designed and built in Salt Lake City

The gardener came in his truck and took them to the dump. The back yard is covered with books, mattresses, and all kinds of things which we have set out to dry in the sun. It is a sad-looking mess."

It took two days to open all the boxes and assess the damage. Among the casualties were a set of *Encyclopedia Britannica* and other books from Howard's extensive collection, including many rare, irreplaceable volumes. "I was heartsick when I discovered my copy of the first edition of the Book of Mormon was completely water-soaked," he noted. "I have prized this book because it has the handwriting of the Prophet Joseph Smith on the front page." He took the water-soaked book to the Church Historian's Office, where the staff managed to save the inside pages, though the cover and binding were ruined. (Later he was able to add another of these extremely rare volumes to his library.)

That fall the Bunkers returned from their mission, and Howard and Claire moved to an apartment three blocks north of the Church Administration Building, on Capitol Hill. Ground was broken that month for their new home, and over the next year they shopped in Salt Lake City and Los Angeles for lighting fixtures, hardware items, carpets, marble and glass, furniture, bookshelves, plants, and other furnishings and accessories.

On July 22, 1963, nearly four years after Howard was called to the Twelve, he and Claire moved into a beautiful, spacious home designed and built to their specifications, with a breathtaking view of the Salt Lake Valley. "We are glad to be in our own home at last," he exulted.

9

Bearing Witness to the World

SECTION 107 of the Doctrine and Covenants, a revelation on the priesthood given through the Prophet Joseph Smith on March 28, 1835, mentions several specific duties of members of the Quorum of the Twelve Apostles. They are to be "special witnesses of the name of Christ in all the world" (vs. 23); to serve as "a Traveling Presiding High Council . . . to build up the church, and regulate all the affairs of the same in all nations" (vs. 33); to go out, "holding the keys, to open the door by the proclamation of the gospel of Jesus Christ" (vs. 35); and "to ordain evangelical ministers," or patriarchs (vs. 39).

As a result of his around-the-world tours with his wife and sons, by the end of 1960 Howard Hunter had already been in some two dozen nations, a good introduction to extensive travels that would take him to nearly every country in the world over the next three and a half decades. As an apostle, he would bear witness of Jesus Christ, build up the Church, ordain and set apart thousands of leaders, and proclaim the gospel to members and nonmembers alike on six continents and many islands of the seas. The imaginary trips he had taken with his father in their living room in Boise had whetted his appetite to see the world and learn more about the peoples and cultures in it, but never could he have imagined such opportunities and experiences as were now his.

With his insatiable curiosity and his penchant for order

and organization in his life, Elder Hunter prepared and studied in advance of every trip, learning all he could about the
places he would visit and the peoples and cultures he would
encounter. He liked to plan his own itinerary, using airline
flight guides and his own knowledge and memory of how
much time to allow and what was the best route to get where
he was going. He wrote detailed reports in his journal on the
places he visited and the people he met—and often supplied
information to other General Authorities when he learned
they would be traveling to places he had been. Once when a
member of the Twelve mentioned that he would be returning
from South Africa at a particular time, Elder Hunter quickly
told him what airline he would be flying on, what time it
would leave South Africa, what stops it would make, and
when it would arrive at its destination, Rome.

Elder Hunter's journal is peppered with entries similar to
this one dated November 30, 1961: "I worked in the office until
late this evening and then went to the library to see if I could
find any material on Iraq and the Holy Land." This particular
research prepared him for one of his most memorable jour-
neys, the Christmas 1961 vacation he and Claire took with
Spencer and Camilla Kimball to Egypt and the Middle East.
The two apostles summarized their experiences and impressions in a letter they sent from Istanbul to their associates in
the Quorum of the Twelve:

> The three weeks have been full and rewarding. We have
> followed our Father Abraham from Ur of the Chaldees
> through his birth, youth, marriage and escape from the idol-
> atry of the great valley between the two ancient rivers. We
> climbed with him the Ziggurat, wandered through the exca-
> vated city where he probably lived, moved with him up the
> valley to the Babylon site which was to become so great long
> after him.
>
> We picked up his trail in the vicinity of Damascus and
> went with him to Bethel and Hebron and Beersheba and to
> Egypt and back to Mt. Moriah to the Sacrifice of Isaac. We

visited the cave of Machpelah where he was buried with Sarah, Isaac and Rebecca, Jacob and Joseph.

We followed Jacob and Joseph and their families into Egypt and the Israelites back to the Promised Land, through their conquests, through their struggles under the judges, through their greatness under the kings and the magnificence of the reigns of Saul, David and Solomon.

We climbed hills like Samaria, which once were the palaces and courts of splendor and now are plowed fields over fallen columns, shattered towers, broken walls and marble, tile, granite in millions of pieces, each of which could tell stories humorous and sad, tearful and glad; stories of plunder, of worship, of idolatry, of conquest, of broken covenants, shattered hopes and penalties suffered.

We followed the covenant-breaker Israelites to Babylon whose ruins we traversed with much interest, and we felt to sit down "by the waters of Babylon" with them and weep for their transgressions (as a people), which brought them into captivity. . . .

We were in Bethlehem on Christmas Eve where Christ was born. There were some 20,000 others there from every land and of every color, race, language and creed. But when we went down to Shepherds' Field, we were all alone in the dark. That is, it would have been dark but for the bright moonlight and the starry sky. We sang softly to ourselves: "Far, far away on Judea's plains, shepherds of old heard the joyous strains: Glory to God in the highest." Here no mosques nor cathedrals marred the scene and we felt a sweet spirit and could well believe that few changes had taken place here since the holy night.

We followed Joseph, Mary and the child, Jesus, down country possibly through the Gaza Strip and to Egypt and visited the spot in old Cairo where tradition says the family lived while in the Nile city. We climbed the hills of Nazareth where He grew up. We followed them over the Judean hills to Jerusalem to the temple. . . .

We wandered over the hills of miracles around the Sea of Galilee, tramped through the areas of silent rocks which once were cities in which He slept and ate, and preached and performed miracles. We crossed the Blue Galilee which He crossed so many times in boats and on which He walked. We followed Him to the Mediterranean, down the Jordan, up to Caesarea Phillippi and back down to Jerusalem. We sat on many hill tops and other important places and read the scriptures. In and around and through Jerusalem we visited most of the traditional places.

We four walked the few miles from Bethany up to the Mount of Olives and down into Jerusalem—the path He followed so many times. We climbed the hill which could well be Calvary—Golgotha, and sat and lingered to read of the cruel arrest, trial, persecution and crucifixion of our Savior.

We went with the sorrowing crowd down the hill and spent considerable time in the tomb and the garden which are claimed to be the excavated places. We had a good spiritual warm feeling here. We felt sure it could well be the authentic place. And the Gospels had a new meaning as we read them on the spot.

And from the Mt. of Olives we read of the ascension. This was a glorious experience. We traveled literally from Dan to Beersheba, from the trans-Jordan to the Mediterranean. . . . We lived again the history of the Middle East, secular and ecclesiastical. We believe these travels will have made us more aware of the realness of the past; the relationship of the past to the present; and our debt to our Lord whose life and death and sacrifice seem even more real.[1]

In Istanbul, the couples parted, the Kimballs to go to stake conferences in Germany and the Netherlands, and the Hunters, to stake conferences in England and Switzerland and meetings in seven missions. Afterwards the Hunters flew to Berlin, where they were taken to East Berlin, on the other side of the massive cement wall that had recently been erected to divide the city. "Soldiers were patrolling both sides of the wall," Elder Hunter noted. "Although I have read about the tyranny of communism, I had never before realized what freedom really means. My heart goes out to those who live under the tension of constant fear."

After living out of suitcases for six weeks, the two apostles and their wives were eager to get home. They flew from Germany to New York, where Sister Kimball left them and went to visit a son in Albany. The other three made it as far as Grand Junction, Colorado, where their plane was grounded because of dense fog at the Salt Lake airport. With no sleepers available when they boarded a westbound train at 2:10 a.m., they had to sit up all night, arriving in Salt Lake City at 8:30.

Elder Kimball and Elder Hunter hailed a taxi to drop them off at the Salt Lake Temple for the Thursday morning meeting of the First Presidency and the Twelve, and to take Sister Hunter home. In his journal Elder Hunter concluded with this comment: "Traveling is interesting, but in all the world nothing can take the place of home."

The Church and the Workload Grow

AS WONDERFUL as home is, Elder Hunter seldom has had time to enjoy it more than a few days at a time. The number of countries opening up to missionary efforts has increased dramatically since 1960, resulting in unprecedented growth of missions and stakes throughout the world, particularly in Latin America and Asia.

Whereas in earlier decades of the twentieth century a member of the Twelve might receive only a few overseas assignments during his entire ministry, apostles in the last half of the century often find themselves visiting many countries each year. Their assignments include meetings with government officials in areas where the Church has not previously been allowed to function, in order to lay groundwork for future proselyting; overseeing missions and temples and providing training for mission and temple presidents; organizing, dividing, and reorganizing stakes; breaking ground for and dedicating new temples; overseeing the Church's temporal concerns; and building up the Church and strengthening the Saints wherever they go.

The ranks of regional officers began to increase rapidly

soon after Elder Hunter's call to the Twelve, with regional representatives and, for a time, mission representatives called to
provide training for local priesthood leaders. Within a few
years the membership of the First Quorum of the Seventy
increased, and in the late 1980s the Second Quorum of the Seventy was organized. Though some programs were simplified
and even eliminated, the burdens of the First Presidency and
the Quorum of the Twelve grew heavier, requiring extraordinary time and effort to keep up with the needs of a church
whose membership was doubling every few years and whose
reach was extending to nearly every part of the world.

Elder Hunter was in the forefront of these exciting developments. He served on many corporate boards and Church
committees and headed or was adviser to major departments
at Church headquarters. When he wasn't traveling overseas
on extended assignments, he presided at stake conferences in
the United States and Canada most weekends. The rare day
when he had no official assignment, he often went to the office
to catch up on his work. Since the Brethren are usually away
on weekends, they are supposed to take Monday off. Periodically in his journal he noted this fact with comments such as
these:

"President McKay asked all of us to take one day a week
from the office. I have never been able to do so, but I would
like to get my affairs in such shape that I can." (February 5,
1962.)

"The First Presidency has reminded us on several occasions that we should not come to the office on Monday. I
thought I would go in for a little while this morning to catch
up on a few things, but it was after six o'clock this evening
before I finished." (March 14, 1966.)

"One of the resolutions I made for this year was not to go
to the office on Monday as we have been asked to do. I broke
that resolution today but hereafter I will try to do better." (January 4, 1971.)

The work only continued to increase, never to decrease,

Elder Hunter presents to King Taufa'ahau Tupou IV of Tonga a check from the Church for a Tongan hospital

and even as late as 1991 he was still resolving not to work on Mondays: "I think I was the only one of the Council of the Twelve in the office today. As General Authorities we are expected to be free on Mondays, but I have not done so. Perhaps I will not come in to the office on Mondays." (November 11, 1991.)

Warm and Unusual Welcomes

DESPITE HIS HEAVY RESPONSIBILITIES, Elder Hunter apparently thrived on and derived great strength from his associations with the Saints. For many, if not most, who attended conferences at which he presided and spoke, he might be the only General Authority they would ever have an opportunity to meet. Long lines formed after meetings, and more than once he missed a plane connection because he remained to shake every hand. He never appeared rushed; every individual he met gained an impression that he or she was the most important person in Elder Hunter's life at that moment.

The joy of the Saints at having a General Authority among them was especially apparent on the islands of the South Pacific. According to one former stake president in Samoa, "Elder Hunter has a special way with the Polynesian people and is particularly sensitive to cultural differences. In that respect he is like President Kimball."

In Tonga to create the Nuku'alofa Stake in 1968, he and Sister Hunter were welcomed by mission leaders and board members, many other Latter-day Saints, radio and press representatives and photographers, and the student band from the Liahona High School. "As we went down the reception line the band played and the crowd gathered to shake hands with us and put leis around our necks," Elder Hunter wrote. "We have never been welcomed by such a crowd. There must have been at least 250 persons."

During that visit, he and Elder Thomas S. Monson, who accompanied him, met Tonga's King Taufa'ahau Tupou IV. Elder Hunter wrote: "At the appointed time we went to the palace and were ushered to the reception room. The King was seated on a sofa at the end of the room. He arose as we entered, greeted and shook hands with each of us as we were introduced. . . . The King is a very large man. We were told that he weighs over 400 pounds, but he is a very pleasant and cordial man with all of the dignity of royalty. We talked about the Church and Brother Monson conveyed President McKay's best wishes."

Until her health made it impossible for her to travel in the late 1970s, Claire usually accompanied Howard when he visited the Saints in various parts of the world. On this trip to Tonga, President Monson recalls, she and Sister Frances Monson visited Relief Society sisters and Primary children. "She would take those sweet little Tongan children in her arms and put one on each knee as she spoke to them," he said, "and then explained to the teachers of the Primary how blessed and privileged they were to have the opportunity of teaching such precious little children. She knew the worth of a human soul."[2]

After one trip to Australia and the South Pacific, Elder Hunter told a *Church News* reporter that a mission president had warned him, "I hope you have a strong neck." The reporter explained, "This observation was thoroughly brought home when the members in Papeete and surrounding islands greeted [Elder Hunter], shaking hands and placing 'shell leis' about his neck. . . . By the time the greetings were over, some 50 pounds of shell necklaces had been draped about the necks of the visitors."[3]

Elder Hunter did not like being the center of attention, but he always enjoyed meeting and being with people. In the South Seas he was honored many times at special ceremonies, such as this one in Fiji in 1969: "By an elaborate ceremony, I was presented with a tabua, which is the highest honor that can be paid to a king or a visiting dignitary. A tabua is a whale's tooth with braided sennit [a braided cord or fabric] to be worn around the neck. They are of such importance that they cannot be taken from the islands without special permission. I was later given a letter from the Secretary of Fijian Affairs in Her Majesty's Service [granting permission] to remove the tabua from the colony."

Another elaborate ceremony, typical of several such ceremonies in the islands, occurred when he was in Samoa in 1974 to organize the Upolo Stake:

"Nearly one hundred warriors sat in the line extending on each side of the prince, who sat at the kava[4] bowl, and about sixty chiefs sat in the group behind the bowl—nearly all of the high chiefs of the south part of the island. . . . The ceremony commenced by the speeches of greeting from the talking chiefs with all the pomp and splendor of the ancient ceremony. After the preparation of the kava, it was served to the visiting dignitaries by the cupbearer. Then came the time for the giving of gifts. A procession formed to display the twenty-five fine mats that were given as well as many other gifts of roast pigs, a cow, baskets, beads and other things. We were told by some of the people that they had never seen such an elaborate ceremony or so many gifts in all of Samoa."

While Elder Hunter was in Tonga in June 1983 to organize a new stake, the Nuku'alofa Mission president, Pita F. Hopoate, and his wife became parents of a baby boy. Two days later, at a dinner at the mission home, President Hopoate announced that the child had been given the name Howard Hunter-i-Ha'apai Hopoate, or "Four H's" for short.

When Elder Hunter returned to Tonga two months later for the temple dedication, Sister Hopoate brought the baby to the airport so he could see his namesake. He commented, "President Hopoate said his initials are H.H.H.H., but H in Tongan is pronounced Ha, so his initials in Tongan are Ha Ha Ha Ha."

Making the Best of It

EXTENSIVE TRAVEL, often with tight schedules, is at times fraught with problems, frustrations, and surprises. Elder Hunter has typically accepted these with equanimity and even humor, as the following experiences illustrate.

In Tripoli in December 1965, he and Claire checked out of their hotel early Sunday morning and took a taxi to the airport for a flight to Tunis. But when they arrived at the checkout counter, they discovered they had left their passports at the hotel. They called the hotel desk clerk, and he sent the passports to the airport by taxi, but by then the plane had taken off, and another one wouldn't leave until the next morning.

They decided to go back into the city to a U.S. military base to attend sacrament meeting with a servicemen's group, but by the time they found the chapel, the meeting was apparently over. At the hotel where they had stayed the night before, no rooms were available, and they were directed to another one. Elder Hunter wrote: "The room was poor and had no bath, but we were glad to have a place to sleep. This was a day when everything seemed to go wrong, from the weather to missing our flight and also sacrament meeting. We just laughed and tried to make the best of it."

On one occasion he was traveling between the islands of Tonga by fishing boat when "a tropical storm came up, the seas became heavy, the boat pitched and rolled and the rain poured down. We took refuge inside. One by one we became seasick, lost our breakfasts, and went to our cabins. All day long the heavy seas continued. Claire and I were too sick to get out of bed and the others were just as sick." The storm finally subsided during the night. When the yacht docked in the morning, though he was still weak, Elder Hunter cheerfully greeted the Saints who had come to meet him and was ready to hike to the chapel he had come to dedicate.

Changes in plans and schedules are always a possibility in the troubled Middle East. In 1975 Elder Hunter needed to fly from Teheran, Iran, to Israel, a direct distance of about 750 miles, but there were no direct flights because of a strike at El Al, the Israeli airline. After going from one airline office to another, he finally managed to get seats on an Iran Airlines flight to Athens, "where there would be more possibility of getting to Tel Aviv. . . . [But] because the fighting in Beirut has increased, the routing was changed and we went south to Abadan on the Persian Gulf, cleared customs at that point, then continued northwest up the Tigris and Euphrates valleys to Baghdad [Iraq]. The course from there was west across Iraq, Jordan, Jerusalem and the Mediterranean Sea to Athens. . . . Our connecting flight [to Israel] on Air France was to leave at seven o'clock but when that time came it was announced there would be a delay until midnight."

Though he didn't arrive in Tel Aviv until well after midnight, a group of Saints was at the airport to welcome him and take him to his hotel in Jerusalem.

Later that year the Hunters were again in the Middle East and flew from Cairo to Beirut, where they met with branch leaders to discuss the future of the Church in Lebanon. "We were nervous being Americans coming into Beirut on an Egyptian airliner," he said. "There were army tanks and soldiers with sub-machine guns guarding the airport. Some of the glass had been shot out and there was damage from the gunfire in the hijacking last week in which fourteen people were killed. Passengers were taken into the city in buses under military escort."

In Belfast, Northern Ireland, stake leaders took the Hunters on a tour of areas where buildings had been bombed and automobiles burned by the Irish Republican Army.

Elder Hunter faced danger of a different sort in 1971 when he and Sister Hunter stopped over for a day in Panama en route home from South America. "Before going to bed we walked down Central Street. As we passed the entrance to an alley, four . . . men swept down on me with the apparent intention of dragging me into the alley. I dropped to the ground and yelled at the top of my voice. In the few seconds they went through my pockets except the one in which I had my wallet, and they could not wrench my hand away from it. A crowd quickly gathered and the men ran into the dark alley. I was not hurt, although I could feel the effects of the encounter, and nothing was missing except my hotel key. This is a rough place."

After a stake conference one weekend, Elder Hunter revealed in his journal his feelings about another kind of danger a General Authority faces:

It's almost impossible for General Authorities of the Church to keep slender. Every weekend we stay at the home of a stake president, and his wife always goes to every effort to cook, bake and spread the table with an abundance of everything. I never object because I have no dislikes—there is nothing I don't enjoy. Most people like baked ham and fried chicken and so do I, but recently I have had so much that I can't look a pig or chicken squarely in the eye without a guilty feeling for the dislike I feel is commencing to creep in.

Take this weekend, for instance. At the Utah Symphony

dinner Friday evening we were served half of a large fried chicken, more than I could possibly eat. On the flight to Chicago Saturday morning we had large slices of ham for breakfast. At noon on the way to Atlanta the stewardess served us deep-fried chicken stuffed with ham. Between Atlanta and Jacksonville we had a light lunch—chicken and ham sandwiches.

When we got to the _____'s home there was a big dinner ready for us and Sister _____ had baked a beautiful southern ham. This morning I got up and sure enough, Sister _____ was preparing a huge breakfast—fried eggs, hot biscuits, grits, peach preserves and, surely you could guess, the biggest slices of fried ham I have ever seen.

On the flight back to Chicago I wasn't very hungry after such a large breakfast, but they served snacks—open-face sandwiches with sliced chicken and ham. I ate the bread and pickles and left the meat. On the evening flight from Chicago to Salt Lake there is always a big dinner. First the liquor service—I had tomato juice—and then the stewardess asked me if I was ready for dinner. "What are you serving?" I asked. "Beef shishkabob," she said. "That sounds good," I replied, but under my breath I said, "Hallelujah, at last something different." Soon the beautiful dinner was served. On the spit there were three large pieces of ham with two small pieces of beef, onions and peppers sandwiched in between. I enjoyed the beef and then commenced to wish that ham and chicken had been mentioned, among other things, in the 89th Section of the Doctrine and Covenants.

I am grateful for the wonderful people with whom we stay each weekend and I appreciate their goodness to us, but as I passed Dee's Hamburger Stand on the way home, I thought, "Wouldn't a hamburger and a malt make a wonderful banquet?"

"Unto the Ends of the Earth"

IN A REVELATION given through the Prophet Joseph Smith concerning the Twelve Apostles, the Lord said, "Thou shalt

Claire and Howard Hunter surrounded by youth
in native costumes on a street in France

bear record of my name, . . . and thou shalt send forth my word unto the ends of the earth." (D&C 112:4.) As an apostle, Howard Hunter has literally proclaimed the gospel "unto the ends of the earth," through sermons transmitted by way of satellite to the farthest regions of the world and through personal visits to many areas that until well into the twentieth century were inaccessible to the Church's leaders and missionaries.

Elder Hunter's travels have taken him to diverse places throughout the world: to Machu Pichu, the Incan archeological site high in the Andes in Peru, and to the wind- and sand-swept deserts of Africa; to Dachau, the infamous World War II concentration camp in southern Bavaria, and to the Taj Mahal in India; to the Great Wall of China and to the Berlin Wall; to Red Square in Moscow and to Tiananmen Square in

Beijing; to war-torn Beirut and Belfast and to quiet villages and country byways in Scandinavia and Scotland; to Victoria Peak overlooking Hong Kong and to Table Mountain overlooking Cape Town, South Africa; to the desolate outback of Australia and to the bustling, crowded cities of Shanghai, Tokyo, Rio de Janeiro, and Bombay. He has sailed on the canals of Venice, on the Mediterranean Sea, and on the Moscow, Seine, Hudson, Nile, Rhine, and Danube rivers; ridden on cogwheel trains, subways, interurban trains, and the Orient Express, as well as in buses, carts, and rickshaws; and climbed onto horses, camels, and donkeys.

There are few places in the world that he hasn't visited, and few modes of travel and kinds of accommodations that he hasn't experienced. And wherever he has gone, he has taught and strengthened the Saints and reached out to them and to others. He is genuinely interested in people and delights to see old friends as well as make new acquaintances. He has met and conferred with heads of state, government officials, and religious leaders in many nations, and he has mingled and made friends with innumerable people of modest means and position.

In Cairo on a Church assignment, he and Elder Neal A. Maxwell walked many blocks through teeming crowds to find the doorman at a hotel where Elder Hunter had stayed many years earlier. He remembered how kind the doorman had been to him, and he was saddened to learn that the man had died.

In Norway in September 1966, he and Sister Hunter visited Hammerfest, the world's northernmost city, far above the Arctic Circle. A *Church News* article described their adventure: "Hammerfest is difficult to reach by normal transportation. It was originally planned that the visitors would fly to Hammerfest by seaplane. A change in the weather eliminated any possibility of using a plane, as is often the case. It was decided that they should travel by car from Alta, the closest city to Hammerfest with a commercial airport. Snow had started to cover the roads. Several times en route Elder Hunter and Pres. [Leo M.] Jacobsen had to push their car through the snow. When it seemed as if further progress was impossible, a truck came by and towed the car over the summit to Hammerfest."

They finally arrived at ten-thirty that night for a meeting that was to have started at seven o'clock, and found that most of the members had waited. "They had come from a number of places along the north cape and from as far as Kirkenes near the Russian border," Elder Hunter said. The newspaper account concluded that as a result of that visit, "missionaries report a more friendly attitude among the people of the town and a new feeling of strength among the local members."[5]

Elder Hunter is a modest man, unassuming and undemanding, a person who thinks first of others' comfort. He prefers to be accepted as part of the group rather than given special treatment. Young people especially relate to him.

When he was asked to accompany the International Folk Dancers of Brigham Young University on a seventeen-day tour of China in May 1975, he might have traveled first class, but he went economy class with members of the troupe and their advisers. "The flight was full and we were crowded," he commented, but he did not complain about any of the conditions, accommodations, or demanding schedule.

He participated in the dancers' excursions and attended most of their performances, and soon became a favorite companion and friend of each person. In his journal he described in detail the group's itinerary and experiences, adding comments such as these: "After a hilarious evening of entertainment, we got to bed about midnight," and "For an hour I answered questions asked by the students." He characterized members of the troupe as "thirty-two of the most considerate, kind, courteous, happy, spiritual and thoughtful young people I have ever been around. It has been a real pleasure to be with them on this trip."

In Hong Kong, at their last devotional, he told the students he would be glad to relay messages to their mothers if they would give him the telephone numbers. Over the next few weeks, back in his office in Salt Lake City, he fulfilled his promise and made every call.

On another trip with BYU students, he showed that he is a good sport, has a keen sense of humor, and is willing to take risks and endure considerable discomfort. In Israel in 1982, he joined a large group of students, leaders, members of the Jerusalem Branch, and others on a journey to Mount Sinai shortly before Israel turned the Sinai over to Egypt.

The students traveled by bus, while Elder Hunter and his party flew in a small plane "over the sands and the rugged wilderness and mountains of the Sinai Peninsula to a little airport in the desert." The airport, he reported, was under heavy guard. "At several places the Israeli soldiers are dismantling installations and the Egyptian army is moving in and building camps. There was the feeling of being in the midst of a war." The students joined them at the airport in the early evening, and the 128 pilgrims crowded into nearby sleeping quarters for a few hours' rest.

At two o'clock the next morning they boarded buses to go to the base of Mount Sinai. There some of the older people mounted camels while the younger ones began the long hike to the summit. Elder Hunter described the scene:

> It was cool and there was a full moon so the rocky trail was visible without lights. The long caravan commenced its trek passing [St. Catherine's] monastery, rounding the base of Mount Sinai, and starting the assent of the steep mountain on the back side. Riding a plodding, swaying, smelly camel is not what one would call a pleasant experience, but neither is the alternative to climb a mountain over a rough, rocky trail. We continued up the mountain and gradually it got colder and the wind commenced to blow. . . . I was wearing a warm jacket and a hood but my legs hanging over the camel were numb in the bitter cold and there was no feeling in my hands as I held to the saddle horn.
>
> Nearly two hours had passed and we were getting closer to the top. The camels were slipping in the rocks and finally

the drivers made motions that they could go no further. They brought them down so we could dismount. I could hardly walk and the wind was heavy. We plodded forward over the rocks, grateful for the moonlight, and were soon at the base of the seven hundred steps that led to the summit. Struggling up the steps, we came to a shoulder where we could see the top. . . .

Suddenly we noticed it was getting light, and we stood in a crevice in the rocks and watched the sun gradually come into view over the rugged mountains at six o'clock—a sight I will never forget. David [Galbraith] asked, "Shall we put our feet on the summit?" I replied, "I've seen it, that's enough. I can't believe that Moses went beyond this point."

The cold and the wind were too much for me, so we started down the steep descent to where we had left the camels. Words cannot adequately describe what it is like to ride a stiff-legged, swaying camel down Mt. Sinai. Most of the students took a short-cut down the other side of the mountain and cheered us as we arrived at St. Catherine's two hours later.

By now it was warm and we sat in the sun on the sand at the back of the monastery and had a spiritual meeting with all of these wonderful young people. We sang . . . and each of us spoke. I read the accounts from the Old Testament that refer to Mt. Sinai and the Ten Commandments, which now become more real and visible since we have climbed where Moses climbed.

Visiting the Homes of the Saints

SOME OF ELDER HUNTER'S most satisfying experiences have come as he has visited in homes of the Saints. One such occasion occurred in Eastern Europe long before the "iron curtain" was parted. In September 1967, accompanied by Rendell N. Mabey, president of the Swiss Mission, and Sister Mabey, he conducted a conference in Poland, which at that time had just one branch of the Church, a group of twenty-four Saints in the tiny village of Zelwagi. There they were guests of the family of the branch president, Erich Konietz. Elder Hunter wrote:

"When we drove into the yard his wife and four little boys came out to meet us, excited to have the mission president and a General Authority come to visit them. They have a humble, crude little house. The grandparents of Sister Konietz lived in this house and now the fourth generation is living here. There are flies, dogs, cats, chickens, and geese in and out of the house, but the family is happy and they are devoted church members. . . . President and Sister Mabey slept on a couch in the dining room, Claire and I stayed in the bedroom, and the family slept in the children's rooms. There are not many accommodations. Water is brought from the well in the back yard in a pail, and because there is no bathroom, one must find his way by moonlight."

The next evening members of the branch met in the first session of the conference. "Two sisters came from Gliwice in South Poland, 22 hours by train, some [came] from the north on the Baltic Sea, about 20 hours by train, another family seven hours by automobile. This is only the second time the branch has been visited by a member of the Council of the Twelve. Ezra Taft Benson was here in 1946. An evening session of the conference was held in the chapel. . . . Except for the language, it was like a meeting at home. The usual friendly greetings, crying babies, and visiting were prevalent."

After the Sunday morning session, attended by thirty-eight persons, "all of those present walked down to the lake and President Mabey performed three baptisms. . . . We returned to the chapel and confirmed them members of the Church."

When it came time for them to leave, the Mabeys distributed gifts of clothing and other items to the adults and toys and candy to the children. "This was like Christmas because they have so little," Elder Hunter wrote. "Most of them cried when they shook hands with us, and it was a sad parting.

They all stood by the chapel waving as we drove away. I wonder if we will ever see this faithful group of saints again."

While on an assignment in Europe for the Genealogical Society in 1972, Elder and Sister Hunter accompanied Fred Barth, an employe of the society, to Jidvei, a small Romanian village. This was the town where Brother Barth was born, and they were the guests of his nephew, Martin Barth. The accommodations were humble but comfortable, Elder Hunter noted, adding, "but none of the houses have indoor bathroom facilities. I wondered about their loyalty when I found the toilet tissue to be the communist party newspaper."

On the last morning of their three-day stay, Elder Hunter wrote, "bells in the church tower and the crowing of the rooster got us up early—the sun was just breaking over the little village. As I came back from the little house at the rear of the chicken coop, I met Martin returning from the morning milking of the buffalo with milk for our cereal. The cold water in the tin basin took the place of a morning shower and we were ready to meet the day. . . . One by one the members of the family came until they were all there. The parting was sad—they have all been good to us and shared everything they have to make our visit enjoyable. We knew, of course, there would be little chance of ever being together."

Making History Come Alive

As A HISTORIAN, Elder Hunter has visited with interest the places where the Prophet Joseph Smith and the other early apostles lived and preached the message of the restored gospel. And as a genealogist, he has done extensive research on his family lines and visited many of the towns and villages in Europe where his ancestors lived.

In October 1963, Elder and Sister Hunter attended a conference of mission presidents and their wives in Nauvoo, Illinois. One evening the sisters stayed overnight in the old home of President John Taylor, while the brethren went to Carthage to sleep on the floor of the jail where the Prophet Joseph Smith and his brother Hyrum were slain by a mob in June 1844. Elder Hunter wrote:

> After we got ready for bed, we sat in a circle on the beds in the main room of the upper floor of the jail and talked about the events which took place in this room many years ago. President M. Ross Richards [of the Gulf States Mission] is a grandson of Willard Richards, who was with the Prophet Joseph and his brother Hyrum on the day of the martyrdom. He told us of what happened on that day and the details of the tragic event. In the dimly lighted room we could see the stains on the floor from Hyrum's blood, and near us was the window from which Joseph fell after the shots were fired. We sang all the verses of the song, "A Poor Wayfaring Man of Grief," which the Prophet loved and which he asked John Taylor to sing for him just before death brought to a close his mortal mission.
>
> I will never forget this occasion with the brethren in the upper room. President Carroll W. Smith [of the Western Canadian Mission] gave the prayer and we retired for the remainder of the night. He and I slept in the inner jail behind the iron bars.

When his schedule has permitted, Elder Hunter has visited the areas in Europe where his and Sister Hunter's ancestors lived before they immigrated to the United States.

In September 1970, with Fred Barth accompanying them as an interpreter, they rented a car in Prague, Czechoslovakia, and drove to Poland to try to find Droskau and other places important to Claire's family history. They stayed in Zary, near the East German border, in what had formerly been the German city Sorau. From there they drove about seven kilometers to Droskau. They could find no one who spoke German, and in the cemetery they discovered that the German headstones had been knocked over and broken or destroyed after the Polish takeover. In Zary, Elder Hunter reported, "we took pictures of the streets, the city hall building at the town square, where we presume Maria [Reckzeh] went with her children to make

*President Thorpe B.
Isaacson, Elder Hunter,
and President Joseph
Fielding Smith at
Liberty jail in Missouri*

arrangements for emigration, and the train station which was
no doubt there at that time."

Two years later, in April 1972, Elder and Sister Hunter
went to Denmark to visit some of the places where his Danish
ancestors lived. Accompanied by President and Sister Paul L.
Pehrson of the Denmark Mission, they stopped in many villages to take pictures, visit parish churches, and talk with
people. At one town they found the church, still well main-
tained and in use after several centuries, where Elder Hunter's
great-grandfather Morten Rasmussen was christened and
members of his family worshipped.

"This has been a thrilling trip to me to have visited every
city, village and church in Denmark where my Danish ancestors, so far as I have been able to secure records, have been
born, christened, married, and died. . . . This visit makes their

history come alive and their lives become real," he concluded at the end of the whirlwind tour.

On another Scandinavian trip, the Hunters visited places in Norway where the family of his great-grandmother Nilla Pedersen had lived for many generations.

In September 1989 Elder Hunter and his son Richard visited Paisley Abbey, founded in 1163 and believed to be the place where his grandfather John Hunter was baptized a member of the Church of Scotland. They then toured Hunterston Castle, on a thousand-acre estate near Largs on the Firth of Clyde.

10

The Apostolic Ministry, Part 1

THE APOSTLESHIP, Elder Bruce R. McConkie wrote, "carries the responsibility of proclaiming the gospel in all the world and also of administering the affairs of the Church."[1]

Almost as soon as he was ordained an apostle, Howard W. Hunter became deeply involved in helping to oversee the affairs of the Church throughout the world. Many of his assignments came because of his expertise in legal and business matters; others opened to him new fields to explore. Each enlarged his vision of the complexities and needs of the rapidly growing international church.

In one typical year, 1971, he served as Church historian, president of the Genealogical Society, area supervisor of the South Seas and Australian missions and then of the South American missions, chairman of the Polynesian Cultural Center, and president of the New World Archaeological Foundation. He was also a member of the Church's priesthood board, magazines committee, board of education, investment advisory committee, area conference committee, personnel committee, meetinghouse library coordinating committee, BYU board of trustees, and BYU law school committee. In addition, he served on the boards of several financial institutions and insurance companies and the Watson Land Company.

In these assignments, Elder Hunter left his mark, showing an openness to new technology, ideas, and ways of doing things, and an awareness of and sensitivity to the needs and feelings of the individuals with whom he associated. His associates in the Twelve, men who have sat in council with him, traveled with him, and worked with him in ecclesiastical and professional capacities, have commented:

• "He has a way of making people feel at ease. He doesn't dominate them. He is a good listener."

• "When you travel with him, he's always watching to be sure that everybody is taken care of and that nobody is being inconvenienced or put out."

• "He is tough when he needs to be tough, and gracious when he needs to be gracious, and forgiving when he needs to be forgiving."

• "We have never seen him distraught or excited or unhappy with anything. He has a way of seeing that everything is done in the right way, according to the scriptures, according to Church tradition and policy. He is concerned with and sensitive to others. He has charity and a forgiving heart. He is loyal to those over him. He is a student of the gospel, of mankind, of human nature. He has all of the qualities needed to be a leader of mankind and to represent the Lord's work."

• "He has extraordinary patience that comes from great inner peace. You have to have the feeling of love and support from our Father in heaven and the Savior to live a life as selflessly as he does."

These character traits, combined with his astute legal mind, have helped him carry out his many assignments. He has been forthright in his stewardship in administering the affairs of the Church. Under his direction, major advances have been made that have helped to speed up the Lord's work among the Saints and facilitate the Church's mission of proclaiming the fullness of the gospel "unto the ends of the world." (D&C 1:23.) A look at some of his assignments illustrates the scope of his leadership and influence.

The Genealogical Society

A SUBJECT CLOSE to Elder Hunter's heart has always been family history. As a small boy he was curious about his roots and listened with great interest to stories of his pioneer ancestors. As an adult he researched the names, dates, and places necessary to connect his family lines. During the months immediately after his call to the Twelve, when he was commuting each week between California and Utah, he occasionally spent an evening at the Church's genealogical library or visiting cousins in the Salt Lake area with whom he could exchange family-history information.

Thus, Elder Hunter had already been involved in genealogy work when he was named to the board of the Genealogical Society, as the Family History Department was then known, on March 4, 1960. He served on the board until June 16, 1961, and was reappointed December 23, 1963. One month later, on January 21, 1964, he was named president of the society, which position he held until May 25, 1972. He was released from the board on February 14, 1975. During the time in which he served, some of the most significant and far-reaching changes in the history of the organization took place.

These changes came in part as a result of the correlation program. On September 30, 1961, in an address at the general priesthood session of the Church's semiannual general conference, Elder Harold B. Lee reviewed the proposed correlation program and the need for "more coordination and correlation between the activities and programs of the various priesthood quorums and auxiliary organizations," looking toward "the consolidation and simplification of church curricula, church publications, church buildings, church meetings, and many other important aspects of the Lord's work."[2]

A major step affecting genealogy work came fifteen months later, in January 1963, when the priesthood was given responsibilities in four primary areas—missionary work, welfare, home teaching, and genealogy—and the head of the

Elder Hunter, president, and Elder Theodore M. Burton, vice president and general manager of the Genealogical Society

Genealogical Society became a member of the all-church coordinating committee.[3]

At the time, Elder N. Eldon Tanner, who had recently been called to the Quorum of the Twelve after service as an Assistant to the Twelve, was serving as president of the Genealogical Society. Though he headed the society less than a year, under his direction several steps were taken to streamline the organization, look toward implementing newly developed computers and other technology, and make the operation more professional and functional. The society was also incorporated as the Genealogical Society of The Church of Jesus Christ of Latter-day Saints, under the laws of the state of Utah.

Elder Tanner was called to serve as second counselor in the First Presidency in October 1963. That December he appointed Elder Theodore M. Burton, an Assistant to the Twelve, to be vice president and general manager of the society. A month later, in January 1964, the First Presidency appointed Howard W. Hunter to succeed President Tanner as president of the Genealogical Society.

One of the major problems then facing the Genealogical Society was a shortage of names for temple work. Latter-day Saints had been encouraged for decades to research their kindred dead and provide completed family group sheets, which were verified by the Temple Index Bureau before the vicarious temple ordinances could be performed. This was a slow and tedious hand-checking process, and often the information provided was incorrect and the sheets had to be rejected.

Exacerbating the problem of insufficient names available for all who wanted to attend temple sessions was the fact that those who submitted names could, if they wished, have those names placed in reserve for their own families. Otherwise the names went into a temple file for use by patrons who had no family names available.

Though the Saints were frequently encouraged to increase their own genealogical research and not depend upon temple files for names, the deficit continued to increase between the number of names available for temple work and the number of members wishing to attend temple sessions. With Church membership accelerating rapidly, particularly outside the United States, and the possibility that several new temples would be announced in the next few years, the situation was critical, and solutions had to be found as quickly as possible.

The Genealogical Society began microfilming documents and records in its collections in 1938. After World War II, negotiations began that would allow the society to microfilm records throughout the United States and in many other countries. Technology was needed to process the information and make it more readily accessible for both genealogical research and temple files.

The answer was found in computers, which by the early 1960s were rapidly being developed and adapted for use in business, industry, education, and other major institutions. The Genealogical Society had long been studying and experimenting with ways to use the new technology, and by 1962 a program was under way to begin using computers owned and operated by the Advance Planning Department, which did computer work for all Church departments.[4]

As president of the Genealogical Society, Elder Hunter determined to learn about computers. He signed up for a week-long seminar, sponsored by IBM, in San Jose, California, in April 1964. The course included classes in finance and inventory control.

After the first day he wrote in his journal: "I was amazed in having been able to write a computer program in one day without previous experience."

After the fourth day: "This was another long day in class spent in learning the many languages of the computer and the mathematics of the operation. We also learned the functions of various types of storage on tapes, drums and discs, and how to draft the different types of programs."

The next day: "The material is so concentrated and given so rapidly, it keeps one under a constant strain to keep up. It has been so long since I have worked complicated mathematical problems or been subjected to the rigors of the classroom that I am under heavy pressure. The work is given to us as fast as we can absorb it. . . . After learning how to direct the computer to go into memory devices for information, we each drafted a program consisting of complicated inventory problems and ran it out on the computer this evening."

Finally, "This was the last day of the school. The morning session covered a great number of programs for which computers can be used, and after lunch the instructors gave us a look into the future and what we might expect in new data processing equipment."

When discussions and proposals concerning computers came up as the society began converting its voluminous records to electronic retrieval systems, Elder Hunter was prepared to speak knowledgeably and with understanding.

Another of the Genealogical Society's needs was a secure,

permanent repository for microfilms. When Elder Hunter became president of the society in 1963, work was well under way on construction of an unusual storage facility: the Granite Mountain Record Vault, a cavernous, steel-reinforced storage complex excavated deep in a mountainside in the canyon southeast of Salt Lake City where the Saints had obtained the granite to build the Salt Lake Temple nearly a century earlier.

On June 22, 1966, General Authorities and other church officials, business, education, and government leaders, and representatives of the news media toured the facility and then assembled in a large open area for the dedication ceremony. Elder Hunter conducted the services, and President Hugh B. Brown, first counselor in the First Presidency, offered the dedicatory prayer.

Entries from Elder Hunter's journals suggest many discussions on ways to help expedite and refine genealogical work:

"Brother Burton came to my office with George H. Fudge [a longtime employee of the society] and we discussed some revolutionary proposals concerning genealogical research" (September 10, 1965). "Today we commenced the microfilming of the eight hundred thousand family group sheets turned in as the result of last year's genealogical program" (March 15, 1966). "At the Genealogical Society we have been working on a program which will eliminate family group sheets and will lead to a new concept in research and temple work" (June 20, 1967). "Brother Burton, Lyman Tyler and I met to make a recommendation to the presidency on libraries in the wards and stakes with correlation to the branch genealogical libraries" (April 10, 1968).

As a result of these and other studies and discussions, several significant and far-reaching changes were made regarding the Church's genealogical operations and temple work. These included the following:

• The order in which vicarious temple ordinances were to be performed became more flexible. Traditionally, ordinances had been done in behalf of a deceased person in the same order in which they were done by the living: baptism, confirmation, priesthood ordination, endowment, marriage, and sealing of children to parents. Under the new guidelines, the greatest importance was placed on having the vicarious work done; thus, children could be sealed to parents even if the names of the parents were not yet known (by using the word *parents* in the ordinance).

• In the past a member had had to obtain a separate temple recommend for each temple visited. This requirement was changed so that worthy members were issued one temple recommend, renewable each year and accepted at all temples.

• Forms for submitting names for temple work were simplified. Under the new Genealogical Information and Name Tabulation program (nicknamed GIANT), members could submit single-entry forms with individual names, without having to wait until the individual could be linked to a family.

• Temple ordinances could now be performed for individuals after they had been dead a year without the necessity of inquiring as to worthiness to determine if there had been an excommunication or other transgression that had not been resolved prior to death.

• The Pedigree Referral Service was developed, to bring together individuals who were working on the same surnames in the same locales.

• The society's research division no longer did research for patrons. Rather, recommendations were made to individuals or family groups from a list of private, accredited researchers.

• The library was converted to open stacks, greatly speeding up the process of finding and obtaining books and, later, microfilms.

• Branch libraries were established in dozens of stake centers outside Salt Lake City.

• The library and offices moved to temporary quarters in downtown Salt Lake City when the old genealogy building was demolished to make way for a twenty-eight-story Church

Office Building. In late 1972, when the new skyscraper was ready for occupancy, the society moved into several floors and one wing.

• Special classes, seminars, and publications were developed to teach people how to research records and do their genealogy. Beginning in 1966, an annual genealogical conference was held at Brigham Young University; the conferences continued until the late-1970s, when the responsibility for training was given to local priesthood leaders.

These and other changes changed dramatically the way the Genealogical Society operated and the services it was able to provide for members and nonmembers alike. By 1969, when the society observed its seventy-fifth anniversary, it was reported that it had collected "more than 670,000 rolls of microfilm, representing the equivalent of three million volumes of 300 pages each. Add to this the society's six million completed records of family groups, a card file index of 36 million individuals, and a book collection of more than 90,000 volumes, and one begins to realize the vastness of its record keeping program. The society also has 80 branch libraries . . . and receives about 1,000 new rolls of microfilm weekly from throughout the world."[5]

Elder Hunter continued to work on his own genealogy during the time he served as president of the society. At a seminar for regional representatives, he described a visit of his home teachers to talk about the importance of preparing family group sheets and pedigree charts. "We wanted to show you our family group sheets that we have prepared," the home teachers explained, adding, "We don't have time to see yours tonight, but next time we come we'd like to take a look at them."

"Now this was quite interesting to me," he told the regional representatives. "I worked a month getting prepared for the next home teachers' visit. When we get people doing these things, it is a great motivation."[6]

To celebrate the Genealogical Society's silver anniversary,

the Church sponsored the first World Conference on Records and a concurrent World Convention and Seminar on Genealogy at the newly opened Salt Palace convention complex in Salt Lake City August 5 through 8, 1969. Over six thousand persons attended more than two hundred seminars. Elder Hunter welcomed the delegates on behalf of the society and gave one of the principal addresses, "setting forth the work and objectives of the Genealogical Society, expressing appreciation to the delegates from the many nations of the world for their assistance, and stating our collective responsibility to preserve the records of the world."

Others who addressed the conference included Lord Thompson of Fleet, distinguished owner of the London *Times* and numerous other newspapers; Dr. Alfred Wagner of Paris, program specialist in archives for UNESCO; Genadii Alexandrovich Belov of Russia, director-general of USSR archives; Dr. Felix Hull, county archivist from Kent, England; and Dr. James B. Rhoads, archivist of the United States.

When the conference was over, Elder Hunter noted in his journal: "It has created much good will for the Church and has opened doors for our work all over the world. . . . Although this has been a tremendous undertaking and has consumed months of hard work, we feel it has resulted in enhancing our position as the dominant organization in genealogy in the world."

The next day he reported, "Many visitors to the conference came into the office today to express appreciation for the proceedings of the week. Each of them was outspoken in praise for the good which has been done in bringing better international understanding in the preservation and exchange of records in the world. Many invited us to visit with them when we come to their countries."

A year later Elder Hunter attended the International Congress on Archives in Moscow, followed by the Tenth International Congress of Genealogical and Heraldic Sciences in Vienna, and in 1971 he assisted in negotiations for the Church to begin microfilming records in Italy. Because of the World Conference on Records "and other information concerning our work," he noted, "doors are being opened to us in many countries where we were previously barred from the records."

Elder Richard G. Scott of the Twelve, who was associated with the Family History Department many years later, summarized the impact of Elder Hunter's leadership in overseeing this vital program: "He dedicated a significant portion of his life to that work and laid the foundations and the direction from which the Church is still reaping the benefits."

Church Historian

In 1970, A YEAR in which many of the changes in the Genealogical Society were being implemented, Elder Hunter received an additional appointment that came unexpectedly at the end of a week that was bittersweet for the General Authorities and the Church.

On Sunday morning, January 18, 1970, President David O. McKay, ninety-six-year-old prophet, seer, and revelator, died after a long illness. Elder Hunter was in Reno, Nevada, to divide the Reno Stake when he heard the news. He cancelled plans to go from there to California and flew home that evening so he could assist the Twelve in planning the funeral services.

On Thursday, January 22, the day of the funeral in the Salt Lake Tabernacle, Elder Hunter wrote: "This was a day we will long remember as one mixed with gladness and sadness— gladness in the life and leadership of President McKay and the joy of having been closely associated with him, but sadness in his passing which will deprive us of his inspiration. . . . Many things have gone through my mind today. I have thought of the occasion when he sent for me to come to his office during conference on October 9, 1959, and called me to serve as a member of the Council of the Twelve; when he laid his hands upon my head the following Thursday and ordained me an Apostle; the many meetings of the First Presidency and Council of the Twelve in the temple; conferences with him in his office; and many other things which I have experienced during the last ten years. I am grateful for this association and the privilege of sitting at his feet and being taught by a true Prophet of the Lord. This brings to a close an important era in the Church under his leadership of nineteen years and an era in my life which has meant much to me."

The next morning, at a meeting of the Quorum of the Twelve in the Salt Lake Temple, Joseph Fielding Smith was set apart as prophet, seer, and revelator and president of the Church, with Harold B. Lee as first counselor and N. Eldon Tanner as second counselor in the First Presidency. President Lee, as the senior apostle, was also set apart as president of the Twelve, and Spencer W. Kimball as acting president.

Afterwards Elder Hunter wrote: "I have never witnessed a greater demonstration of complete unity than there was in the meeting this morning. The Spirit of the Lord whispered to each of us a confirmation of divine approval of the action which was taken, and we knew it was the will of the Lord."

Elder and Sister Hunter were scheduled to fly to the South Pacific on Saturday evening, so he went to the office early that morning to finish up some work. The First Presidency also met that morning, and during their meeting, they called Elder Hunter to their council room and asked him to serve as Church Historian and Recorder. He would be the seventeenth person to hold that office in this dispensation, succeeding President Joseph Fielding Smith, who had served for forty-nine years.

In an interview for publication in the *Improvement Era*, Elder Hunter said of his call, "I was taken so completely by surprise that I didn't at the moment feel the impact of the awesome responsibility of this assignment. President Smith had been the Church Historian for so many years that I could hardly visualize myself in that position. . . .

"The assignment as given by the Lord through revelation is tremendously challenging—both in fulfilling the task of col-

Church Historian
Howard W. Hunter,
October 1971

lection and writing and in making the material of use to the members of the Church. I think that most people have an interest in history, and I, too, have had a very deep interest in history. I have a 20–volume work containing the history of civilizations, which I have enjoyed reading and rereading. I believe that when we understand what has gone on in the past, we can make better plans for the future."[7]

With typical zeal, Elder Hunter began learning as much as he could about the Historian's Office—its history, its responsibilities, its organization, and its vast holdings. At the time he was appointed, according to a report in the *Church News*, the office had a staff of forty-eight and the holdings included "in excess of 260,000 bound volumes and nearly a million pamphlets, photos, recordings, and documents. The Church historian is responsible for all the record keeping of the Church including minutes, temple records, all ordinations, patriarchal blessings, and all media produced by the Church such as motion pictures, slides, tapes, etc."[8] In addition, the Historian was in charge of the Church Library Coordination Committee and the Church's record management program, which evaluated materials for microfilming and permanent preservation.

These duties were all mandated by revelations given through the Prophet Joseph Smith, as in the first verse of section 85 in the Doctrine and Covenants: "It is the duty of the Lord's clerk, whom he has appointed, to keep a history, and a general record of all things that transpire in Zion."

At the time Elder Hunter received this call, the Quorum of the Twelve was seeking ways to relieve the apostles from some of their heavy administrative burdens. Thus, in addition to learning all he could about the Historian's Office, he also began counseling with members of the professional staff and other respected LDS historians on how the office might be reorganized. During a trip to Boston, he met with one historian who, in addition to sharing his ideas, took him through the archives and library system of Harvard University.

At the temple meeting of the Twelve on January 6, 1972, Elder Hunter wrote, "It has been decided to release the Twelve from serving as heads of departments or organizations so they can devote more time to policy matters."

After a meeting of the General Authorities the following week, he reported, "It was announced that I would be released as Church Historian and a full-time professional historian called to that office. . . . The Historian's Office was reorganized with Alvin R. Dyer [then an Assistant to the Council of the Twelve] as the managing director under the direction of Spencer W. Kimball and me, Leonard J. Arrington as Church Historian, and Earl E. Olson as Church Archivist. This will leave me in a position of direction but relieved of the operational function."

The next day, after President Tanner announced the changes in a meeting of the department's employees, Elder Hunter concluded, "In my opinion this marks a new era in the

Historian's Office." He continued to serve as adviser to the department until February 1978.

New World Archaeological Foundation

THE OPPORTUNITY to learn about an entirely different type of history came to Elder Hunter on January 26, 1961, when he was appointed chairman of the advisory board for the New World Archaeological Foundation (NWAF), a professional research organization based at Brigham Young University and involved in archaeological work on Mesoamerica (southern Mexico and northern Central America).[9]

In the late 1940s a group of Church members interested in the Book of Mormon as it might relate to archaeology was conducting studies in Mesoamerica in an effort to establish possible ties with sites mentioned in the Book of Mormon. One of them, Thomas Ferguson, developed contacts with prominent archaeologists at the Carnegie Institution and Harvard University on the need for expanded research on civilizations in ancient America, and their support resulted in the organization of the NWAF. It was incorporated as a nonprofit organization in October 1952, with financing through individual LDS donors, though much of the fieldwork was done by non-LDS scholars.

Exploratory work was begun in 1953; then, with Church financing, large-scale excavation commenced in 1955 at a major site at Chiapa de Corzo in southern Mexico. Investigations later expanded to other areas of Mexico and to Guatemala. In March 1959 the BYU board of trustees approved incorporating NWAF within BYU, and two years later the name of the foundation was changed to BYU–New World Archaeological Foundation.

Elder Hunter took an active interest in the foundation, meeting often with board members and personally inspecting the archaeological sites two or three times a year. He also took a strong fatherly interest in the staff workers and their families. His expeditions, often combined with Church assignments, took him into primitive—at times even dangerous—areas, and he immersed himself in learning as much as possible about the ancient civilizations and artifacts.

Many entries in his journals, such as the following, illustrate the sense of adventure he received from this assignment.

"Pierre came to the motel before daybreak with six saddle horses. . . . [We] left before six o'clock for a ride up the mountain to see the ancient ruins of Tonala. The trail was very steep and rocky and we traveled five or six miles to an elevation of over 2000 feet. The ruins consist of many walls, terraces and large structures overlooking the coastal plain and the Pacific Ocean. . . . It was one o'clock when we got back to the motel. This was a long time in the saddle for one who doesn't get more exercise than an office chair." (December 12, 1964.)

"We went to Chiapa de Corzo . . . an extensive site of about 140 mounds dating from approximately 1000 B.C. to the Classic period. The large structure which we have restored was in use at the time of Christ. We returned to Tuxtla Gutierrez, went to the laboratory, and discussed plans for digging in the sites of Izapa, Mirador and Chiapa de Corzo this coming year." (December 14, 1964.)

"We left Comitan at six o'clock. . . . Before getting to the border we took a road south to the Grijalva River and followed down the river. The river road was very poor, rocky, ungraded and wound through the trees and bush. . . . As we drove along we had to stop at every fence, open the wire or pole gates and close them after us. . . . As we continued down the river from San Felipe we passed through an area known as the archaeological site of Las Briscas. For a distance of about five kilometers there are terraces in the hillside and many platforms indicating a large concentration of people in this area at the time of Christ." (February 16, 1967.)

"This day was spent on the Usumacinta River [separating Mexico from Guatemala]. A little plane took us . . . to a clearing in the tropical forest on the river at a place called Agua Azul. From there we were taken down the river in a native

New World Archaeological Foundation group at Chichen-Itza:
Gareth W. Lowe, John Hale Gardner, Leo P. Vernon, Howard W. Hunter,
William P. Bradford, and Martin B. Hickman

dugout canoe, forty-two feet long and about thirty inches wide, hewn out of a mahogany log. . . . The trip was through beautiful tropical forest. Yaxchilan is one of the largest of the early Mayan sites. In addition to the many mounds, there are temples and other structures in fairly good state of preservation. . . . This site has never been dug nor has any reconstruction been done. For centuries it has been inaccessible except to the few who have gone in by boat. We spent several hours walking through the dense forest and climbing to the high points to see the temples. . . . This was a rewarding day . . . although the vigorous activity and heat of the day here in the tropics almost exhausted us." (May 9, 1967.)

"The 22–kilometer trip [by jeep] is over the worst road I have ever been on. For an hour we climbed over rocks and hills, through bush and canyons before arriving at the ancient Mayan site of Xcalumkin. . . . We went with the crew into the Mayan Indian Village of Cumpich. An Indian woman cooks for them in her hut, and they wanted us to have Sunday dinner: eggs, beans and tortillas. The hut has a dirt floor, and while we ate, cats, dogs, turkeys and pigs wandered in and out. I didn't mind that too much, but I didn't appreciate having the chickens fly on the table while we were eating." (April 14, 1968.)

At El Mirador in Guatemala, "they took us to some of the excavations and to the top of El Tigre, one of the highest of the temple mounds. On the way back we watched hundreds of spider monkeys swinging through the tops of the trees. The parrots and tucans were screeching and the whole jungle seemed to be alive. We kept a lookout for snakes. The rains earlier in the month have driven them into the trees and several workers on archaeological sites have died from their bites. We saw three snakes on the trail. One was the deadly bushmaster, one a coral, and the other we couldn't identify. About four o'clock the howler monkeys came, yelping and howling in the trees. . . . We had dinner in the mess tent—rice and beans. Brother Bradford [Elder William R. Bradford of the First Quorum of the Seventy] and I slept on top of sleeping bags in a tent with net siding to keep out the mosquitos and bugs of the jungle." (March 8, 1980.)

According to one noted archaeologist, "By 1967 the BYU-New World Archaeological Foundation was recognized both in Mexico and abroad as the most active and most respected non-Mexican institution working in Mesoamerica."[10]

Elder Hunter served as chairman of the foundation for some twenty-four years, and in all those years, he never tired of visiting archaeological sites. An entry in his journal after one trip in February 1979 summarized his feelings: "I have been here several times, but this famous site never ceases to be interesting."

Setting a Record for New Stakes

ONE VISIT THAT Elder Hunter made to Mexico in November 1975 raised some eyebrows at home and apparently established a record unequaled in the history of the Church. Assisted by Elder J. Thomas Fyans, who was then serving as an Assistant to the Twelve, Elder Hunter had been assigned to divide and realign several stakes in Mexico. After meeting with the regional representatives and the mission president and reviewing information provided by the stake presidents, he determined that the five existing stakes, together with some branches from the Mexico City Mission, should be made into fifteen stakes.

"Our purpose," he wrote in his journal, "was to reduce the size of the stakes, to better align them, to reduce travel of members, and also to provide for the rapid growth that is taking place in Mexico. It was the consensus that smaller stakes can be better trained, that leadership can be more effective, and the anticipated growth of about 1,000 members commencing by March will be better fellowshipped."

The two General Authorities called F. Burton Howard, legal counsel for Mexican affairs, in Salt Lake City, to get his opinion on one of the proposed stakes, and he said he would discuss the matter with President Marion G. Romney and call them back. "When the call was returned," Elder Hunter reported, "President Kimball and President Romney were on the line with Brother Howard. I am sure they were shocked when we explained our proposal, but after our explanation, they authorized us to proceed."

Elder Hunter and Elder Fyans interviewed leaders for an entire day and into the late evening, and "by eleven o'clock, fifteen stake presidencies had been selected and called." Then, in typical laconic understatement, Elder Hunter concluded: "I doubt there has ever been such a mass organization in the Church, and we were tired by the time we got home."

Actually, before they returned to Salt Lake City a few days later, he and Elder Fyans attended a three-day seminar for presidents of missions in Mexico and Central America, organized the Poza Rica Stake from a district of the Mexico Vera Cruz Mission, visited an archaeological site of Mayan ruins, and stopped over in Houston to divide the Houston Texas Stake.

After Elder Hunter reported on the stake organizations at the next temple meeting of the Twelve, he wrote, "I think the brethren were somewhat shocked, but I know time will prove that my decision was right."

That wasn't the last he heard of the matter; several times he was the object of good-natured ribbing by his associates. The next year, after he reported on another visit to Mexico, President Kimball asked him why he had created only three new stakes. And in May 1977 he wrote, "Bruce McConkie has returned and reported that he had organized five stakes in South America in the past ten days. President Kimball asked if he was trying to catch up with my record. Comments are still made about the fifteen stakes I organized one weekend in Mexico City."

Time proved Elder Hunter right. The Church continued to grow rapidly in Mexico, and within two years some of the fifteen stakes were ready to be divided. In fact, only fourteen months after he had organized the Poza Rico Stake, he was back in Mexico to divide it. The next day he divided the Vera Cruz Stake, the Church's eight hundredth stake, and one week later he organized the Merida Mexico Stake, the first stake in Yucatan. This particularly pleased him as chairman of the board of the New World Archaeological Foundation, for, he wrote, it was "in the heart of the Mayan area of Mesoamerica which has such great significance in the Book of Mormon history."

11

The Apostolic Ministry, Part 2

IN HONOR OF Howard W. Hunter's fifty years as a member of the California State Bar, the United States Court of Appeals for the Ninth Circuit in California honored him at a special session in November 1990. On that occasion, John S. Welch, a longtime friend and prominent Los Angeles attorney, remarked that Howard Hunter "epitomizes the practice of law in the classic style: honor, ethical conduct, courtesy, gentility, the art of making the adversarial system work while sticking to the rules, and . . . integrity." Another lawyer and longtime friend, Judge J. Clifford Wallace, commented on Elder Hunter's keen lawyer-like analysis and legal problem-solving talent.

When the Howard W. Hunter Professorship in Law was established at the J. Reuben Clark Law School at Brigham Young University, a biography in a commemorative booklet stated that Elder Hunter's "ability and capacity to give useful service [as an apostle] have been greatly influenced by his study and practice of the law." He was then quoted as saying, "The process by which conclusions are drawn is similar in both the law and in church administration."

President Thomas S. Monson recalled a comment President Harold B. Lee made after a long discussion on a Church matter in which Elder Hunter took a stand that prevailed: "If ever I am in need, before a jury, of an effective defense attorney, I would like it to be Howard Hunter. The judge would feel good, and I would win the point and I would feel good, and Brother Hunter would feel good."

These are qualities that have uniquely qualified Elder Hunter for special assignments in administering the world-wide Church. Many of these assignments have required extra-ordinary negotiating skills, the ability to listen to diverse points of view nonjudgmentally, to analyze complex issues and cut through to the heart of a matter, and to resolve prob-lems and find solutions that result in agreement and good feel-ings among the parties involved. The ways in which Elder Hunter has handled assignments in two areas half a world apart—Hawaii and the Holy Land—illustrate well these spe-cial strengths.

The Polynesian Cultural Center

IN FEBRUARY 1955 President David O. McKay spoke at the groundbreaking ceremonies for a new college to be con-structed by the Church in Laie, Hawaii.

Listeners were startled (and some perhaps even skeptical) to hear him say that Laie had the potential of becoming "a missionary factor, influencing not thousands, not tens of thou-sands, but millions of people who will come seeking to know what this town and its significance are."[1] At that time Laie was a small village surrounded by farmland, mountains, and ocean on the north shore of the island of Oahu. The only building of significance was the Hawaii Temple, where the 15,000 Latter-day Saints in Hawaii and others on the islands of the South Pacific could perform saving ordinances for themselves and their kindred dead. It was certainly not a des-tination for "millions of people." In fact, Hawaii itself was still not a major tourist destination: in 1955, there were only about 110,000 visitors, almost all from the U.S. mainland.

The Church College of Hawaii opened that fall with 153 students, mostly Polynesians from the islands of the Pacific. For many of the students, just getting to Laie by plane cost an enormous sum, and they needed employment in order to stay there. In 1959, after the students staged a highly successful production of Polynesian songs and dances at a theater in Honolulu, the dream many college leaders had had of a center where students could present similar shows and share their native customs began to come true. The Polynesian Cultural Center (PCC) was completed and dedicated in October 1963—a sixteen-acre complex where some 1,000 Polynesians demonstrated the culture and customs of their islands at six different villages and a 750–seat dinner theater.

But tourists did not immediately flock to the center. The first year, average attendance at the evening show was 324, and tour operators in Honolulu, as well as convention and tourism officials, had to be convinced that the PCC could become a major tourist attraction.

On January 13, 1965, fifteen months after the PCC opened, Elder Howard W. Hunter received a letter from the First Presidency appointing him president and chairman of the board, the first General Authority to hold this position. Up to that time, the center had been governed by a twenty-seven–member board that included stake and mission presidents and representatives from the cultures showcased in the six villages. Under new by-laws, a smaller, more manageable board was appointed.

Elder Hunter and his board had their work cut out for them. They had to deal with many challenges in managing a program that brought together peoples of diverse cultures and temperaments—Hawaiians, Tahitians, Tongans, Maoris, Fijians, and Samoans (islanders from the Marquesas were added later)—and many points of view on the mission and programs of the center. Even some of the Brethren did not comprehend President McKay's vision of the center as a major force in introducing visitors not only to the peoples of Polynesia and their cultures, but also to the Church and the saving principles of the gospel of Jesus Christ.

As with all his assignments, Elder Hunter plunged into a thorough study of the center and its strengths and needs. Just a week after his appointment, he spent three days in Laie, and he went often over the next decade. After a trip to Hawaii on February 18, 1966, he wrote in his journal: "Several of us spoke [at a student assembly] and reviewed the purposes and objectives of the Cultural Center in helping students receive an education which would otherwise be impossible. . . . We are now in the third year of operation. Loss for the first year amounted to over $600,000, for the last year about $70,000. This year we hope to bring it to the break-even point. . . . Even though the loss was $70,000 last year, we paid the sum of $150,000 to apply on students' tuitions."

Eventually island tour operators began promoting the PCC, and attendance picked up. Awareness of the center increased in August 1966 when the show was presented for four nights at the Hollywood Bowl in California. "In the 50 years of its history," a Los Angeles *Times* music critic reported, "it is unlikely that the Hollywood Bowl has ever been the scene of a more uniquely beautiful spectacle than 'Festival Polynesia!'"

Portions of the show were taped for "The Ed Sullivan Show" and seen by millions of television viewers nationwide. Within a year attendance at the PCC increased dramatically, and the theater was expanded to accommodate 1,400. And it wasn't long before most performances were sold out.

By 1968 the center was reporting a profit, resulting in substantial assistance for students at the college. In 1971, after noting that profits continued to increase, Elder Hunter recorded, "We are pleased with these results although we are concerned about the future. Capacity has been reached and expenses are increasing."

By that time, nearly one million people were visiting the center annually. To provide greater capacity and meet rising costs, plans were made to expand the PCC to encompass forty-two acres, with a new 2,500-seat theater, an enormous dining hall for a nightly buffet, several new cultural attractions, and service and administrative buildings.

*Elder Hunter
at the Polynesian
Cultural Center's
tenth anniversary
in October 1973*

The expansion program was nearly completed when Elder
Hunter was released as president and chairman of the board
in April 1976, and Elder Marvin J. Ashton of the Quorum of
the Twelve was named to succeed him. In his journal Elder
Hunter summarized his involvement with the center:

"This brings to a close the period of twelve years I have
headed this enterprise. During that time we have converted
from a substantial operating loss to a very profitable operation. Thousands of students from the South Pacific have been
assisted in getting their education, most of whom would not
have been able to leave their islands to go to school except for
this assistance. The center has given large sums to the BYU-
Hawaii campus, has become a major factor in building the
image of the Church and promoting a missionary effort, has
improved the community of Laie and has become the most
patronized tourist attraction in Hawaii. It is a viable unit of the

Church, and I have enjoyed the assignment given me by the First Presidency to make it successful."

On Sunday, July 4, 1976, Elder Hunter returned to Laie for the dedication of the new buildings. "This was an important day for two reasons," he wrote. "The United States now enters the third century of its history, and the Polynesian Cultural Center commences its fourteenth year in newly expanded facilities."

He could look with satisfaction on the center's accomplishments. President McKay's prophecy uttered at the dedication of the Church College of Hawaii in 1955 had indeed come true. The college, now renamed Brigham Young University–Hawaii, the adjacent Polynesian Cultural Center, and the temple on the hill to the northwest of the campus were now "influencing not thousands, not tens of thousands, but millions of people."

Building a Bridge

"A CABINET MINISTER of Egypt once told me that if a bridge is ever built between Christianity and Islam, it must be built by the Mormon Church," Elder Hunter told an audience at Brigham Young University in 1979. "In making inquiry as to the reason for his statement, I was impressed by his recitations of the similarities and the common bonds of brotherhood. Both the Jews and the Arabs are children of promise, and as a church we do not take sides. We have love for and an interest in each. The purpose of the gospel of Jesus Christ is to bring about love, unity, and brotherhood of the highest order. . . .

"To our friends of Judah, we say: We are your brethren of the house of Joseph—we feel a close relationship to you. We are messengers of the true covenant and bear a message that God has spoken in this day and time. To our kinsmen of Abraham, we say: We are your brethren—we look upon no nation or nationality as second-class citizens. We invite all men to investigate our message and to receive our fellowship."[2]

Elder Hunter first visited the Middle East during his world tours with his wife and sons in 1958 and 1960. By 1965, six years after he was called to the Twelve, he noted, "We have now visited all of the major Moslem countries of North Africa and we have been in nearly all of the major cities. This area is rich in contributions to world history." By 1993 he had visited nearly every Islamic nation in the world—and some of them several times. He had also visited the Holy Land more than any other General Authority, making some two dozen trips to conduct Church business.

Intensely interested in ancient history, he described in his journal extensive details of each place he visited, such as this entry after a visit to Shiraz, Iran, in 1975:

"There was little change since Claire and I were here on April 28, 1966, but since that time I have read the story of the Persian Empire and this visit was like a walk through ancient history. After spending some time in the ruins of the fabulous palace, we went to see the tombs of Darius the Great, Xerxes I, Artaxerxes I, and Xerxes II at Nagsh-i-Rastam, cut into the sides of a vertical rock cliff. Persepolis and the tombs date back to about 500 years before Christ, and the place was burned by Alexander the Great about 330 B.C. in revenge for the burning of Athens by the Persians."

When he visited a historical site, Elder Hunter often reviewed what happened there. For example, though he visited many times the Garden of Gethsemane, the Mount of Beatitudes, and other sites associated with the Savior, on each occasion he or a member of his party read what was said about that place in the scriptures, and they sat and contemplated the significance of those events.

In the Middle East, Elder Hunter met heads of state and other government leaders, yet he also conversed with camel drivers and servants. He was entertained in palaces and in Bedouin tents; rode in limousines and on mules and camels; ate sumptuous meals and simple peasant food. He related to individuals in all walks of life because of his genuine interest in people. He attended lectures and read extensively about the Middle East, and his knowledge of these countries opened doors and resulted in valuable friendships for the Church.

Whenever Arab and Israeli officials and citizens visited Salt Lake City, Elder Hunter typically represented the Church in meeting with them. One such visitor was George M. Mardikian, an Armenian emigré and restaurateur in San Francisco. When he came to Utah in May 1967 to receive an honorary doctorate from Brigham Young University, Elder Hunter took him to the Hotel Utah apartment of President David O. McKay. Mr. Mardikian, he wrote, "is personally acquainted with the heads of the Arab nations, and the discussion of this meeting was centered about Arab affairs in the Middle East. Mr. Mardikian stated that the greatest need of the Middle East is an understanding of the doctrines taught by the Church— work, free agency, the dignity of man and others."

A few months later, when Elder Hunter was in the Bay Area of northern California on a stake conference assignment, he talked with Mr. Mardikian on the phone "for half an hour, principally about conditions in the Middle East. He thanked me for taking him to see President McKay and said, 'I have met nearly every patriarch and head of most of the Christian churches in the world, also the heads of Islam and other religions, but I have never been in the presence of a man who radiated such a spirituality as President McKay. I had the feeling as we talked that he was truly a prophet of God.'"

On several trips to Israel, Elder Hunter met with the long-time mayor of Jerusalem, Teddy Kollek, and they became good and trusted friends. He also associated with other city and state officials.[3] Through his extensive experience in the Middle East, he developed strong feelings about the peoples there and their rich heritage in religious and secular history. During one visit to Jerusalem in 1979, he alluded to those feelings as he described his surroundings:

"From my [hotel] window I can see the area below the south wall of the Old City from the junction of the Kidron and the Hinnam Valleys to Bethany. . . . I walked out in the garden in front of the hotel and watched darkness fall and the lights come on in Old Jerusalem. A full moon rose and cast a glow over the city below, which is steeped in meaningful history. Words don't very well express the feelings that came to me, alone and in the quiet of the cool evening."

As a result of Elder Hunter's understanding of this special place, the First Presidency assigned him to spearhead two significant undertakings of the Church in the Holy Land: the Orson Hyde Memorial Garden and the Jerusalem Center for Near Eastern Studies.

The Orson Hyde Memorial Garden

ON OCTOBER 24, 1841, Elder Orson Hyde of the Quorum of the Twelve Apostles was in Palestine, as the Holy Land was then known, on a special mission for the Church. "A good while before day," he recorded, "I arose from sleep, and went out of the city as soon as the gates were opened, crossed the brook Kedron [sic], and went upon the Mount of Olives, and there, in solemn silence, with pen, ink, and paper, just as I saw in . . . vision, offered up [a] prayer to Him who lives forever and ever." As he stood on the hillside across the Kidron Valley from Jerusalem, he offered a prayer, dedicating the land of Palestine for the building up of Jerusalem and the gathering of Abraham's posterity.[4]

On October 24, 1979, President Spencer W. Kimball stood on that same hill to dedicate a memorial garden commemorating Elder Hyde's prayer. Elder Howard W. Hunter was present on that occasion, having taken a major role in raising funds and in the negotiations leading to the construction of the garden.

Groundwork for this project was laid when President Harold B. Lee, Elder Gordon B. Hinckley of the Twelve, and President Edwin Q. Cannon Jr. of the Swiss Mission visited Israel in September 1972. They met with representatives of the Israeli ministries of religion, foreign affairs, and tourism, and explored the possibility of a monument to Orson Hyde in Jerusalem.[5]

Three months later, on December 19, 1972, Elder Hunter wrote in his journal: "Because I am going to the Holy Land next week, the First Presidency called me to their meeting this morning and asked if I would meet with the group leader [for the Church] in Jerusalem and with the mayor, if necessary, regarding a monument to the prayer of Orson Hyde in Jerusalem."

In Jerusalem on New Year's Day, Elder and Sister Hunter looked at possible sites for the monument. He reported to President Lee on his impressions of the sites visited, but nothing was decided at that time. Two years later, the City of Jerusalem invited the Church to participate in a green-belt park development surrounding the walls of the Holy City. After a visit to Jerusalem, Elder Hunter reported that the proposed site, located on the Mount of Olives, would be the largest single tract in the park. Thus the Orson Hyde Memorial Garden began to be a reality.

Elder Hunter and Elder LeGrand Richards were assigned to oversee the project and to find ways to raise funds for it. In May 1976, they recommended to the First Presidency that a foundation, to be known as the Orson Hyde Foundation, be organized, with President Tanner, Elder Hunter, Elder Richards, and five great-grandchildren of Orson Hyde as the incorporators. Elder Richards was named president and trustee of the foundation.

A major responsibility of the foundation was to raise one million dollars from private donors. In March 1977, two days after the incorporation was completed and the Church's official participation in the park was assured, Mayor Kollek sent a cable stating, "A commitment from the Mormons is better than a commitment from the U.S. Government, as the Mormons will keep their promise."

Elder Hunter traveled to Jerusalem several times to negotiate the contract for the memorial and oversee the construc-

Elder James E. Faust, Elder Hunter, and BYU President Jeffrey R. Holland
at the Orson Hyde Memorial Garden in March 1981

tion of the garden, which was described in an *Ensign* article as "an amphitheater in a grotto-like setting [with] seating for visitors with a view of the Old City and numerous landmarks of Jerusalem. A heroic-size plaque in the garden inscribed in English and Hebrew contains excerpts of Elder Hyde's prayer. The plaque is accessible by winding pathways through groves of trees, plants, and other shrubbery."[6]

A sealed copper box containing a list of the 30,000 donors was inserted in the rock wall of the amphitheater, along with memorabilia related to the Church, Elder Hyde, the construction project, and the dedicatory services.

Seven General Authorities, led by President Kimball, joined more than a thousand other Latter-day Saints in Jerusalem for the dedication services. Many of them, including Elder Hunter, traveled to Israel by ship as participants in a BYU travel-study tour. On the morning of Wednesday, October 24, Mayor Kollek hosted a reception in the city council chambers for more than one hundred guests, including government officials, education leaders, and heads of religious groups. "Several made remarks," Elder Hunter wrote, "and LeGrand Richards delivered a check to Teddy Kollek for the balance of the $1,000,000 which we had agreed to pay."[7]

After the reception, the guests were taken to the upper entrance of the garden and formed a procession to walk down the switchback path, lined with spectators, to the amphitheater. Elder Hunter conducted the services and introduced Mayor Kollek, who presented a medal of the City of Jerusalem to President Kimball, Elder Hunter, and Elder Richards.

"We are very grateful that all of you made the effort to come to the other Jerusalem," the mayor said, referring to the Church's teaching of a "new Jerusalem" to be built on the American continent. "Everybody who knows about the history of Jerusalem in comparatively modern times knows about the prophecy of Orson Hyde. And here the Jews are back in Jerusalem again. We have political arguments, but nobody doubts that the city today is a more beautiful city, a better city united than divided by barbed wire and mine fields and concrete walls."[8]

It was a long day, with a buffet luncheon and visits to other sites the Church might be interested in developing in Jerusalem, followed by dinner, lectures, and programs aboard the ship. "All of the passengers were excited and pleased by the great event that took place today," Elder Hunter wrote.

One of the most excited and pleased participants was Howard Hunter himself. Late that night he joined several of those who had assisted in developing the Orson Hyde Memorial Garden for a midnight supper. Their efforts and the completion of the garden, he concluded, "will have a great impact for good in extending a favorable image of the Church."

The Jerusalem Center

WHILE PLANS WERE PROCEEDING on the Orson Hyde project in Jerusalem, Elder Hunter was also searching and negotiating for a site for a center to house the Brigham Young

University semester-abroad program and the Jerusalem branch and district of the Church.

However, finding a suitable site, coming up with a suitable architectural plan, and negotiating the way through countless bureaucratic requirements would not be easy. On each visit in connection with the Orson Hyde project, Elder Hunter, with leaders of the study-abroad program and the branch, looked at possible sites for a center.

As he explained later to a BYU tour group, "things move slowly" in Jerusalem. "First you design what you want to build. Then you go through a study of the plan and of zoning regulations. Finally, after the plans are approved, the land is leased. Ordinarily this takes ten years to get where we have gotten in four." At that time completion of the center was several years away, and some of the most difficult and perilous problems still lay ahead.

The search for a site began in earnest in 1979, when the Orson Hyde Memorial Garden was nearing completion. On February 8, 1979, Elder Hunter met with a group of General Authorities and BYU officials to determine if the Church should consider building in Jerusalem.

Two months later Elder Hunter, Elder James E. Faust, and Church Commissioner of Education Jeffrey R. Holland met with the First Presidency and, Elder Hunter wrote, "recommended the purchase of land in Jerusalem and the construction of a building for a branch chapel, . . . also housing and classrooms for the BYU studies-abroad program." The proposal was approved, and Elder Hunter was "authorized to seek out and negotiate for a parcel of property."

That decision set in motion countless meetings, telephone calls, and trips to Israel, as Elder Hunter learned about Israel's complex laws governing transfer of property and other requirements that must be met before construction could start. He had qualified and capable individuals to work with, such as Fred Schwendiman, a BYU vice president who had overseen construction of the Missionary Training Center in Provo and who would become project director for the Jerusalem Center; Robert Thorn, former president of the South African Mission, who had expertise in property negotiations; David Galbraith, president of the Jerusalem Branch; Dallin H. Oaks, BYU president until 1980, and Jeffrey R. Holland, who succeeded him in that position; and Robert C. Taylor, head of the BYU Travel Study Department.

The site the Church favored was one that President Kimball had visited when he was in Jerusalem to dedicate the Orson Hyde gardens. Owned by the Israeli government, it was on the Mount of Olives, adjacent to Hebrew University's Mount Scopus campus and near the site of a proposed Israeli Supreme Court building. Brother Thorn was authorized by the First Presidency to see if he could obtain that site, and for more than a year he pursued the matter, tracking the requirements for obtaining the land through four different government ministries. But as sometimes happens in delicate negotiations in the Middle East, the road wasn't smooth. On September 10, 1980, Elder Hunter wrote in his journal: "Robert Thorn has reported to us from Jerusalem that the negotiations for the parcel of land he has been working on have broken down with the real estate agents and we are now on our own to attempt the purchase. This is a most difficult problem."

Finally, in January 1981 Elder Hunter received word that the registration of Brigham Young University in Israel had been approved, paving the way for the acquisition of land there. Four months later the Israel Lands Authority agreed to lease to BYU approximately five acres of the land the Church had sought, for a term of forty-nine years with an option to renew for an additional forty-nine years.

However, the lease agreement could not be completed until architectural plans were submitted for the review of various Israeli committees and agencies. In addition, public notice of the Church's intention to lease the property had to be posted. Architect David Resnik was authorized to begin drawing up the plans immediately, and after the First Presidency

*Elder Hunter and Elder Mark E. Petersen inspect the site selected
for the Jerusalem Center, October 1983*

approved them, they were submitted to the Israel Lands
Authority.

After nearly three years of negotiations and lengthy reviews, David Galbraith called Elder Hunter on September 27,
1983, and told him that the plans had been approved by the
Jerusalem District Council. That afternoon at a meeting of the
Church Board of Education, the center received an official
name: Jerusalem Center for Near Eastern Studies—Brigham
Young University.

The proposed lease arrived within a few months, and a
few days after it was approved by the First Presidency, Elder
Hunter, Elder Faust, and President Holland flew to Israel to
complete the negotiations. On April 2, 1984, President Holland, representing BYU, signed the documents, climaxing
what Elder Hunter described as "a long time and endless
work." The building permit was issued in December, and construction began the day before Christmas.

But that did not end the problems in getting the center

built. Though the Church's intention to build an educational center had been posted much earlier, opposition by both Jews and Arabs escalated dramatically as soon as construction work began at the site. "The Jews have a fear that our presence in Jerusalem is a means of proselyting, and the Arabs are concerned because we are building on what they consider to be occupied land," Elder Hunter reported to the First Presidency after a trip to Jerusalem in February 1985 to try to defuse the opposition.

Articles in Jerusalem newspapers called on the Knesset to rescind permission to proceed with the project, and protestors increased their pressure on public officials and threatened violence at the construction site. The author of a biography of Mayor Kollek wrote:

It was only when the construction started that the orthodox sat up and took notice, and the outcry began. The prospect of an ostentatious Mormon presence in Jerusalem infuriated not only the Jewish orthodox but the veteran Christian communities of the cities, to say nothing of the Palestinian militants who said that if the Jews wanted to be so generous to the Mormons, they could allot them ground in west Jerusalem and not that expropriated from the Moslems. The Apostolic Delegate registered a formal protest on 'environmental grounds' alone; privately, however, Christian churchmen spoke of the new campus as 'an outrage'. Said one, 'They are not Christians, and they have no traditional community in the city.' Even secular Jews were troubled by the fact that the Mormons, who baptize the living in the name of the dead, had asked the Israel Holocaust Authority, Yad Vashem, for lists of those who had died in the concentration camps (the request was turned down).

Kollek (who was only one of those backing the project) was the target for most criticism because he had stood up for the Mormons as a matter of principle, and he was in an awkward position. The other officials tried to dissociate themselves from the project. . . . [Mayor Kollek] and his supporters argued that the business was a storm in a teacup, and that

Mormon students had been visiting Jerusalem for years without a single conversion. . . . In November [1985], the haredim [ultra-orthodox Jews] staged another of their huge demonstrations, and Kollek had to write to the Mormon leaders in Salt Lake City explaining the sensitivity of the issue, and insisting that they provide a written guarantee that no attempts would be made on the campus to convert the Jews of Jerusalem.[9]

The issue of proselyting was central to the position of the Jews. The Church had agreed, as a condition for building in Jerusalem, not to engage in proselyting, a position reiterated in a *Church News* article in which a Church spokesman pointed out, "Where missionary work is against the law, we don't do it."[10] However, the protestors refused to accept this assurance, and the controversy continued to rage.

Meanwhile, construction of the center moved ahead. Elder Hunter and Elder Faust flew to Jerusalem again in May 1986. "The afternoon [of May 21] was spent touring the building," Elder Hunter wrote. "The heavy construction work is nearly all completed and by October the student quarters will be ready for occupancy. . . . We have delivered to each of the 120 members of the Knesset a copy of a letter signed by 154 members of the U.S. Congress from both parties making a joint appeal to allow the completion of the BYU Center for Near Eastern Studies in Jerusalem.

"The members of Congress state that Israel's commitment to democracy and plurality is one of the main motivations for their long-standing support for Israel. [They have stated,] 'By allowing this center to be built and used as intended, Israel will be reaffirming its commitment to pluralism and to the special nature of Jerusalem. We believe that rather than hinder U.S.–Israeli ties, the BYU Center will be a further source of understanding and cooperation between our two countries.'

"The other good news," he added, "was the opinion handed down by the attorney general of Israel to the ministerial committee on the Mormon university that there is no way

Jerusalem Mayor Teddy Kollek welcomes to his office Howard Hunter,
accompanied by Richard Hunter, in January 1987

of halting the construction of the center, that the procedures
were legal, that the permit was obtained legally, that the agreement was given legally."

When Elder Hunter returned to Jerusalem in January 1987,
Mayor Kollek assured him that inspection approvals of the
center would be available within a few weeks, permitting the
BYU students and faculty to move into the completed portion
of the building. Two months later David Galbraith sent a
telegram to Elder Hunter with this message:

> Today we made history! Today, March 8th, our eighty stu-
> dents at Kibbutz Ramat Rachel picked up everything that
> was not nailed down and walked on to the bus with it. In a
> little over half a day and in only one trip involving three
> moving vans and two passenger buses, we made the big
> move. . . . The day passed without incident. Either our Ortho-
> dox friends were sleeping or we give them too much credit!
> In any case, we are finally into our new building. This marks

a whole new phase to our presence in this land. All these many months we have labored on a building of cement and stone, and as impressive and grand as this building is, it now takes on added meaning as it assumes the measure of its creation. The students breathe into it the breath of life and those stone-cold corridors and lifeless rooms now take on an air of happiness. In place of the sounds of construction, there is shouting and whispering, laughing and crying, and the very walls absorb it all and at last, they are content.

It would be more than a year before Elder Hunter could return to Jerusalem. That summer he underwent serious back surgery, followed by many months of recuperation and rehabilitation. The Israeli Cabinet voted on May 8, 1988, to allow the Lands Authority to issue the lease. Elder Hunter heard the news at 3:30 the next morning when Jeffrey Holland called to tell him "that the ministerial committee of the Knesset approved yesterday the execution of the Jerusalem Center lease with some minor modifications and that television and the press have made the announcements."[11]

Six days later Elder Hunter, accompanied by his son John, Elder and Sister Faust, and President and Sister Holland, arrived in Jerusalem to sign the lease.

"This journey," according to a Jerusalem Branch history, "marked the first time Pres. Hunter was able to see the Center since its occupation. To honor this great man for the vision and energy he had devoted, not only to the center but especially to the members of the Jerusalem Branch over the years he had been visiting them, a small reception was planned with a choir of the spring-term students and branch members. . . . Still recovering from back surgery, Pres. Hunter was wheeled through the main entrance by Pres. Holland as the choir greeted them by singing 'The Holy City.' "[12]

At 3:00 P.M. on Wednesday, May 18, Elder Hunter and his party went to the office of the Lands Authority to sign the documents. Yehuda Ziv signed for the Lands Authority, Jeffrey Holland signed for Brigham Young University, and Elder

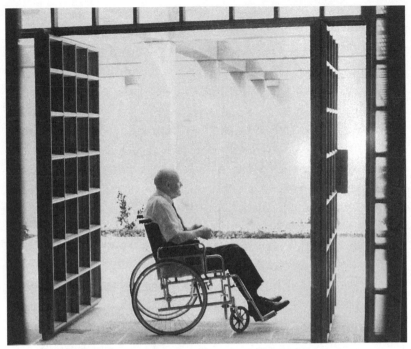

President Hunter awaiting the arrival of Mayor Teddy Kollek
for the dedication of the Jerusalem Center

Hunter signed for the Church under a power of authority. Elder Hunter wrote afterwards in his journal, "We came out of the Lands Authority feeling that a big load had been taken from our shoulders."

The next day, he noted, "was a special day for the administration, faculty, and students of the Jerusalem Center. Mayor Teddy Kollek of Jerusalem and his secretary, Noemi Teasdale, paid an official visit to the center. He has been a good friend and has helped us in many ways since the beginning of the project. The securing of the land, approval of plans, and the endless problems of construction would have seemed impossible had it not been for his help and advice.

"A large delegation greeted them as they arrived at the front gates at ten o'clock. President Holland escorted them through the domed gallery to the main auditorium, where he gave an explanation to the mayor of all the physical facilities of the building, the living facilities, food services and a demonstration of the impressive pipe organ. All of the windows look down to the Old City. As they toured the building the mayor repeatedly said, 'It is magnificent,' and he said to President Holland, 'I wasn't prepared to see such a magnificent building.'"

Elder Hunter refused to let health problems keep him from returning to Jerusalem for the center's dedication in May 1989. On the eve of his departure he fell in his office and cut his head, resulting in several stitches, but he and his son Richard left for Israel as scheduled. On the day of the dedication, he and other Church officials, including President Thomas S. Monson and Elder Boyd K. Packer, visited with Mayor Kollek and then returned to their hotel for lunch. Afterwards Elder Hunter went to his hotel room to have the stitches removed.

"When Dr. [Poulson] Hunter closed the cut on my head with seven stitches," he wrote, "he said they would need to come out in about eight days and that I should go to the Hadasa Hospital in Jerusalem. Boyd Packer said he has a doctor's degree and he came to my room with his daughter-in-law, Sue Packer, who is a registered nurse and took out the stitches in about five minutes."

At four o'clock that afternoon, about fifty invited guests gathered in the auditorium of the Jerusalem Center for the dedication services. President Monson, second counselor in the First Presidency and chairman of the BYU board of trustees, conducted the services. This was an emotional occasion, a dream come true, for the speakers: Robert C. Taylor, who had directed the first BYU travel-study tour to the Holy Land more than two decades earlier; Fred J. Schwendiman, resident director of construction for the center; Elder Holland, recently called to the First Quorum of the Seventy after nine years as BYU president; and Elder Packer, a member of the BYU board of trustees.

The final speaker was Howard W. Hunter, president of the Quorum of the Twelve Apostles, member of the BYU board of trustees, and the agent for the First Presidency in supervising the Jerusalem Center project from its inception. After his remarks, he offered the dedicatory prayer, in which he summed up his own feelings as well as the feelings of those who had labored and waited so long for this day:

> This building wherein we are seated has been constructed for the housing of those who love thee and seek to learn of thee and follow in the footsteps of thy Son, our Savior and Redeemer. It is beautiful in every respect, exemplifying the beauty of what it represents. O Father, we thank thee for the privilege of building this house to thee for the benefit and learning of thy sons and daughters.
>
> We pray, Father, that thou wilt bless this house in every way. Bless the land on which it rests, and the beautiful grounds that surround it. Bless its foundation, the walls, the roof and all of its details. We pray that it will be kept from damage or destruction from the hands of men or from the ravages of nature, and that it will remain beautiful and representative of that which is sacred and pertains to thee.
>
> We thy children, therefore, dedicate to thee, Father, that which we have built with our hands in love, this beautiful building, the Jerusalem Center for Near Eastern Studies, with all of its appurtenances, praying that it will be acceptable in every respect to thee. May all who enter herein to teach, to learn, or for whatever purpose be blessed of thee and feel thy Spirit.

12

"We Took Sweet Counsel Together"

AFTER THE TEMPLE meeting of the First Presidency and the Twelve on October 4, 1972, Elder Hunter recorded in his journal: "President Lee made reference to the 55th Psalm: 'We took sweet counsel together, and walked unto the house of God in company.' "

Special feelings of brotherhood are shared by those whom Latter-day Saints sustain as prophets, seers, and revelators. Each has been called of God to bear witness to the world that Jesus is the Christ, that he is the author of the gospel, that he conquered death, that through him comes the universal resurrection, and that those who are obedient to the gospel may be saved and exalted in the kingdom of God. Each has consecrated his life and talents to the Lord's service and to oneness with his brethren. Each brings to the council his own unique perspective and experience, which they meld as they take "sweet counsel together."

Elder Hunter has never ceased to marvel at the privilege he has had each week to meet with the First Presidency and the Twelve in the temple to partake of the sacrament, petition the Lord in prayer, and discuss the affairs of the Lord's kingdom. "The meeting of this council in the temple is an experience which makes one feel he should be better and do better," he wrote in 1967. "There is kindness, unity and love."

Many such expressions are tempered with feelings of wonder at being so blessed, such as these: "Sitting with this group

Elder Hunter confers with Elder Theodore M. Burton before general conference session in October 1970. In the background are Elder Gordon B. Hinckley and Elder Thomas S. Monson

of my brethren makes me feel my inadequacies, but always brings a resolution to try harder." "Times like these make me feel my own insignificance and unworthiness to be allowed such privileges and blessings." "These meetings are highlights in my life and always leave me with the question as to why I was selected and why I am privileged to sit in this council." "I left the temple today, as I have on previous occasions, feeling my inadequacies and wondering why I was selected for this association. I always resolve to attempt to do better and strive to be the example of what is expected."

Part of the answer to this question may lie in his patriarchal blessing, which he received when he was twenty-two, in which he was told: "Thou art one of those whom the Lord foreknew. . . . Thou shalt lend thy talents to the church and shall sit in her councils and thou shalt be known for thy wisdom and thy righteous judgments."

In 1960, as a member of the Twelve, President Kimball

expressed the feelings of Elder Hunter and the other Brethren regarding their association and their support of the living prophet:

"When in a Thursday temple meeting, after prayer and fasting, important decisions are made, new missions and new stakes are created, new patterns and policies initiated, the news is taken for granted and possibly thought of as mere human calculations. But to those who sit in the intimate circles and hear the prayers of the prophet and the testimony of the man of God; to those who see the astuteness of his deliberations and the sagacity of his decisions and pronouncements, to them he is verily a prophet."[1]

Elder Hunter has felt especially blessed as he has had an intimate, almost daily, association with five prophets—David O. McKay, Joseph Fielding Smith, Harold B. Lee, Spencer W. Kimball, and Ezra Taft Benson—and their counselors.

The apostles shared a tender experience just before Christmas 1968 when as a group they visited President McKay, who was confined to his apartment in the Hotel Utah. Starting with the newest apostle, Thomas S. Monson, each spoke a few words and, Elder Hunter wrote, "bore testimony of the Prophet of the Lord. This deeply touched the President, and he wept as he made the statement that in all the world there is no other group like this, brethren who love each other and love the Lord. With tears streaming down his face he prayed that the Lord would make him worthy of the confidence of the brethren. It was a moving occasion, and the Spirit bore witness to me that we were sitting in the presence of the Lord's Prophet upon the earth."

On another occasion, this time in 1977, Elder Hunter wrote: "During the course of the day I had a short conference with each of the members of the First Presidency. I never cease to be amazed at their vigor and ability to carry the heavy load that falls on their shoulders in the rapidly growing Church. President Kimball will soon be 83 years of age and he is as active as a young business executive, and in spite of the physical problems he has had in the past, he works night and day without ceasing. . . .

"President Tanner will be 80 years old in May. He, too, is vigorous and has a keen active mind. I am always amazed at how quickly he can sort through a maze of facts, find the essential kernels and make decisions that are unquestionable.

"President Romney was 80 years of age last September. . . . [He] became very sentimental when he talked about his wife's failing health and said it will not be long until they will both be where the problems of old age will be taken from them. . . . He is one of the sweetest, kindest, and most spiritual men I have ever known. I sustain these three brethren with all my heart."

Two years later Elder Hunter stopped at the hospital late one afternoon after President Kimball had undergone serious surgery and was still under intensive care. "I spoke to Sister Kimball," he wrote, "and she invited me to step in and see the president. I was reluctant to visit him so soon after surgery, but I was pleased that I did. He had just asked her if any of the brethren had been in and apparently I was the first. He vigorously took my hand and pulled me down beside him, pushing away the oxygen mask, and kissed me.

"I couldn't believe that he could be so energetic and sharp after his ordeal. He jokingly asked if I had brought some work for him to do. I replied that I would get some for him if he wanted to work. This is typical of the president—never an idle moment or a time of relaxation from anxiously pursuing the challenges of extending the kingdom."

Concern for Others

EACH MAN ORDAINED to the apostleship and sustained as a prophet, seer, and revelator brings to his quorum and to the Church unique strengths and gifts. Among his associates, Howard Hunter is described as a man of sound judgment and quiet wisdom. He rarely talks about himself and his accom-

*Elder Marvin J. Ashton
and Elder Hunter
on the grounds of the
New Zealand Temple in
November 1979*

plishments or shares his personal feelings. His concern is for
the accomplishments and feelings and comfort of others.

In a training meeting for General Authorities, Elder Marvin J. Ashton once recounted an experience Elder Hunter had
shared with the Brethren: "He [Elder Hunter] said he had just
had an enjoyable visit with a couple. He married them in the
temple about thirty years ago. He said, 'I enjoyed hearing
about their children, their homes, their activities, and where-
abouts.'" Elder Ashton concluded, "He could have taken all
the interview time talking about his thirty-two years as a
member of the Twelve had he chosen to."

Elder Dallin H. Oaks recalls the first time he met Elder Hunter, in February 1963. At the time Elder Oaks was living in Chicago, and Elder Hunter had accompanied Elder LeGrand Richards on an assignment to divide the Chicago Stake, create two new stakes, and select the stake presidencies. Shortly after they arrived on Friday afternoon, Elder Hunter learned that his father had just died in California.

"But there was no announcement of that," Elder Oaks said. "He went through the interviews in a stalwart fashion, not drawing any attention to himself." On Sunday evening, after the conference sessions (at which Elder Oaks was sustained as second counselor to the president of the new Chicago South Stake), Elder Hunter flew to Los Angeles to be with his mother and sister. On Tuesday, after services in the Walnut Park Ward, he offered the dedicatory prayer at his father's grave.[2]

The Twelve and those who work with them have learned that Elder Hunter weighs matters carefully before jumping in with opinions, conclusions, or solutions, undoubtedly a result of his legal training. He listens carefully as others express their opinions and feelings. If consensus isn't reached or anyone in the group still has strong feelings about a matter, he will table it rather than force a vote. But when the time comes for a decision, his associates know that Elder Hunter's recommendation will be honest and forthright. And sometimes, after listening carefully to others' opinions and recommendations, he will turn the discussion in a completely new direction to point out important considerations and consequences they need to be aware of before making a final decision.

At one of their meetings, several of the apostles were lamenting the absence of Elder LeGrand Richards, who was critically ill in the hospital. The prognosis was that he probably wouldn't survive the medical crisis. Elder Hunter listened without comment as each one around the table expressed dismay and a great sense of loss that their beloved brother might be taken from them. Then suddenly Elder Hunter slammed his hand down on the arm of Elder Richards's chair next to him and declared forcefully that Elder Richards would be back in their midst, sitting in that chair.

Some time later, Elder Richards did return. His work on earth was not yet finished, and he resumed his place in the council room with his brethren.

Times of Camaraderie

WHILE MEMBERS of the First Presidency and the Quorum of the Twelve bear heavy burdens, they also enjoy relaxing and talking about lighter matters—and no one likes a good story more than does Elder Hunter. After one of the weekly temple meetings, he commented, "We have lunch together in the little dining room on the same floor of the temple. This is always a pleasant occasion. Not only is the food good, but the conversation as well. The stories, humor, and other expressions are choice."

Many comments and stories from these and other informal occasions have found their way into his journal. Once he described a luncheon discussion in which one of the Brethren told about a woman who felt that women should hold the priesthood. When she approached Elder John A. Widtsoe about this matter, the storyteller said, Elder Widtsoe supposedly told her that the Prophet Joseph Smith was about to have a revelation on that subject when he was martyred. Amid the laughter of the brethren, President McKay quipped, "Did he tell her this was the reason the Lord took him?"

President McKay's quick wit was evident when he told the brethren after he turned eighty-eight, "I have learned to appreciate old age—he has been an enduring companion. I haven't always thought so, but if he hadn't been, I wouldn't have seen seventy-five, eighty, eighty-five, or my eighty-eighth birthday, so I am learning to live with him." A few weeks later, Elder Hunter wrote, President McKay "said to us in the temple meeting that he guessed he was growing old, and then added: 'I know that my youth is far spent because my get-up and go has gone and went.'"

On one of his own birthdays, Elder Hunter made a comment that President McKay would have appreciated: "This is my seventieth birthday. I have always thought that one was very old who had obtained that age, but now I feel that I should reconsider my former opinion." Two years later, on his seventy-second birthday, he noted, "Attaining this age makes me realize the shadows are lengthening. I would be pleased to have future birthdays pass me by."

Elder Hunter loved to retell a story on himself that he received in the following memo from Gary Gillespie, who worked in the First Presidency's office at the time: "One of the branch presidents down in Mississippi indicated to the members of his branch that a real treat was in store for them because Apostle Hunter would be visiting their forthcoming stake conference. After the meeting an excited little boy was overheard reporting the news to one of this friends, 'Guess who's coming to our next stake conference!' When his friend did not respond, the little boy beamed, 'A possom hunter!'"

During their visit to the Holy Land in 1961, Spencer Kimball and Howard Hunter forged a special bond of friendship, one that remained firm through the twenty-four years they served together in the Twelve and continued for the twelve and a half years President Kimball presided over the Church. In his journal Elder Hunter mentions several times when they and their wives went to dinner and a show together.

On one occasion, in 1964, the Kimballs, who were vacationing for a few days at a friend's cabin in Big Cottonwood Canyon east of Salt Lake City, invited the Hunters and the N. Eldon Tanners to join them for dinner. Elder Hunter described the evening:

"I went home early from the office and got Claire. We stopped for President and Sister Tanner and drove up the canyon. Sister Kimball had a delicious dinner ready when we arrived. After dinner the six of us hiked to Donut Falls and

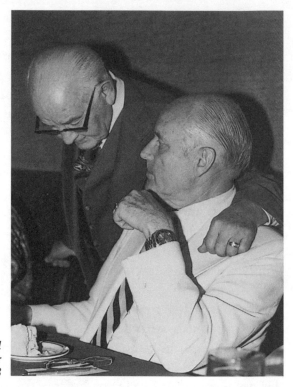

*President Kimball
and Elder Hunter
in 1978*

back. It was nearly dark when we returned, and we couldn't get in because the key was locked inside. Spencer drove to a telephone and learned where we could get another key." Later, back in the cabin, "We spent a pleasant evening around the table singing songs, accompanied by Spencer on the harpsichord, and hearing about the Kimballs' recent tour of the missions in South America."

"Therefore, Brethren, . . . Be of One Mind"

IN HIS SECOND epistle to the Corinthians, the Apostle Paul concludes, "Therefore, brethren, farewell. Be perfect, be of good comfort, be of one mind, live in peace; and the God of love and peace shall be with you." (2 Corinthians 13:11.) These words, written nearly two millennia ago, aptly describe the leaders of the Church in this dispensation.

Perhaps no greater examples of the unanimity and unity of the Brethren in the latter days can be found than at the time when the Brethren unitedly confirmed the 1978 revelation that "all worthy male members of the Church may be ordained to the priesthood without regard for race or color," and the times when one prophet is called home and another one is set apart to carry on as the Lord's mouthpiece on earth.

Prior to the day the revelation was received, President Kimball talked at length, over a period of several months, with the members of the First Presidency and the Quorum of the Twelve as a group and individually. Elder Hunter noted in his journal one such occasion when the prophet invited him to his office and they discussed the subject for about an hour. "I could feel his deep concern and his desire to follow strictly the will of the Lord," he said.

Elder Bruce R. McConkie wrote concerning the meeting at which the brethren all "heard the same voice and received the same message from on high":

"It was on a glorious June day in 1978. All of us were together in an upper room in the Salt Lake Temple. We were engaged in fervent prayer, pleading with the Lord to manifest his mind and will concerning those who are entitled to receive his holy priesthood. President Kimball himself was mouth, offering the desires of his heart and of our hearts to that God whose servants we are.

"In his prayer President Kimball asked that all of us might be cleansed and made free from sin so that we might receive the Lord's word. He counseled freely and fully with the Lord, was given utterance by the power of the Spirit, and what he said was inspired from on high. It was one of those rare and seldom-experienced times when the disciples of the Lord are perfectly united, when every heart beats as one, and when the same Spirit burns in every bosom."[3]

"Following the prayer," Elder Hunter wrote, "there were many expressions of love and appreciation among the brethren. Comments were made about the feeling shared by

Members of the Twelve help their quorum president, Ezra Taft Benson, celebrate
his eightieth birthday on August 4, 1979. From left, David B. Haight,
L. Tom Perry, Bruce R. McConkie, Marvin J. Ashton, Ezra Taft Benson,
LeGrand Richards, Mark E. Petersen, Thomas S. Monson,
Howard W. Hunter, Boyd K. Packer, James E. Faust

all, that seldom, if ever, had there been greater unanimity in the council."

After the written copy of the revelation was read to the brethren the following week, Elder Hunter wrote that "there were expressions from several of the brethren about the powerful witness of the Spirit last Thursday, and how this confirmed the divine origin of the revelation." The next day—Friday, June 9, 1978—the document was read to all of the General Authorities at an early-morning fast meeting, "a highly spiritual meeting with much emotion and some tears, and the brethren expressed love for all of God's children and bore testimony that President Kimball is a Prophet of God. This is a meeting we will never forget."

Within hours the word had spread through the media to the world, and Saints everywhere felt many of the same emotions and joy as those who had participated in this glorious manifestation.

Some of the most spiritually affirming experiences Elder Hunter and his brethren in the Twelve have shared have come at times of sorrow when a beloved prophet has passed away and one of their number is set apart and sustained as the new president, prophet, seer, and revelator.

The passing of President David O. McKay in January 1970 had not been totally unexpected, since he had been in failing health for several years and his decline had been gradual. (See chapter 10.) However, news of the deaths of the next two prophets came suddenly, without warning.

On Sunday, July 2, 1972, Elder Hunter wrote that since he had no stake conference assignments, he spent his free time working on his genealogy. Shortly before ten o'clock that evening, a Church spokesman called to tell him that President Joseph Fielding Smith had passed away at nine-thirty. "This was shocking news because he has not been ill," Elder Hunter wrote. Then, after describing what he had been told about President Smith's final few hours, he concluded, "I have often wondered about the condition of persons who are translated, and tonight I have had the feeling that this was the course the President has followed from mortality to immortality without tasting of death."

President Smith had been Elder Hunter's file leader in the Twelve for more than ten years and then president of the Church for two and a half years. "My life has been enriched by this close association," Elder Hunter wrote. "I am grateful."

The apostles met in the temple the day after the funeral, and Harold B. Lee, as senior apostle, was sustained by his brethren as president of the Church, with Nathan Eldon Tanner and Marion G. Romney as counselors in the First Presidency. After these brethren were ordained and set apart, Elder Hunter wrote, "the Spirit . . . bore witness to each of us that what was done was the will of the Lord."

Only eighteen months later he again witnessed the transfer of the presidency, after the unexpected death of President Lee. When they received the news on Wednesday evening, December 26, 1973, the Hunters were spending the Christmas holidays with their family at John's home in Ojai, California.

Elder Hunter conferred by phone with Presidents Tanner and Romney and assured them he would return early the next morning. Then he and Sister Hunter, John and Louine, and Richard and Nan talked until well after midnight.

"I told them of the deliberations of the Council of the Twelve after the death of President McKay and President Smith and the way in which their successors were chosen," he wrote. "Claire and I then told them of our plans for sharing our estate with them and their children. . . . We were pleased by the way they expressed their love for each other and their plans for the future and eternity. This was a great and rewarding experience."

On Saturday, December 29, a cold, rainy day, Elder Hunter joined the other General Authorities for the funeral services in the Tabernacle and graveside services at the Salt Lake City cemetery. "The shock of the passing of President Lee has not worn off," he wrote in his journal that night, "and it is hard to believe he is gone. Although he served as president for only eighteen months, his leadership and vigorous programs will long be remembered."

The next afternoon in the Salt Lake Temple, the apostles again met to select a president. Spencer W. Kimball, the senior apostle, was ordained and set apart as president of the Church, with President Tanner and President Romney as counselors. "Never had I heard the Council more in unity and harmony," Elder Hunter wrote, reflecting later on the proceedings. "I will always remember the sweetness of this occasion and the great love and courtesy shown by the brethren for each other."

As president of the Church, President Kimball set a pace for the Brethren, and for all Latter-day Saints, that was extraordinary, as he challenged everyone to lengthen their stride. He himself set the example. At a temple meeting in December 1980 it was announced that by the time all of the stakes then approved had been organized, there would be 1,244 stakes in the Church. Elder Hunter commented in his journal, "When it was mentioned that about one-half of these [1,244 stakes] had been created in the years since President Kimball became president of the Church, he said, 'Shall we keep on?'"

Though President Kimball suffered from ill health for the last few years of his presidency, he continued to inspire the Church, and particularly his associates in the leading quorums, as they lengthened their stride. Thus, when Elder Hunter and the other members of the Twelve were notified on Tuesday, November 5, 1985, that his condition was grave, the news "cast a gloom over the offices." At about 10:30 that evening, Elder Hunter received a message informing him that President Kimball had passed away.

The next morning the apostles met in the Salt Lake Temple. President Gordon B. Hinckley, who had been serving as second counselor in the First Presidency (President Romney, President Kimball's first counselor, was ill and unable to attend the meeting), resumed his place in the Twelve next to Elder Hunter, beside whom he had sat for twenty years, from 1961 to 1981. These two apostles were assigned to meet with the family and then with departments responsible for various aspects of the funeral services.

A storm predicted for the day of the funeral, Saturday, November 9, held off until just before the graveside services began in the Salt Lake City cemetery, when heavy hail pelted the area. In his journal for that day Elder Hunter wrote: "A great oak has fallen. During his administration and under his leadership, there have been gains in every department of the Church membership, missionary work, temple building and Church administration. His phrase 'lengthen our stride' became synonymous with his life."

The next afternoon at the meeting of the brethren in the temple, Ezra Taft Benson, the senior apostle, was sustained as president, prophet, seer, and revelator, and trustee-in-trust of the Church, with President Hinckley and Elder Thomas S. Monson as his counselors. As the senior apostle, President Romney was now the president of the Quorum of the Twelve

Apostles, but because of his ill health, the next senior apostle, Howard W. Hunter, was sustained as the acting president. In the temple that day, President Hunter ordained and set apart President Benson, after which President Benson set apart his two counselors. Then, with President Hinckley as voice, President Hunter was set apart to his new calling and given a blessing.

At the end of that year, President Hunter summarized his activities and concluded: "With a change in duties, I don't know what my assignments will be, but I do remember the pledge I made before the general conference when I was sustained as a member of the Twelve, and that will be fulfilled to the best of my ability." That pledge was: "I am willing to devote my life and all that I have to this service." This willingness to devote his life and all to the Lord and the Church had been put to the test several times in the years before he was set apart as acting president of the Twelve. In the years to come, he would be tested even further.

13

Family and Neighbors

WHEN PRESIDENT McKAY set Elder Hunter apart as a member of the Quorum of the Twelve Apostles, he prayed that Elder Hunter would be blessed in his home life, that it would "continue to be sweet and wholesome."

Many times in his journal, after he had completed a mission tour or an extensive trip to the far corners of the world, Elder Hunter would add, "It's good to be home." The gracious and comfortable home he and Claire built in Salt Lake City soon after he was called to the Twelve was designed to fit their particular needs and was a haven, a refuge, a place of peace. There he could relax away from the strenuous—at times relentless—pace of his calling, and pursue personal interests or just do nothing in particular. At the end of one year, after summarizing extensive trips throughout Europe, northern Africa, South America, and the United States, he added, "It is good to start this new year at home. . . . We spent a lazy and quiet New Year's Day at home."

Elder Hunter has extensive collections of books and of classical music recordings, and among his first projects in his new home was completion of his library and installation of a stereo system. Less than a month after he and Claire moved in, he purchased some plywood and cut out the enclosures for the stereo speakers to be installed in the library. The next day, he wrote, "Richard and I completed the hookup on the stereo equipment, and by early evening we were able to test it."

*Photo of Howard
with granddaughters
Kathleen and Anne
appeared on the cover
of the October 1964*
Instructor *magazine*

That evening they also viewed slides projected on a screen mounted in the library bookshelves.

In his journal he noted many of his projects, such as the following:

"I stayed home today, worked in the yard and in the basement putting up wallboard and drapery rods."

"I spent most of the day cleaning up my workshop, mounting my power tools, sorting out an accumulation of hardware, and installing some electrical wiring."

"The motor on our furnace was in need of repair so I took it to a shop and had the work done. I spent part of the day tearing down the garbage disposal, getting new parts, and putting it back together."

"I started a project of copying the tapes of the conferences of the Pasadena Stake from the time of dedication of the stake center to my release as stake president. These were made on miscellaneous tapes, and I want to put them in order on four-track tapes."

In high school Howard had excelled in his woodworking classes, and now he had opportunities to put into practice the skills he had acquired. His sons describe how well his workshop is organized. According to John, "I'll say, 'Dad, I need a wrench,' or whatever else I need to work on something at his house, and he'll tell me, 'Go downstairs, to the third door, third drawer, in the middle,' and that's right where I'll find it."

The location of the house, high on the east bench of Salt Lake City, brought the Hunters both blessings and challenges. The neighborhood was quiet and the views spectacular, with the entire Salt Lake Valley and glimpses of the Great Salt Lake to the west, and the mountains rising majestically to the east. With good traffic conditions, Howard could be downtown in about ten minutes. And even a snowfall could bring peace and tranquillity, as this description of New Year's Eve in 1970 illustrates:

"We spent a quiet evening at home. As midnight approached, I walked out on the deck. The night was clear and cold, everything was covered with a white blanket of snow, and the lights of the city cast a reflection to softly light the darkness. A few snowflakes commenced to fall, and out of the stillness I heard a horn blow, and a skyrocket burst with loud report into a thousand stars."

The occasional downside to the foothill location could usually be attributed to weather conditions. In his journal on various dates, Howard wrote: "It was snowing so hard when I left the office this evening that I parked the car at the bottom of the hill and walked home. Cars were stalled all the way up the hill." "It snowed most of the day and I stayed home from the office." "Snow fell during the night and there was a white blanket over everything this morning. I never shovel snow from the walks and driveway that I don't wish we were back in California, at least for the winter."

Some of the worst problems came from heavy rainstorms.

In September 1963, rain washed away grass seeds and some of the top soil. The landscapers returned the next day and replanted. The following day a cloudburst destroyed their work and caused serious erosion. Elder Hunter, who was scheduled to leave for Kansas City that Friday afternoon, rushed home and worked in the downpour to get the water diverted. Then he caught a late-evening flight, arriving in Kansas early Saturday morning. The next week he had a concrete deck with curbing around it constructed to redirect future runoff.

One Saturday he wrote, "I spent most of the day digging up the flower beds, . . . leveling, spreading topsoil, and planting grass seed." The next day, "A rainstorm came up that reached cloudburst proportions where we live. It washed away the seed I planted yesterday and took the peat moss and dirt down the hill. This is a discouraging state of affairs." On Monday, "On my way home [from the office] I bought more grass seed and peat moss and spent the remainder of the day regrading and planting the lawn east of the driveway that was washed away by the cloudburst."

One spring, two days after he planted vegetable seeds and set out tomato plants in a grow-box (which he described as his "little farm"), a late-season snowstorm killed all the plants. "This gives me a better understanding of the problems of a farmer," he commented.

In June 1979, the Hunters had some unexpected visitors: "While we were in Samoa, a family of skunks moved into our yard and burrowed under the concrete slab that forms the back steps of our house. This morning we looked out and saw two adult skunks in the backyard and six bush-tailed little ones frolicking on the grass. Apparently they have established a new home, and I've got to figure out some way to get them out without incurring their displeasure."

Howard called the city animal-control department and was told that skunks do not like mothballs. "I left the office early, purchased a supply of mothballs, and rolled some of them into the hole under the slab when I got home. After dark the skunks came out and the little ones played on the lawn." The next day, after the skunks romped on the back lawn again, he put more mothballs in the hole. That did the trick; they left.

Five years later the skunks returned. "I still have some of the mothballs that encouraged them to leave the last time," Howard wrote, "so I put them in the hole. The next day they had thrown them out, and I put them back. Apparently they have moved, because the last three days they have not been there." He concluded, "I'm glad they left without leaving a reminder."

Friends and Neighbors

THE SUNDAY AFTER they moved into their home, Howard and Claire spoke in sacrament meeting in their new ward, the Monument Park Thirteenth Ward. "After the meeting many people came up to meet us and introduced themselves as our neighbors," he noted in his journal. "I am sure we will enjoy this ward."

Because of heavy travel schedules, particularly on weekends, Elder Hunter often attends Sunday meetings in his own ward only once or twice a year. At tithing settlement one year, he told the bishop that he "would be happy to accept the assignment to do home teaching, perhaps in substituting where the regular teacher could not do his teaching for some reason."

Talmage and Dorothy Nielsen, who built a home across the street from the Hunters and moved in about the same time, served for a time as their home teachers. Sister Nielsen says that Elder Hunter "was always humble and teachable." She remembers an occasion when, after someone in their Sunday School class raised a question, the teacher turned to Elder Hunter and asked, "What do you think?" He declined to respond, explaining, "You must remember, I'm just a General Authority."

Claire was active in Relief Society, attending meetings and

socials whenever she wasn't traveling with her husband. One entry in his journal describes a craft she learned in the early 1960s that many Relief Society sisters will remember: "Claire went with some of the Relief Society sisters this evening to learn how to make glass grape decorations." The centerpiece she made was displayed in their home for many years.

The Hunters moved into an area with friendly neighbors who looked out for one another and who enjoyed socializing with each other at block parties. Preston Adams, a fellow ward member, frequently cleaned their walks and driveway after snowstorms. When the wind blew out their large front window, Howard reported, "Some of our neighbors came with plastic, cloths, and other things to help cover the furniture and carpeting from the driving rain." At Christmas, a steady procession of people visited the Hunters, brought treats, and presented special programs.

Howard did his part to keep the neighborhood safe and clean. One day, after a house-cleaning spree, he put the garbage bags out on the curb for pickup by city sanitation crews. That night some teenagers in a jeep rammed into the bags, scattering garbage down the street for two blocks. A neighbor saw Howard outside early the next morning, cleaning up the garbage and putting it in new bags.

On another occasion, Talmage Nielsen was installing a speaker system on his boat, which was parked in his driveway across the street. Howard insisted on helping, and immediately crawled under the boat to see what needed to be done. Since he had installed his own stereo system, he understood the process.

While the Nielsens were serving a mission in Ecuador in 1992–93, Elder Hunter saw their son in their front yard, repairing a broken sprinkler head. Within moments he was on his way across the street, offering to help.

The Nielsens shared many special memories with the Hunters. Once they all went to the family's lakeside ranch in the Wasatch Mountains on the Fourth of July. When one of the

Nielsen children threw a firecracker that started a grass fire, threatening the home, Claire grabbed a blanket off the back of a horse, ran down to the lake and soaked it, and beat the fire out.

Another neighbor and close friend, who also served for several years as their stake president, is Jon Huntsman, a prominent industrialist and philanthropist. One Christmas he called Howard and told him that a mutual friend from Southern California, Roland Rich Woolley, had for several years phoned the Huntsman children every Christmas Eve, identified himself as Santa Claus, and explained that he would come during the night to leave presents if they had been good children during the year.

"Brother Woolley died recently," Elder Hunter wrote, "and I was pleased to have the invitation to be Santa this year. I called and talked with each of the five littlest ones, and it was a real pleasure to hear them tell how hard they have tried to be good and how much they will appreciate whatever Santa leaves for them." He continued to make the annual calls during the three years the children lived in Washington, D.C., while their father served as a mission president.

Family Activities

IN JULY 1969 Howard and Claire, John and Louine, and Richard and Nan met in Boston to begin a twelve-day Church history tour by rental car. Richard had prepared ahead of time and provided commentary, drawing from the Prophet Joseph Smith's words in *History of the Church* and from other historical sources on events that took place in the areas they visited.

The six vacationers stopped often as they wound through New England, New York, Pennsylvania, Ohio, Illinois, and Missouri. At the Sacred Grove, where the Prophet had prayed and had had a vision of God the Father and His Son, Jesus Christ, Howard wrote: "The grove was beautiful after the showers of the past few days. The sun shone through the trees in ribbons of light, and the quiet of the grove gives one a feel-

Richard and Nan, left;
John and Louine,
Howard and Claire
at Adam-ondi-Ahman
in July 1969

ing of serenity. I can better understand what took place on that spring morning in the year 1820."

History was also in the making that July. While stopped at a traffic light in Farmer City, Illinois, they listened intently to the car radio as American astronauts circled and then landed on the moon. "It was a breathtaking experience to listen to the instructions from the ground for the landing," Howard recorded. "People all over the world were listening and nervously awaiting the result of this crucial moment. After a few seconds the words of Neil Armstrong came from the spacecraft, 'The Eagle has landed.'"

That night they checked into a motel at Nauvoo, Illinois, headquarters of the Church in the early 1840s, and immediately turned on the television sets in their rooms. Like viewers all over America and the world, they watched in awe as the astronaut took his historic walk on the moon and planted the American flag in moon soil. "The whole thing seems incredibly fantastic, but we saw it with our own eyes and listened to the whole procedure with our own ears," Howard marveled. "Walking on the moon by earth man is now a fact."

While traveling, Howard liked to keep on the go from early morning until late at night, and he didn't always take time to stop at mealtimes. One day, after they had visited several sites, he commented, "Well, I think we really should eat two meals a day." The others immediately responded, "That's fine. Let's decide right now which two we'll have and make sure we get them!"

Before he was called to the Twelve, Howard had planned to practice law in California with his sons. Though they both graduated from Brigham Young University and John also completed a master's degree at the Provo school, they elected to attend California law schools and to practice law there.

John received his LL.B. from the University of Southern California, where he was on the staff of the *Law Review.* He served as a deputy district attorney in Ventura County, northwest of Los Angeles, for four years and then became a partner in a law firm. In 1970 he was appointed judge of the Ventura County Municipal Court by then-Governor Ronald Reagan, and in 1992 he retired from that position and accepted an appointment as judge of the Superior Court in Ventura. His wife, Louine, received a bachelor's degree in elementary education from BYU. They have made their home in Ventura County and now reside in Ojai in a Spanish-style hilltop home surrounded by orange groves.

Richard graduated in law from the University of California in Berkeley and established his practice in the San Francisco Bay Area. He and Nan lived for a time in Denver while he completed work on a CPA degree. After practicing law for several years in various Bay Area communities, he established his own firm in San Jose. Nan received a degree from BYU in zoology in 1961, and has been active in education as the owner and director of a private elementary school. A gifted musician, she wrote the words to a hymn in the LDS hymnal, "Father, This Hour Has Been One of Joy." Richard and Nan built their home in a wooded area in San Jose.

Howard ordained both of his sons as high priests in the

Family members enjoy lunch in Howard Hunter's office between conference sessions in October 1984: Howard, left; Anne Hunter, Richard's daughter; Dorothy Hunter Rasmussen and her husband, Marvin; Richard Hunter; and Robert Hunter, John's son, and his wife, Kenna. Richard's eldest daughter, Kathleen, took the photograph

Church at age twenty-three, when each was called to serve as counselor in a bishopric, and a few years later he ordained each to the office of bishop. When he stopped over in San Francisco, while en route to an assignment in the South Pacific, to ordain Richard a bishop in 1971, he wrote in his journal: "He [Richard] called our attention to the fact that John, he, and I were each ordained a bishop at thirty-two years of age. I don't know how our family could be more blessed, and I don't know how I could be more blessed as a father than to have both of my sons faithful in their priesthood and raising families in faith and devotion." John and Richard also served in stake presidencies.

Both sons, usually with their wives and often some of their children, attended most general conferences after Howard was called to the Twelve, sitting in a reserved section near the front of the Tabernacle. Between sessions they went to Howard's office in the Church Administration Building for a lunch prepared by Ruth Webb, his secretary for more than two decades. When she was ill or away, other secretaries or daughters-in-law and granddaughters packed picnic baskets for the traditional gatherings.

Howard and Claire welcomed their family and looked forward to visiting into the late evenings and sometimes viewing home movies. In his journal Howard described his sons' visit in October 1972: "Arriving home [in Salt Lake City], they raided the cookie jar and sorted through the refrigerator—not much change from the routine of earlier years. It was a comfortable feeling for the family to be kneeling together again for prayer at bedtime."

A Proud Grandfather

IN HIS ASSOCIATIONS with the Saints throughout the world, Howard has often been asked if he is related to this or that person named Hunter. His grandfather, John Hunter, did not join the Church, and Will Hunter was John's only son who had a male heir to carry on the Hunter name. The odds doubled in the next generation, when Howard had two sons who married and had families, and those families have ensured that the name will live on. John and Louine have eight sons and two daughters, and Richard and Nan have four sons and four daughters.

When each of their children was born, Louine and Nan received a pad of one hundred one-dollar bills from the proud grandfather. The new mothers had fun tearing off the bills as they spent them. The last of the eighteen grandchildren was born in October 1979. Since this was also Louine and John's tenth child, Howard had his bank make up a pad of one hundred ten-dollar bills. "I hope she enjoys spending them," he wrote in his journal.

Many of Grandfather Hunter's visits with his grandchildren had to come on the run, such as brief layovers while traveling through California on Church assignments. One story repeated in the family and media told how, because John's children went with their father to the Los Angeles air terminal

Howard and Claire's descendants flank them in photo taken at the beach in July 1974. John's family is on the left, Richard's on the right

to meet their grandfather, they came to know Howard as "the grandpa who lives at the airport."

Howard and Claire looked forward to visiting their family in California in July and during the Christmas holidays, when General Authorities have no official assignments. They alternated these brief vacations between Southern California and the Bay Area. Usually both John's and Richard's families managed to be together for at least part of the time. All eighteen grandchildren were born between 1959 and 1979, resulting in many little ones underfoot, with more structured activities in the earlier years, and teenage activities and competitive sports as they grew up.

Summers were a time for outings in the mountains or at the beach. In July 1975, the family enjoyed a few days at the Aspen Grove family camp, a BYU facility in American Fork Canyon twenty-five miles south of Salt Lake City. One evening the entire family crowded into Howard and Claire's cabin at the recreation area for a talent show. "The nights are cool and there is no heat in the cabins," Howard wrote. "We are glad we brought our electric blankets."

Some of the most relaxing times came at rented beach homes on Monterey Bay and at Mussel Shoals near Santa Barbara. In July 1976 Howard wrote: "Everything at the seashore seems alive and moving, especially the seventeen children with the last name of Hunter, who are busy digging, building, swimming, throwing, jumping, running, screaming, chasing, climbing, wrestling and eating, but seldom ever sitting, sleeping or anything of a quiet nature. The cousins are having the time of their lives."

One year, under Nan's direction, the children worked out a mystery story, assembled costumes, rehearsed, and then filmed a story they titled "Kidnapped," which their proud grandfather claimed "must be the most exciting production ever filmed." An annual tradition was a sand-castle building competition, which was judged by the adults, and each year the children presented a talent show.

On Sundays, the entire family would either attend a local ward, where they filled two long benches, or conduct Sunday School and sacrament meeting at their rented beach house, times that brought the family even closer. Once as the priesthood holders in the family were driving into town for priesthood meeting, their car broke down. They managed to get back to the beach house, where they called taxis to come take the family to Sunday School. But only one taxi showed up, "intending to take half of us and come back for the others," Howard remembered. "This would have made us miss Sunday School so we stayed and held our own meeting. Richard, our bishop, conducted. We sang hymns, John administered the sacrament, and it was passed by Robert and Steven. Testimonies were borne by everyone except the tiny children. It was a joy to hear the children express their feelings about the Church and their gratitude for being members of our family. How blessed we are to have our sons, their wives and children actively devoted to the Church. It may be that there was a reason why we were not able to get to church this morning."

On a memorable summer evening in 1983 he wrote: "The children wanted me to tell them how I was called to the Council of the Twelve and what my assignments are. When the evening's program ended we went out on the beach and watched the grunion come in. Hundreds of wriggling, shining, silver fish, glistening in the lights from the house, came in on the beach with the breakers. The boys gathered several buckets full and put them in bags in the freezer to be used for fish bait."

Howard, who as a youth had collected birds' eggs in the marshes along the Boise River, was fascinated by the birds at the beach. One summer he wrote: "On most beaches there are many people and few birds, but here there are few people and therefore hundreds of birds of many varieties. . . . I have always thought there was something peculiar about bird watchers, but since reading about the birds that live near the water and migrate from one hemisphere to the other, I have become very interested. All morning long strings have been going up and down the beach, skimming along the breakers. The most common birds are various species of sandpipers, plovers, curlews, willets, oystercrackers, dunlines, snipes, gulls and pelicans. They become fascinating to one who doesn't have anything to do."

He also enjoyed the solitude of early-morning walks: "Not a person could be seen when I got up and went for a walk this morning. The ocean was beautiful and the tide was out. I walked along the beach for the length of Mussel Shoals. . . . A lonesome dog joined me. He led the way and we watched the sand birds as they search for sea food at the edge of the water where the waves washed the beach." The next day, "Again I was up early and retraced my steps of yesterday along the beach, watching the birds follow the water as it washed up on the sand and fell back to leave sand crabs and other little creatures exposed for prey to the hungry sea birds."

Christmas at his sons' homes brought respite from the typically cold, snowy season in Utah. It also brought considerably less peace and quiet than Howard experienced at home, such as Christmas day at John's home in 1968:

"The children were up early, and it was not long before the

John and Louine Hunter's family, Christmas 1983

house looked like it had been struck by a tornado, but I suppose this is to be expected from five excited little boys. . . . About seven o'clock Richard, Nan, and their four children arrived from San Jose, so all of our family is together and we had a second Christmas. It was soon bedtime. The two little ones were put in cribs and the other seven in sleeping bags, and before long all was quiet again. This has been a nice day and enjoyable to be together."

In 1971 Howard and Claire were again at John's home. "Blast-off time was seven o'clock. The children were up, dressed, and ready for the dash to the living room when the word 'go' was said. Bedlam reigned, but out of the noise and confusion emerged seven children from the shredded wrappings and ribbons, with their arms loaded with Christmas plunder."

For the holidays in 1975, the family had a special Christmas at Richard's home in honor of their Danish heritage. "Nan prepared a big turkey dinner for Christmas Eve," Howard reported. "The table was beautifully set with Christmas tree

Richard and Nan Hunter's family, Christmas 1983

plates, candles and Danish delicacies." The next morning "the children were up early. Bedlam reigned supreme in the excitement of opening gifts. Later in the morning we had a Danish smorgasbord breakfast that was delicious. . . . We had a late supper by candlelight with cold turkey and more Danish specialties. Nan has made this Christmas a little bit of Denmark."

The entire family was together at John's home in 1983, which, Howard noted, with the older grandchildren now receiving mission calls and attending college, "could well be the last time."

Just before Christmas in 1987, Howard recorded in his journal, "Richard had asked that I have a talk with each of his eight children, so after dinner I had the pleasure of a little private chat with them individually. We talked about their progress in school, their feelings about the Church and their testimony, their family relationships, and many other things. I am so pleased with their successes, maturity and ambitions."

Having their grandfather perform their temple sealings has been important to the grandchildren. As those who are married have planned their weddings, they have consulted him to work out any scheduling problems, according to Richard, "knowing that his schedule was difficult and that he would not ask for any special favors to alter it."

With the relentlessly demanding life Howard led most of the time, it wasn't always easy for him to relax on vacations. "When Grandpa came for Christmas," Nan says, "we recognized that if he were going to be happy in our home, we had to have something for him to do." She began saving projects and repairs for his visits.

One year Howard helped Richard rake leaves and trim shrubbery, clean the garage, and haul a load of rubbish to the dump. Then they drew up a design for a puppet theater for the children and went to a building materials company for the lumber and hardware. The next morning, while Richard conducted tithing settlement at his ward, Howard cut out the materials. That afternoon he and Richard assembled the theater and Nan and Claire made puppets and clothes for a manger scene.

Another Christmas, Howard wrote: "Richard went to the office for part of the day, and while he was gone I cut out and made stick horses for the little children's Christmas. When he returned, we disconnected the kitchen range and replaced some of the electrical parts."

The next year, while Richard was at work, Howard began the projects Nan had planned: "First I tore down the clothes dryer and removed the heating element that had burned out, then commenced the construction of a plywood dollhouse for Merrily from plans Nan had obtained." The following morning he raked the leaves, cleaned the yard, and completed the dollhouse.

During one visit, he and Richard hauled lumber home from a lumberyard, then framed in and built a deck complete with a roof (it took every available person to raise the roof, including Nan's parents, Sol and Florence Greene), laid out a sprinkler system, and installed water lines and valves. Once,

*Howard carves turkey
for Christmas dinner
at John's home in 1983*

after taking apart the salt machine for the soft-water system and cleaning the deposits, he commented in his journal: "This should qualify us for merit badges in home repairs."

As the grandchildren went on missions, Howard kept in touch with them by letter, and occasionally an assignment would take him into their area, where he could visit with them personally. During a 1990 stop at Colonial Williamsburg, Virginia, he spent a few minutes with Richard's daughter Merrily, who was serving in the Virginia Roanoke Mission. "Today in Williamsburg was a special day to write about in my journal," she reported in a *Church News* article. "My grandfather enjoyed the review of the history of our nation. He is avidly interested in history, and his patriotism is something his whole family is always aware of."

The love his grandchildren have for him is expressed in a 1979 Father's Day message signed by Richard, Nan, and their eight children: "We will honor you this day by striving our hardest to keep the commandments, loving each other and all others, working hard at our assignments, studying the scriptures, praying together and individually, planting a garden, serving others and keeping the Sabbath day holy plus more! We thank you for your part in our family, for all your love and care for us, and we appreciate and love you for it. We are proud of all you have done in your life, and it is an honor for us on this day (and all others) to know we belong to you forever and you to us. Love and 1,000 kisses."

Extended Family Relationships

HOWARD HUNTER is a family man. He takes great pride in his descendants and he feels close to his ancestors, those who sacrificed so much to join the Church and helped to establish communities and families in Zion. In his journal he once quoted novelist George Eliot: "I desire no future that will break the ties of the past."

In March 1957, two and a half years before Howard was called to the Twelve, he visited Mount Pleasant, Utah, where his pioneer great-grandfathers had settled, and wrote: "Even though I have never lived here, this is my home because my roots are here. How grateful I am for the heritage that means so much to me that comes from the settlement in this valley by those of faith who left loved ones behind, trusted the winds to make the Atlantic crossing, and endured the hardships of the great American desert to come to this place yet untamed by the hand of man."

For many years he took an active role in extended-family organizations, where he compared, exchanged, and verified genealogical information. In 1973 he noted, "The whole day

was spent on my genealogical records. I have now completed
the record of all of the descendants of my great-grandfather
Anders Christensen, which now number 288 families to the
end of 1973. I am also doing research on his progenitors' lines
and have extended some of them beyond what the family has
done in past years."

A few years later, when the Church asked members to prepare four-generation family-group sheets and submit them to
the Genealogical Department, he attended workshop sessions
of the Christensen family and "gave out family-group sheets
on Anders Christensen and his four wives and gave instructions on the preparation of four-generation sheets."

Christensen family reunions in Mount Pleasant usually
extend over two to three days, drawing participants from far
and near. Whenever possible, Howard has attended. The
reunions are highlighted by visits to the old Anders Christensen home and the Morten Rasmussen home, which is listed
on the federal register of historic homes; family grave sites in
the Mount Pleasant cemetery; visiting and sharing genealogical information; enjoying a talent show; and attending a session at the Manti Temple.

One year Howard attended a Thanksgiving dinner for
members of the Rasmussen family in the Mount Pleasant
School cafeteria. "It was a delightful occasion," he said. "I took
my genealogical book of the Rasmussen family and was able
to get much missing information."

The Hunter family genealogy has been more difficult to
find, as Howard's great-great-grandmother Nancy Hatch
Nowell was the only ancestor active in the Church. In
Philadelphia in 1974 he met a cousin of his father, Dorothy
Carousso, who was an officer of the Pennsylvania Genealogical Society. She showed him through the society's archives and
library and gave him copies of her research on the Nowell
family line. She also told him about the book titled *Testimony of
Nancy Nowell*, comprised of what she described as "a daily
account of the devotional and devout exercises of my heart

and the testimony of the truth." He was able to obtain a copy for his own library, which he would occasionally pull off the shelf to read.

Claire Hunter also was interested in genealogy. She compiled information on her German ancestors, though many records that would have been helpful were destroyed during World Wars I and II. And she traced records of the Jeffs family and wrote family histories.

Though their parents and siblings all lived in California, Howard and Claire kept in close touch with them, visited them whenever possible, and looked forward to their visits to Utah.

When Howard's name was read in the 1959 general conference, one of the first persons to respond was his mother, who sent a telegram from her home in Southgate, California: "Proud of you. Speeches all wonderful. Such a thrill. I am covered with goose pimples. Most sincere. God be with you all. [signed] Mother."

Nellie was her son's proudest booster and supporter. In a Mother's Day article in the *Deseret News* in 1983, Howard reminisced that when he became bishop of the El Sereno Ward, she told him: "It's nice to be important, but it's more important to be nice."[1] The article described how Nellie "had a strong personality, she had charisma, but she always loved people, and everyone loved her. She was not the show-off type, but they always said she was the life of the party at [Relief Society] work meeting; she always had a story to tell."

In addition to her activity in the Church auxiliaries, Nellie was a member of the Daughters of Utah Pioneers. She sang with the "Memorial Chorus of California DUP" at the dedicatory services of the DUP Memorial Building in Salt Lake City July 23 and 24, 1950.[2]

Howard had been in Chicago when he learned of his father's death in 1963, and he was in Chicago September 4, 1971, when he learned that his mother was seriously ill and had been taken to the hospital. He and Claire were changing planes at the Chicago airport, en route from Frankfurt, Germany, to a conference assignment in Milwaukee, and the president of the Chicago Stake intercepted him to give him the news. He called his sister, Dorothy, in Los Angeles, and learned that Nellie, who suffered from a heart ailment, had developed pneumonia but was responding to treatment. He went on to fill his assignment, as he had done eight years earlier when his mother told him, after he learned of his father's death, "You are on the Lord's errand and should finish the assignment first."

Nellie's condition declined rapidly, and on Thursday, November 11, while Howard was attending the temple meeting of the Twelve, he received a message that she had just died peacefully in her sleep. "The brethren extended their sympathy," he recalled. "President Kimball asked if I would like to be excused. My thoughts went back to the day in Chicago when I got the message that my Father had passed away. When I called Mother, she encouraged me to stay and finish the Lord's business before leaving. I told President Kimball I would stay and take care of my duties."

The next day Howard attended the inaugural of Dallin H. Oaks as president of Brigham Young University, then accompanied other General Authorities to St. George for a solemn assembly in commemoration of the one hundredth anniversary of the ground breaking for the St. George Temple. His official duties now completed, he flew with Claire to Los Angeles for his mother's funeral and burial. "This was a sad day for us, yet one of rejoicing," he wrote. "Mother has lived a long and useful life, and each one of her posterity are active in the Church. Her physical body had given out and it was time for her to go, her work accomplished. How thankful I am to the Lord for my inheritance."

Claire's mother too welcomed visits from Howard and Claire whenever they were in Southern California. For many years she took in boarders at her big home in Los Angeles. She served in many Church callings, including temple worker,

*Will and Nellie Hunter
celebrated their fiftieth
wedding anniversary
in Hawaii in 1956*

counselor in Primary and Relief Society presidencies, and religion class teacher. In April 1967, after she had suffered several
strokes, she lived with Howard and Claire for a few months,
and then her family moved her to a retirement home near the
Salt Lake Temple. She died on December 22, 1974, at ninety-
two, and was buried in Inglewood, next to the graves of her
husband, who died in 1933, and her infant grandson, Howard
William Hunter Jr., who died in 1934.

14

"A Full Share of Ups and Downs"

LIFE—EVERY LIFE—has a full share of ups and downs. Indeed, we see many joys and sorrows in the world, many changed plans and new directions, many blessings that do not always look or feel like blessings, and much that humbles us and improves our patience and our faith."[1]

When Howard W. Hunter spoke these words in his October 1987 general conference address, he was speaking from experience. Over the previous fifteen years he had had a full share of ups and downs, joys and sorrow, and had seen many changed plans and new directions. He went on to explain:

"Being childlike and submitting to our Father's will is not always easy. President Spencer W. Kimball, who knew a great deal about suffering, disappointment, and circumstances beyond his control, once wrote: 'Being human, we would expel from our lives physical pain and mental anguish and assure ourselves of continual ease and comfort, but if we were to close the doors upon sorrow and distress, we might be excluding our greatest friends and benefactors. Suffering can make saints of people as they learn patience, long-suffering, and self-mastery.'"[2]

Patience, long-suffering, and self-mastery. These became guiding principles in Elder Hunter's life, as first Claire and then he experienced major health problems.

In the early 1970s Claire started to exhibit occasional memory loss, severe headaches, and disorientation. Howard wrote in his journal in October 1972 that he had taken her to the doctor's office and then the hospital for tests. When the results were in, the doctor "diagnosed her condition as hardening of the arteries and prescribed medicine to help overcome the problem."

But the problem didn't go away. Three months later, in February 1973, she was back in the hospital for more tests, including dye injected in the arteries of her neck and traced through her head. A blood clot was located, and new medications were prescribed. Again there was no improvement.

Over the next few years many more tests were conducted, other medications were prescribed, and specialists were consulted, but no one knew exactly what was causing Claire's illness nor how to treat it successfully. During a business trip to Southern California, Howard talked with a neurological surgeon at a hospital in Hollywood. On another occasion he and Claire's physician consulted by phone with deans at the Harvard University and the University of California medical colleges. When they described the symptoms, the neurologists were not encouraging.

After she experienced sudden and severe pains in her left chest and arm, Claire was hospitalized in July 1975. Part of her left lung had collapsed. That problem was corrected, but six months later, on December 29, she was back in the hospital for a cisternagram—an injection of a radioactive isotope in the spinal fluid. Afterwards the surgeon discussed the options with Howard, including possible surgery.

"Although the indications for surgery are not strong," Howard wrote in his journal, "he [the doctor] said this is the last avenue available. He also told me that if it was his wife, he would proceed with a shunt operation. This was a most difficult decision to make. If it will help Claire, it should be done. If no good will result, it will be terrible to subject her to this ordeal. I felt the need to go to the temple where I could be alone, and after returning, I called Dorothy, Richard and John. Each of them expressed the opinion that if this is the only thing that might give relief, the risk should be assumed; otherwise we would always feel that there was something that might have been done."

The morning after New Year's Day in 1976, Howard went to the hospital before dawn and sat with Claire until she was taken to surgery. "I went with her as far as the doors to the operating room, gave her a kiss, and she was taken on through the doors. As time went by, I waited and wondered and thought of the times outside the delivery room doors years ago. Suddenly the tense anxiety turned into a feeling of peace. I knew the right decision had been made and that my prayers had been answered."

The surgeon reported that he "had placed a shunt from an area in the brain above and back of the right ear to a vessel in the neck to relieve the pressure. If pressure has been the problem, this may provide relief."

Every day until she was released nearly two weeks later, Howard visited Claire in the hospital: early in the morning, at noon, and after work until she went to sleep. One evening, by the time he left the hospital, heavy snow made the roads nearly impassable. It took more than an hour—at least five times as long as usual—to get to the street leading up to his home from the boulevard down the hill. "I could not get up the hill to our house because it was blocked by dozens of stalled cars," he wrote, "so I left the car and walked home. . . . Sometimes I wish we were still in Southern California."

Ten weeks after Claire's surgery, Howard took her to the doctor for a check-up. "He said there should have been greater signs of improvement by this time, which may indicate that the accomplishment will be minimal."

Before Claire was released from the hospital, tests were taken that indicated she was developing adult-onset diabetes. The doctors said it was a mild case that could be easily controlled, and Howard learned how to perform necessary tests at home. But it was soon obvious that she could not be left alone, and so he arranged to have a woman come stay with her during the day. A few months later he prepared a small apartment in the basement of his home for a live-in companion/housekeeper. He, however, still took care of her at night, which meant that he got little sleep.

Despite his constant worries about Claire, Howard continued to carry a heavy load in the Twelve. He was released from one or two of his assignments, but the Church was growing rapidly, particularly in Latin America and Asia, and he was determined to do his full share of the work. Whenever he could, he took Claire with him, particularly in the early stages of her illness, but as it became more difficult to give her adequate care away from home, he traveled alone or took another member of his family. Most of his grandchildren attended BYU, and they accompanied him to social and official functions on campus. At general conferences, Claire would sit with Dorothy near the front of the Tabernacle in the rows reserved for family members and special guests, rather than in her assigned seat with the other wives of General Authorities.

When he was away from Salt Lake, Howard called home often to check up on Claire's condition, which continued to deteriorate. Small strokes took their toll, and it became difficult for her to speak or to use her hands. When her left lung collapsed, she was taken back to surgery to have tubes inserted through the chest wall to extract the air around the lung so it could inflate again. Several times she had fainting spells, possibly caused by small strokes. Her companion would call Howard at the office, and he would dash home as quickly as he could. Often she would have revived by the time he got there, but sometimes she had to be taken to the hospital for observation and treatment.

In May 1981 Claire suffered a cerebral hemorrhage. The doctors' prognosis: she probably would not be able to walk again. When she was released from the hospital two and a half weeks later, she was in a wheelchair, still unable to walk. Two weeks later Howard wrote hopefully, "Although the doctors have said she would not be able to walk again, she is now able

to stand if she is supported, and this morning by [my] holding her hands and leading her, she was able to walk from the
bedroom to the kitchen."

Dorothy Nielsen, Howard and Claire's dear friend and
neighbor across the street, remembers being present when
Howard returned home from the office or a trip. He would
help Claire to her feet from her wheelchair and, supporting
her tightly, whirl her around the room just as he had done
when they went dancing so many years before. He took her
regularly to her favorite hair dresser for permanents and
shampoos, and even though she couldn't communicate, he
would talk to her and tell her about his day and share news
with her about family and friends.

"The Tenderness Which Was Evident"

EACH MINOR VICTORY and hope for Claire's recovery
seemed to be followed by even more debilitating setbacks. In
April 1982, she had another cerebral attack, and this time she
didn't respond. She went into a deep slumber that lasted for
several days, and when she finally did open her eyes occasionally, there was no sign she knew where she was or what
was happening. This time the doctors insisted that she be
released to a care center where she would have twenty-four-
hour nursing service.

Howard had strongly resisted having Claire taken care of
any place but in her own home. But because he too was experiencing major health problems by this time, it was no longer
possible for him to care for her and also keep up the pace of
his ecclesiastical calling. And so, on April 22, 1982, some ten
years after Claire's health had begun its relentless decline, she
was admitted to a nursing home about five miles from their
home, in the East Millcreek area of Salt Lake County.

Howard now began a routine of visiting Claire once or
twice a day. If he was out of town on assignment, he would go
to her bedside from the airport before going home. "Each day
I have the hope that she will be better, but the progress is

slow," he wrote on May 3, 1982. "Most of the time her eyes are closed, and she doesn't seem to recognize me." Three weeks after she was admitted to the nursing home, he removed her diamond engagement ring, but because her finger was swollen, he had to clip her wedding ring to get it off—"the first time it has been off since I put it on her finger in the temple the day we were married."

For eighteen months Claire remained in the nursing home, with little change in her condition from day to day. And for those eighteen months, Howard and other family members, as well as Lucy Thomas, the elderly woman who had taken care of her at home, visited regularly, hoping against hope that she would awaken from her deep sleep and recognize them.

Following the afternoon session of general conference on Saturday, October 1, 1983, Lee Child, Claire's niece who had been like a daughter to the Hunters, went with Howard to see Claire. "She did not recognize anyone at this stage of her illness," Lee remembers, "but my uncle and I talked to her as though she heard. We made her comfortable and told her of our love for her. That was a special 'sharing time.'"

The following Thursday Claire developed pneumonia. Because she seemed to be a little better on Saturday, Howard left to fulfill his assignment to divide the Caldwell Stake in Idaho. After the stake conference meetings on Sunday, he called home and was told that Claire's condition was "about the same." He returned to Salt Lake City on a late-afternoon flight and was met at the airport by Dr. J. Poulson Hunter, their family doctor and dear friend.

"As soon as I saw him, I knew something was wrong," Howard remembered. "He said, 'Claire has left us. She passed away just an hour ago.' I was heartsick. We walked out of the terminal together and he drove me to the Church Administration Building where I had left my car. On the way he talked about how much better this was for her and, of course, I knew this if she could not get well, but it did not take away the pain I felt knowing that she was gone."

*The Hunter family on the front lawn at Howard's home
following Claire's funeral, October 12, 1983*

He drove directly to the nursing home, where the nurse who had been with her said that Claire had passed away peacefully, "from deep breathing to soft, quiet breathing which gradually stopped." He called the funeral home and then remained with Claire until after the hearse left. "As I drove home," he wrote, "the full impact of what had happened commenced to make an impression on me [that] this was the last trip I would make to see her at the nursing home after going there at least once a day for the past eighteen months. When I got home the house seemed cold, and as I walked about, everything reminded me of her."

On Wednesday, October 12, friends and family members filled the Monument Park Stake Center for the funeral services. Howard took comfort from the words spoken and the prayers offered by close friends and associates: President Gordon B. Hinckley, President Thomas S. Monson, and Elder James E. Faust; J. Talmage Jones, his former bishop and counselor in the stake presidency in Pasadena, and Daken K. Broadhead, also a former counselor in the stake presidency. Richard Hunter offered the family prayer and John Hunter delivered a tribute to his mother. After the services, the cortege drove to the Salt Lake City cemetery, where Richard dedicated the grave on a hillside overlooking the Salt Lake Valley.

For more than a dozen years, Howard had cared tenderly for his beloved companion as her health went continually downhill. Elder Faust, in his funeral sermon, summarized what many felt that day: "This queenly woman must have been one of God's great and noble women to have commanded so much love and so much cherishing—so much respect, devotion, admiration and loving care from her eternal companion. This was reciprocated by Clara even though after a time she became diminished. At times she would smile and respond only to Howard. The tenderness which was evident in their communication was heart rending and touching. I have never seen such an example of devotion of a husband to his wife. It has been a many-splendored love affair."

After the family had all left that evening, Howard sat alone for about an hour, reflecting. "It seemed lonesome," he wrote in his journal. "Claire hasn't been home for a long time, but I am commencing to realize that she will not be back."

A Not-So-Patient Patient

FOR MOST OF his life, Howard enjoyed good health, except for the bout with polio when he was a child. In fact, he noted in his journal, it wasn't until October 1965, just before his fifty-eighth birthday, that he consulted a doctor because of illness. An infection, which caused a high fever and flu-like symptoms, kept him home for two weeks. Up to that time, and for a dozen years afterward, he was relatively healthy. Any necessary medical care was given in his doctor's office.

In February 1977, he went from the temple meeting to the hospital for tests, then returned to the office to await the doctor's call with the diagnosis. He was shocked when he was told he had mumps, probably contracted on the day he organized two new stakes in Mexico. "I never thought I would have the honor of having 'Mexican' mumps," he mused. He gathered up some files and papers and went home to bed.

"Everyone seems to think it is funny that I have the mumps, but I don't think so," he wrote in his journal. "President Kimball says maybe I haven't yet grown up."

Not having had much experience with illness, it was difficult for him to stay down. After spending most of the second day "with the adding machine, ledgers, papers, statements and checks" to take to the accountant in connection with the large cattle ranch he and Gilles DeFlon had purchased in northwestern Utah, he reported that he "got a good day's work done without too seriously violating the instructions to stay in bed. Dr. Hunter came by to see me in the evening—no doubt to see if I was in bed." After the doctor checked again two days later, Howard commented, "I think he really comes to see if I am following his instructions to stay in bed. Fortunately that's where I was when he arrived."

The year 1980 was not a good year so far as Howard's health was concerned. On June 4 he entered the hospital, where he underwent four and a half hours of surgery to remove a tumor. He was grateful when his surgeons told him they had found no cancer cells in the lymph nodes, which meant he would not have to undergo radiation or other treatment. The day he was released from the hospital, he reported that his home teacher brought him a bowl of beautiful strawberries. "I'm commencing to believe that it's not so bad to be sick after all," he wrote.

Just a few weeks later, on July 23, he arrived home in the evening and sat down to read the newspaper when he felt a severe pain in his chest. He called Dr. Hunter, who came quickly and took him to the hospital for an electrocardiogram. Within an hour Howard was admitted to the intensive care unit of the hospital for a heart attack. He was on a heart monitor in the ICU until July 28, and extensive tests were done before his release from the hospital August 7. One of the cardiologists told him that the damage to his heart had been minimal, and with caution and care, he should be able to return to normal activities soon.

At the time Claire was still at home, her condition gradually deteriorating, so Dorothy took her for a few days so that Howard would not have to worry about her. The doctors ordered him to rest and give his heart time to heal, though at times he chafed at the prescribed regimen. At the end of the first week home he noted, "This was the most quiet day of all—I was home alone. I have had surgery, a heart attack, and the next may be a nervous breakdown for not being allowed to do anything." One week later he wrote, "With nothing to do, nothing was done all day." By the end of August, he found the inactivity "becoming unbearable."

One activity that the doctors encouraged was walking. In the evenings, when the sun started to set and cool breezes floated down the canyon above his home, he walked around the neighborhood, listening to tapes of BYU devotional talks, general conference sessions, and other gospel-related information. In his journal he wrote, "By increasing exercise each day I will be able to walk a mile [within three weeks] if in the meantime I don't have a nervous breakdown thinking of all the things that need to be done and not being able to do them." When he reached his goal of one mile a day, his doctor challenged him to increase it to two miles within another three weeks, though, Howard admitted, "I don't become enthusiastic about walking."

On Friday, September 5, Howard wrote, "This is a red-letter day—going back to the office even if it is only for two hours each day." When he flew to Los Angeles two days later to attend the Watson Land Company board meeting, he took advantage of a wait at the airport to walk a mile and a half around the corridors. Gradually, as he followed the regimen recommended by his doctors and physical therapists, his heart healed and he was able to resume his full share of assignments. But he also continued to guard against further problems. One year after he returned to work he wrote, "Each week-day morning I get up at five-thirty and go for a walk for at least a mile, not because I enjoy it but because the doctors insist."

"The Sand Runs Faster"

THE YEARS IMMEDIATELY after his heart attack found Howard traveling almost as much as ever: to Mexico, Europe, the Middle East, South America, the Far East, the islands of the South Pacific, Australia, and many parts of the United States and Canada. He visited some places several times, such as Israel, where the Jerusalem Center was nearing completion.

By year's end he was usually content to stay home and rest. One New Year's Eve he wrote in his journal: "Although many stay up to see the Old Year out and the New Year in, I went to bed early. About midnight I woke up. Automobile horns were blowing, sirens were wailing, and it sounded like people were beating on tin pans. Above the noise there were shouts of 'Happy New Year!' I pulled the sheets over my head and went back to sleep."

The next year he reflected, "The year just closing seems to have rushed by much faster than the one before, and the one before that, shorter than the year that preceded. The thought becomes a reality and not just an illusion that the sand runs faster as each year passes into the twilight. . . . Job said: 'With the ancient is wisdom; and in length of days understanding.' I hope this is true. In any event, there is much for which to be thankful at the close of this year, even though there are conditions I would change if it were possible. Perhaps it could best be summarized by the simple but expressive prayer of George Herbert: 'Thou that has given so much to use, give one more . . . a grateful heart.' "

A blessing for which he was grateful was that, after recovering from the heart attack, he had no other major health problems in the early 1980s, particularly as these were the years when Claire needed the most constant care. He continued to walk when the weather was good. When it was cold or stormy, he went to the Church Administration Office early in

Howard and his sister, Dorothy, at the Temple of Luxor in Egypt. During Claire's illness and the years after her death, Dorothy accompanied him on overseas trips

the morning to work out in the basement exercise room. "Before coming up to my office," he wrote one day, "I have been working out with one hundred strokes on the rowing machine, then jumping on the trampoline and finishing with another one hundred strokes on the rowing machine. I believe this gives me better exercise than walking a mile as I did before."

Though he kept busy after Claire's death, he missed her greatly. Family members, associates in the Twelve and the First Presidency, ward members and neighbors, and friends near and far kept in touch, but there were many lonely times when he returned home after a busy day at the office or a long trip away.

In February 1987, nearly three and a half years after her death, he wrote: "This would have been Claire's eighty-fifth birthday. I left the office early and drove to the City Cemetery. It was a clear, cold day and the snow on the grass was about four inches deep. As I made a path through the snow and stood at her graveside, I had a feeling of loneliness and then thought how alone she must feel away from her family and the grandchildren she loved. Those feelings still persisted after I got home and saw the things that bear her touch."

Howard went to the doctor for periodic checkups after his heart attack, and he watched his diet and exercised regularly. He was pleased when, after each examination, his heart was found to be healthy. Thus, he and his doctors were shocked when, in October 1986, it was discovered that there were blockages in his coronary arteries, and immediate surgery was recommended. At six-thirty the morning of Sunday, October 12, he was anesthetized and taken to the operating room, where he underwent four aorta coronary bypass grafts in five hours of surgery.

His sons alternated staying with him while he was in the hospital. Within two days he was able to take a short walk, and by the tenth day he could walk a mile through the hospital corridors. When he returned home the next day, Dorothy was waiting to help him, but she came down with the flu after a day and had to go home. Independent as always, he didn't let family members know about this complication. He chose to stay alone, with a church security officer there twenty-four hours a day to answer the phone and doorbell and see that he wasn't disturbed while he was regaining his strength.

Howard was determined to recover as quickly as possible so that he could resume his duties in the Twelve. At the time he was serving as the acting president of the quorum, since President Marion G. Romney, the senior apostle, was unable to preside because of failing health. Howard went to a cardiac rehabilitation center regularly to work out on the exercise machines. "I am sure this exercise routine will speed up recovery time if it is followed," he commented in his journal, adding, "although the procedure makes a person tired and taxes his strength."

Soon Dorene Beagles, who had replaced Ruth Webb as his secretary, began bringing him papers from the office, and some of the Brethren stopped by to bring him up to date on what was happening in the Church. "Overall there is progress," he wrote about his recovery, "but I wish it was faster."

By the end of the year he had apparently made full recovery from his heart surgery. "I am grateful that I will be able to go forward into the new year without any limitations," he wrote in his journal. "There is every reason to believe that 1987 will be a good year."

"The Opening and Closing of Doors"

THE NEW YEAR did start out well. Howard was able to return to a full schedule of assignments and duties. On January 22, accompanied by Richard, he went to Europe for conference assignments and then to Jerusalem for meetings on the Jerusalem Center. Five days after he returned, one of his doctors gave him a treadmill test and commented that he was amazed at the condition of his patient's heart—"better than the average of sixty years old." This pleased Howard, who was looking forward to his eightieth birthday in the fall.

But by now he was feeling increasing discomfort, this time in another part of his body. For some time he had had pain in his lower back, and it seemed to be increasing. An X ray in February indicated possible deterioration of a disk and accompanying arthritis. In March he underwent several tests in the hospital. Everything seemed to be within normal limits except for the deteriorating bones in his lower back, resulting in pinched nerves and pain in his lower back and legs. The doctors decided to watch carefully before recommending treatment.

On April 6, the day after general conference, Howard had to cancel plans to go to Burma when tests taken to determine the cause of a persistent pain in his stomach—unrelated to the pain in his back and legs—showed that he had a bleeding ulcer. He was admitted to the hospital for treatment. Two days later, after efforts to stop the bleeding failed, he was admitted to the intensive care unit and then taken to surgery. After administering to him, his three surgeons began operating at nine o'clock that night and did not finish until midnight. He had to be given nine pints of blood.

For the next few days Howard was heavily medicated and not conscious of what happened. But for the medical staff these were days of crisis. He later learned that he was under constant care and the supervision of five doctors, as he had to be given more blood and his kidneys began to fail. Finally his condition was stabilized and he was moved out of intensive care. On April 18 he recorded in his journal: "On April 6 I came into the hospital for an examination which was to take an hour, and this morning I was released. That was a long hour and much has happened. Surgery was successfully accomplished, and I have sufficiently recovered to leave the hospital." Richard's daughter Anne, who had just completed the semester at BYU, came to stay with him while he recuperated at home.

Though Howard's ulcer problem was now under control, the back pain was becoming worse. After one particularly "miserable night," he wrote, "I got no sleep and was more tired when I got up than when I went to bed." He went to the office once or twice to catch up on paperwork, but he was unable to attend the temple meetings of the Twelve because it was difficult to sit that long.

On May 11 Howard was readmitted to the hospital, where the doctors hoped to build him up for back surgery. Two weeks later he was released and sent home for further recovery. He still wasn't strong enough for surgery. The pain by now was almost unbearable, and his family made arrangements for twenty-four-hour nursing care. After a week at home he was readmitted to the hospital. "The doctors have concluded that surgery is necessary even though I am still in a weak condition as the result of the ulcer surgery in April," he wrote.

On Thursday, June 4, Howard returned to surgery, where the surgeon enlarged the opening of the vertebra through which the nerve creating the pain passes. The surgery itself went well, but the prognosis for relief from the pain remained uncertain.

The next several days in the intensive care unit were a blur. As Howard later wrote in his journal, "I was under heavy medication and was not in touch with reality." On June 11 he was moved from the ICU to a private room, and the next day, he said, "The disorientation commenced to clear today and I was able to be up and go for a short walk." But he was still in considerable pain.

Louine and Nan took turns staying with him, so that a family member was there most of the time he was in the hospital and after he returned home. When California schools let out for summer vacation in late June, the two mothers brought their children to Utah to stay in dormitories at BYU and participate in activities on campus. They alternated between staying with Howard in Salt Lake City and supervising their children in Provo.

Richard believes this was a time when his father had to learn a great lesson—to let others take care of him. "Dad has been fiercely independent all his life," he said. "If he could do something, he would do it. Some of that was because there was a way he liked to have things done. And some of it, I think perhaps the greater reason, was that he didn't want to inconvenience someone else to do what he could do himself." Thus, Richard adds, "he was not very willing for others to help him. But this was an opportunity and a blessing for the family and other people to really serve him the way he'd served them."

Once Richard said to his father, "You know, Dad, the doctrine of the Church is that we 'shouted for joy' at the chance to come to this earth and have a body. Do you really think that's true?" Howard paused a few moments, then replied, "Yes, I think it is, but I'm not sure we know the full story."

Howard's back healed well after the surgery, but because of the deterioration of the nerves, a complication of diabetes, he experienced constant severe pain in his legs. A physical therapist came to the house twice a week to give him exercises for his legs, and he was able to walk around the house with the aid of a walker, but the doctors told him that because the pain had not diminished after the operation, he might soon have to be in a wheelchair.

"I do exercises each day," he wrote in his journal under the date of July 27. "I have arm exercises holding a bean bag, leg exercises pedaling a device like a bicycle, walking on the walker, and other routines to help strengthen my arms and legs." But the nerves in his right leg were seriously damaged, and it became increasingly difficult and painful for him to walk. Within just a few weeks he began using a wheelchair.

Beginning in mid-August, Howard was able to rejoin the Brethren for their weekly temple meetings. It was tiring, but it was also invigorating to be back with his associates and the work to which he had consecrated his life and energy. On September 29 he noted, "This is the first time I have spent all day at my desk since April general conference, and this weekend commences the October conference."

On Sunday morning, October 4, 1987, to the amazement of all who knew of his struggles through surgery and rehabilitation, Howard Hunter addressed general conference. In his journal he described what happened:

"I had great apprehension about being able to fill the assignment, but my brethren encouraged me to try. Boyd Packer and Russell Ballard had made arrangements to have casters put on my tabernacle chair and to have a shelf-like pulpit built which was hinged on the top and attached to the rail of the stand near the pulpit so it could be lifted up when used and then lowered. I was the second speaker in the first session. Brother Packer and Brother Ballard pushed me up to the rail and raised the hinged pulpit so I could speak seated in the wheelchair. I spoke on the subject of 'The Opening and Closing of Doors,' the effect of adversity in our lives. The fear I had seemed to leave me and I felt I had overcome my disability."

His opening words immediately caught the congregation's

Four months after his back surgery, Howard, sitting in a wheelchair, addressed general conference

attention: "Forgive me if I remain seated while I present these few remarks. It is not by choice that I speak from a wheelchair. I notice that the rest of you seem to enjoy the conference sitting down, so I will follow your example."

He was back where he belonged, teaching the Saints by both example and word.

Reasons for Celebration

HOWARD'S RECOVERY from his two major surgeries, combined with his eightieth birthday on November 14, was cause for celebration that fall. Family members came from far and near to help him celebrate. Nan and Louine prepared a big birthday dinner and set the dining room table in his home with elegant china, crystal, and silver.

After dinner, the family sat around the table and took turns telling Howard what they most admired about him and how he had influenced their lives. It was, according to Nan, a

Howard with friends and neighbors Talmage and Dorothy Nielsen, who hosted his eightieth birthday party in November 1987

tender time, with many tears shed. Then someone said, "Tell us, Grandpa, what you think we should know—what advice do you have for our lives." After a brief pause, and demonstrating his characteristic sense of humor, he replied solemnly, "Well, when you take a shower, keep the curtains inside the tub."

The next morning they all attended stake conference, where front-row seats had been reserved for them. The stake president, Jon Huntsman, invited Howard, his sons, and his two oldest grandchildren, Kathleen and Robert, to speak. After the benediction, the choir and congregation sang "Happy Birthday," and many came up to shake Howard's hand. The celebration continued later that afternoon with a reception across the street at Dorothy and Talmage Nielsen's home. "There was a constant stream of friends coming for two hours," he wrote. "I have been to many receptions, but none as lovely as this. . . . This was an occasion to remember."

The birthday celebrations concluded a few days later when the First Presidency and Council of the Twelve and their wives honored Howard at a dinner party at Elder and Sister Packer's home.

On New Year's Eve Howard summarized the major things that had happened to him and concluded: "The year of 1987 draws to a close, and as I look back, it has been one of pain and suffering for me, yet there has been joy and a few accomplishments. I am grateful that my health has been sufficiently restored to permit me to carry on the work which has been assigned to me."

Sometimes progress comes in slow increments, so slow that we scarcely notice them until we look back later and see where we were and where we have come. At times Howard's progress seemed that way. He was determined to walk again, and so he continued to push himself to the limits of his endurance in therapy. If he could possibly avoid it, he did not intend to spend the rest of his life in a wheelchair.

At the University of Utah Rehabilitation Center, he was fitted for a leg brace to give his weakened legs more stability. After wearing it for the first time while practicing walking on the double bars, he commented, "I didn't do very well, but I will get used to it." Two days later he wore the brace while walking with a walker and was able to go three times as far as before he had it. "This progress is encouraging," he acknowledged.

His next challenge came in mid-February, when he started to learn how to use forearm crutches. The second time he used them, he was able to walk five hundred feet without assistance. On April 29 he reported: "For the first time I was able to walk at therapy with a walker and without a brace. I was not very steady, but I did manage to walk the 500-foot course through the hospital halls. This gives me the hope that the time may come when I will have greater use of my legs."

Less than two weeks later he was on his way to Hong Kong for a Beneficial Life Insurance convention, with side trips to the island of Macau and to Canton, China. From Hong Kong he flew to Israel by way of Bangkok, Munich, and

Frankfurt, to sign the Jerusalem Center lease. John and a Church security officer were at his side constantly, to lift his wheelchair in and out of buses and other vehicles and help him get around. It was a strenuous trip, but Elder Hunter returned home exhilarated, mainly because the Jerusalem Center was at last ready for occupancy, but also, perhaps, because he had proved he could still travel overseas.

That summer and fall Howard continued to go to therapy and to practice walking with the walker and leg brace, and eventually he was even able to forgo the brace as long as someone walked beside him in case he started to fall. Before his operation, the doctors had told him the pain would last about six months. After a year he still had it, but it was lessening somewhat, for which he was grateful.

The greatest triumph came on Thursday, December 15. In his journal under that date he wrote:

"There was a last and a first today. The temple meeting was the last for the year 1988, and it was the first temple meeting since August 13, 1987, that I have not been in a wheelchair. Today I went to the temple on a walker. It was slow and laborious, but I was able to do it with Neil [Neil McKinstry, a Church security officer] walking by my side to catch me if I would fall. When I came into the council room, the brethren stood and clapped. This is the first time I have heard clapping in the temple. They have been extremely kind and solicitous of me, and in nearly every prayer that has been offered in the last year or so, I have been prayed for. Most of the doctors have told me that I would never be able to stand or walk, but they have failed to take into consideration the power of prayer."[3]

In mid-February of 1988, one of Howard's therapists came to the Tabernacle to help him practice walking up to the stand and back. "I was surprised to be able to do it, and it may be possible to stand and speak, something the doctors told me I would not be able to do." The Church maintenance department modified his seat on the podium, extending the arms forward and raising the cushion so he could stand more easily. With other sessions of practice, including the long walk through the tunnel from the Church Administration Building to the Tabernacle, he finally felt ready for conference.

On Sunday morning, April 1, 1988, all eyes in the Salt Lake Tabernacle were focused on Howard W. Hunter as he slowly stood and began to move, with his walker, to the pulpit. The hearts of the Brethren, family members, and others who knew of his struggles to get to that point were beating a little faster, and silent prayers were being said.

In his journal he recorded what happened: "I got along well today until about the middle of my talk, when I lost my balance and fell backwards into an arrangement of flowers and landed on my back on the podium of the [choir] conductor. President Monson, Boyd Packer, and Dale Springer [a Church security officer] quickly lifted me up on my feet and I continued my talk."

Those who were listening to conference over the radio and those who weren't paying close attention in the Tabernacle or to the television coverage could scarcely detect that anything had happened. There was only a brief pause, and then President Hunter continued speaking as though nothing had happened. At the conclusion of his talk, President Monson commented, "All who have witnessed him coming to the podium have witnessed a miracle." Then, referring to President Hunter's quick recovery from his fall, he added, "Perhaps not one miracle, but two."

At noon, members of the Hunter family gathered in his office for their traditional conference lunch together. The grandchildren, who feel free and easy around their grandfather, teased him about his performance. "Yeah, Grandpa, you just wanted more attention," one said. Another piped up with, "Your talk wasn't good enough so you had to do something to make it better." Grandpa Hunter sat back in his chair and roared with laughter.

He wasn't laughing three weeks later when a CAT scan

revealed that he had broken three ribs. "I have no pain except when I twist," he recorded. "Because they are healing well, I elected not to be taped."

In his October 1987 general conference address, President Hunter said, "Doors close regularly in our lives, and some of those closing cause genuine pain and heartache. But I do believe that where one such door closes, another opens (and perhaps more than one), with hope and blessings in other areas of our lives that we might have not discovered otherwise."

A few months later a *Church News* reporter asked him about the reaction to that talk. The reporter wrote:

> President Hunter said he had had a lot of correspondence and comment regarding that conference address from people "who appreciated the thoughts that were expressed."
>
> "Adversity," he declared, "touches many, many lives. What makes the difference is how we accept it. It's important to know it's all within the purposes of the Lord, whatever they are for us. If we can submit ourselves to that, we can go forward in faith and understanding."
>
> In speaking of the experiences he has had as an apostle, President Hunter softly said: "I've learned patience. I've learned to have confidence. I think I've learned something about the principle of faith. I've learned compassion.
>
> "Those . . . years, as far as I'm personally concerned, have been a refining influence in my life."[4]

15

President of the Quorum of the Twelve

ON FRIDAY, MAY 20, 1988, Marion G. Romney, president of the Quorum of the Twelve Apostles, died at his home in Salt Lake City. Thirteen days later, at the weekly temple meeting on June 2, Howard W. Hunter was sustained and set apart as president of the Twelve.

Though it had been one year since his back surgery and he was still struggling to regain the use of his legs, President Hunter was determined to let nothing deter him from fulfilling his responsibilities in presiding over the quorum. Having served as acting president of the quorum for more than thirty months, he was well aware of what those responsibilities were. And as chairman of the Assignment Committee, he made sure that he carried his full share of the heavy burdens imposed by the rapid growth of the Church. He also served as chairman of the Correlation Executive Committee and was a member of the Church Board of Education, the Church Investment Advisory Committee, and several other committees. In addition, he was chairman of the board and of the executive committee of Beneficial Life Insurance company and on the boards of nine other corporations.

"Serving in these capacities, being President of the Council of the Twelve, having assignments to stake and regional conferences and area training meetings, will keep me fully occupied," he wrote.

For a few days after he had been called to the Twelve

*The new president of
the Quorum of the
Twelve*

nearly twenty-nine years earlier, he may have wondered how
soon he would be fully occupied, but that didn't last long. He
soon had numerous assignments, and as the Church grew, so
did the workload for the Brethren. At the end of 1959, the year
he became a General Authority, Church membership was
1,616,088; by the end of 1988, it totaled 6,721,198, with congre-
gations in 97 nations and 25 territories, colonies, and possessions. The number of stakes increased from 290 in 1959 to
1,707 in 1988, and the number of missions, from 50 in 1950 to
222 in 1988. There were 5,500 full-time missionaries in 1959
and 36,132 in 1988. The Church had 12 operating temples in
1959; by 1988 there were 42, and several others were under
construction or had been announced.

In nearly twenty-nine years as a General Authority, President Hunter had visited stakes and missions throughout the
world—many of them several times—and indeed, he had
organized many of them. He had also participated in nearly

all of the thirty temple dedications. When he was called to the Twelve, two General Authorities visited quarterly stake conferences; by the time he became president of the Twelve, stakes were holding conferences twice a year, and members of the Twelve usually visited only when a new stake president was to be called. The number of General Authorities increased from thirty-four in 1959 to ninety-six in April 1989, with the organization of the Second Quorum of the Seventy.

The period in which he had been a General Authority up to the time of his call as president of the Twelve, he told a *Church News* reporter, "has been an enjoyable time. There has been a lot of work. We expect that, however. But there is no sacrifice in connection with this work," he said, adding that "the work is being pushed forward all over the world. . . . I don't think there has ever been a time in the history of the Church when its officers and leaders have worked harder than right now. The enthusiasm of the leadership, of course, has been a great motivating force, but today there's also a special enthusiasm that's stimulated by the membership of the Church itself. We're all moving forward together. I think it's that unity that has brought about such great success."[1]

President Hunter, who had honed his administrative skills in major assignments with most of the departments and general committees of the Church, now presided over the quorum most directly involved in setting policy and overseeing the tremendous growth of the kingdom.

Though President Hunter still had health problems, he didn't cut down much on his travel schedule. Two weeks before he was set apart as president of the Twelve, he returned from Jerusalem, where he signed the lease of the Jerusalem Center. Two days later he was admitted to the hospital, where he spent six days on intravenous feeding to balance the fluids in his body.

In May 1989, accompanied by his son Richard, he was once again in Israel, this time for the dedication of the Jerusalem Center, whose planning and construction he had

Charles Hunter presents framed picture of Hunterston Castle in Scotland to Howard Hunter, October 1987 (see chapter 1)

overseen for so many years. From there he went to Jordan to visit with members of the small branch of the Church there. He and others in his party were entertained by Oli Ghandour, chairman of the board of Royal Jordanian Airlines and Hotels and a former prime minister of Lebanon, and by General and Mrs. Hamaidy El-Fayez, aide-de-camp to Jordan's King Hussein. The travelers then flew to Rotterdam for a regional conference, stopping briefly en route to visit the Frankfurt Temple.

In July, President Hunter went to Cancun, Mexico, for a Beneficial Life Insurance Company convention, and the day after he returned, he attended the Anders Christensen family reunion in Mount Pleasant, Utah.

Early September found him in France, Scotland, and England for two weeks of mission, regional, and area meetings and leadership training sessions, with Richard again as his travel companion. They managed to squeeze in sightsee-

ing at cultural and historical sites, including a visit in Scotland
to Hunterston Castle.

Traveling with a wheelchair did little to dampen President
Hunter's enthusiasm for sightseeing. He visited many places
where he had been several times before, such historic land-
marks as the old city of Jerusalem and the Sea of Galilee in
Israel; the ancient Roman city of Jerash in Jordan; the
Aalsmeer Flower Auction in the Netherlands; the ruins at
Chichen-Itza in Mexico; the Eiffel Tower and Notre Dame
Cathedral in Paris; the Highlands of Scotland; and the verdant
countryside in England. And everywhere he went, he fulfilled
Church assignments, renewed acquaintances with the Saints,
and made new friends.

"I've Decided to Be Married"

EACH THURSDAY MORNING the Twelve meet in the temple
at eight o'clock to discuss matters of concern to them, and at
nine-thirty members of the First Presidency join them for the
rest of the morning. Near the end of the Twelve's meeting on
Thursday, April 10, 1990, after all agenda items had been covered, President Hunter asked, "Does anyone have anything
that is not on the agenda?" Having been forewarned privately
that their president had something he wanted to bring up if
there was time at the end of their meeting, none of those present said anything. "Well, then," he continued, "if no one else
has anything to say, I thought I'd just let you know that I'm
going to be married this afternoon."

One of the apostles who was there that day said, "My jaw
went clear down to the floor, and everyone wondered if they
had heard correctly. Then President Hunter, in his very modest way, explained, 'Inis Stanton is an old acquaintance from
California. I've been visiting with her for some time, and I've
decided to be married.' He explained that President Hinckley
was going to marry them in the Salt Lake Temple and added,
'I've invited President Monson to be one of the witnesses and

Inis's bishop will be the other one.' And then he told us that no one else was invited."

In his journal, President Hunter wrote his version of what happened that morning: "At the conclusion of the meeting of the Twelve in the temple, I made the announcement that I intended to be married that afternoon. This came as a surprise, and each expressed his delight and best wishes. The Presidency joined us and we took up the business of the day. After the meeting, we had a nice lunch together."

Three days earlier Elder James E. Faust, who had been informed of the coming nuptials, had arranged to have the county clerk come to President Hunter's office to issue the marriage license so he could avoid any publicity that might occur had he gone to the clerk's office. President Edgar M. Denny of the Salt Lake Temple had also come to the office and made the necessary arrangements for the temple sealing and ceremony.

At two o'clock that Thursday afternoon, Howard W. Hunter and Inis Bernice Egan Stanton knelt at the altar in one of the sealing rooms in the temple, and President Hinckley performed the sealing ceremony and pronounced them husband and wife.

Afterwards, the newlyweds went back to President Hunter's home, where they would live. The Sunday before the wedding, he had ridden to church with his neighbor Dorothy Nielsen and had confided his plans to her. "I was so surprised that I had to pull the car over to the side of the road and stop," she recalled. On Wednesday afternoon, the day before the wedding, she arranged for some Relief Society sisters in the ward to clean his house. While the couple were at the temple on Thursday, she set their dining room table with sparkling china, sterling silver, candles, and a centerpiece of fresh flowers, and left dinner for them in the kitchen.

Sister Nielsen wasn't the only one who was surprised. The bridegroom-to-be confided his plans to very few people. His sons and daughters-in-law had told him earlier that they would be pleased if he were to remarry. They had even suggested some possible "candidates." He had smiled at such suggestions but didn't seem interested in following through on them.

A few days before the wedding, when Richard was visiting in Salt Lake City, his father asked him, "What would you think if I got married?"

"We think it's not only appropriate, but it's the right thing for you to do," Richard assured him.

"Well, I've been thinking about it," his father continued.

"Do you have somebody in mind?"

"Yes." President Hunter then told him a little about Inis.

Richard said he would like to meet her, and President Hunter invited her to come have dinner with them that evening.

Afterwards Richard asked Howard if he and Inis had talked about when they might be married. "Yes," his father replied. "It's this Thursday." He explained that they wanted the ceremony to be small and private, with no publicity. Inis had two daughters and a son from a previous marriage, and they too were taken by surprise—and were not invited to the wedding. The only persons there besides him and Inis, Howard said, would be someone who had the sealing power and two witnesses.

On Easter Sunday, three days after they were married, Howard and his bride attended church in his ward, which would now become her ward. "The bishop announced our marriage," he wrote, "and after the meeting people swarmed about us with congratulations and good wishes. Inis was well received. . . . Easter was a pleasant day."

The following week members of the First Presidency and the Council of the Twelve and their wives honored the couple at a dinner at the home of Elder and Sister Packer. "The dinner was delicious," President Hunter said. "In the center of the table was a large wedding cake that Inis cut and served. . . . This was an evening we will never forget."

Inis and Howard

While the marriage surprised his family and associates, the couple had known each other for many years and had been seeing each other quietly and discreetly for several months. The new Mrs. Hunter had been a member of the El Sereno Ward in California when he was bishop. In the early 1970s she became the receptionist for the high-rise Church Office Building soon after it opened, and their paths crossed occasionally through the years.

An articulate woman with a sparkling personality, Inis brought joy and light back into her new husband's life. They made a few changes in the home, adding some new furniture and accessories that reflected her taste and personality. One noticeable addition was the large and impressive array of dolls she had made, with expressive faces and meticulously designed costumes. She delighted the wives of the General Authorities when she discussed her dolls at one of their monthly Lion House luncheons. She had taken up the art of dollmaking after moving to Salt Lake City, and after she had become skilled in making the classic faces and forms, she was asked to teach classes on the art. Her work could command large prices were she to offer them for sale, but she preferred to keep them for herself and for close family members and friends.

Becoming the wife of a General Authority, particularly of one who had been in the limelight for more than thirty years, brought challenges for Inis. When the Brethren attend area and regional conferences, their wives usually accompany them and are called upon to speak. Two weeks after her marriage, she accompanied Howard to a regional conference in Norfolk, Virginia, where she spoke on the subject "Bloom Where You Are Planted"—"the importance of doing what we are asked to do to the best of our ability, thus helping to build the kingdom and furthering our way on the way to eternal life," he reported. "It was a good talk and well delivered. I was proud of her."

A few weeks later they went to a Beneficial Life Insurance Company convention in Vail, Colorado, where the guests could test their skills in horseback riding, canoeing, and other mountain sports. "Inis was the horseshoe-pitching champion," he proudly observed.

Sharing the Pleasures of Travel

INIS HAD NOT traveled extensively before she and Howard were married, so his assignments to widespread places throughout the world were a blessing for them both—for him because he would have a constant travel companion after many years of loneliness, and for her because she would see the world with a loving guide who took great pleasure in everything he saw and who willingly shared these pleasures with her. They both loved meeting people, the Saints who crowded around them after conferences and the people they met along the way.

Five weeks after their wedding, they began a delayed honeymoon, a cruise on the Nile River from Luxor to Aswan with a BYU travel-study group. Each day they had opportunities to visit ancient sites, such as the Temple at Karnak, the Valley of the Kings and the Valley of the Queens, and the statues and temples of Ramses II. After docking at Aswan, they flew to Cairo for additional sightseeing, then went on to Israel for nine days of tours and Church assignments. The newlyweds were the focus of attention at a Jerusalem Center concert one evening. A male double quartet sang a song entitled "Two Silhouettes on the Shade," which they dedicated to Howard and Inis.

From Israel, the Hunters flew to London. Again they toured historical sites Howard had visited several times before, but this time he was seeing them through the eyes of Inis, to whom it was all new and exciting.

Three weeks after they returned home, Howard and Inis flew to Hawaii, where he was honored as the first president of the Polynesian Cultural Center. "Those who were invited were largely 'old timers' who contributed to the planning and building of the Center, and those on the program were the early performers in the shows," he wrote. "It was a wonderful evening and I was pleased to see many old friends."

That November Howard celebrated his birthday in Australia, where he and Inis attended regional and stake conferences in New Zealand, Australia, and Fiji. On his birthday, November 14, they were honored at a dinner at the Sydney Opera House in a dining room overlooking the city and harbor. "Dinner was formal and beautifully served," he commented. "For dessert, the waiters in formal dress brought in a birthday cake and served it to us while everyone at the table sang 'Happy Birthday.' Today I became eighty-three years old."

Marriage seemed to agree with him, for he ended the year with only one major illness, a bout with pneumonia that put him in the hospital for six days. He continued his therapy sessions, still determined that he would regain greater strength in his legs. On August 3 he wrote in his journal: "Three years ago today, in 1987, I commenced the use of a wheelchair, and it was not until the end of 1988 that I began to use a walker. For nearly two years I have continued to use a walker although the doctors told me I would never be able to walk. I am going to continue therapy with the hope that I may be able to walk without assistance."

In October he was able to stand, "with a little help," in the prayer circle of the General Authorities for the first time since April 2, 1987. It was a major milestone in his recovery.

Howard and Inis continued their jet-speed pace in 1991. He was pleased to introduce her in January at a special sacrament meeting of the South Pasadena Ward, the former El Sereno Ward, commemorating the fiftieth anniversary of the ward's creation. He reported: "There have been fourteen bishops serve since the ward was organized in 1940. I was the first. . . . Many of the original members of the ward were present and a large number of those who have moved away came back for the meeting. . . . As the first bishop, I was the principal speaker. At the close, the bishops [eleven were present] formed a receiving line in the Relief Society room and we shook hands with most of those present. It was a glorious occasion to see many old friends and reminisce about the happenings of years gone by."

In February, accompanied by Elder and Sister M. Russell Ballard, they flew to Merida, Mexico, to visit the ancient archaeological sites of Uxmal and Kabah. From there they went to Cancun, then back to Merida to drive to the Mayan city of Chichen-Itza. At a regional conference in Merida, more than one thousand priesthood leaders attended a Saturday priesthood leadership session, and more than four thousand members from the four stakes in the region attended the Sunday morning conference session. "At the conclusion everyone stood and sang 'As I Have Loved You' and waved white handkerchiefs. It was a scene we will never forget," Howard wrote.

The visit to Merida was a homecoming of sorts, for not only had he been there many times as president of the New World Archaeological Foundation, but he had also organized the first Merida stake in January 1977. Now there were four stakes. Many Saints crowded around him before and after the meetings, eager to shake his hand and show him their children.

A much longer trip came in May when Howard and Inis went to conferences in Santiago, Chile; Buenos Aires and Iquasu, Argentina; and Sao Paulo, Brazil. In Alaska for a regional conference the next month, they enjoyed a five-hour cruise on Prince William Sound, which he described in his journal: "We saw 26 glaciers, fjords, waterfalls, and wildlife sea lions, porpoises, seals, sea otters, countless types of fish, birds, and mammals, and many species of the wildlife of Alaska. Near the end of the cruise we stopped near cliffs where thousands of kittiwakes and other seabirds were flocking. We had a nice dinner en route as we watched the glaciers calve from the ice walls and plunge in the ocean. The cruise was spectacular."

Not even a medical emergency could keep him from taking another trip two weeks later. Mayor Teddy Kollek of Jerusalem had come to Salt Lake City for his first visit to Utah, and prominent church, government, business, and industry leaders had been invited to a dinner in his honor. Just as Howard stood up to speak, he began to choke. He was rushed to the hospital, where it was discovered that food had been aspirated into his lung. On the third day in the hospital, he reported, "I called Dr. Hunter and told him I did not want to remain in the hospital any longer. He said he would come and talk with me about it. I called Inis to come and get me. She and the doctor arrived about the same time, and I told them I was going home and going to Hawaii tomorrow. He objected, but when he found out I was serious, he made arrangements for my release."

The next morning Inis and Howard flew to Los Angeles, where Richard and Nan joined them, and the foursome flew on to Honolulu. John and Louine had gone on ahead and met them there. The three couples were feted at the Polynesian Cultural Center and toured other places of interest on Oahu before flying to Kauai for the annual Beneficial Life Insurance Company convention.

August found the Hunters in Guatemala and Panama for regional conferences. In Panama, President Hunter wrote, "We went to the summit of Ancon Hill for a dedicatory service. . . . It was a beautiful, clear morning and all was quiet except for the occasional chirp of a bird. . . . I gave the dedicatory prayer dedicating the land of the Republic of Panama to the Lord and for the preaching of the gospel." In Guatemala, in addition to participating at a regional conference, they visited the Mayan ruins at Tikal and other sites.

Eleven days after they returned home, they were on their way to more meetings and conferences, this time in Japan, Hong Kong, and South Korea, with a side trip to Guangzhou (Canton), China.

The last few days of this hectic year were surprisingly quiet. In his journal Howard described some of these days: "It was a quiet day at the office. . . . This evening we listened to music from tapes and compact discs on the new equipment we have incorporated into our stereo system." "There is nothing to write about today—nothing was done and nothing accomplished." "I was in the office all day and we spent the evening at home." (This was a Monday, the day the General Authorities were not expected to go to the office.) And finally, on New Year's Eve: "Dorene and I worked in the office this morning, but there was little activity so after lunch we closed the office and went home. Inis prepared a nice dinner, and after listening to music we went to bed early and didn't wait up to see the new year ushered in. Thus another year came to an end."

"We Have Enjoyed Traveling Together"

IN THE FIRST twenty months of their marriage, Howard and Inis traveled to and met with the Saints in Africa, Asia, Europe, North America, South America, and several islands of the sea. In February 1992 they went to Africa for a regional conference in Johannesburg with Elder and Sister Packer. They arrived a few days early so they could visit the famed wildlife preserve, Kruger National Park, about 250 miles from Johannesburg. Their party of nine, including the two apostles and their wives, drove to the park in two vehicles—a car and a van—and stayed at a compound of thatch-roofed African huts.

Within a short distance from their compound they spotted a giraffe, several herds of impala, hippopotamuses, elephants, lions, leopards, rhinoceroses, and water buffalo. They had been told they must keep their doors and windows closed in the park, but while they were on a bridge, someone in the van rolled down a window to photograph a leopard on the riverbank. "A baboon quick as lightning jumped through the window, lifted the lid from the ice chest and grabbed some bags of fruit and the chips," Howard reported. "He sat on the bridge, peeled the bananas and ate the fruit and the chips. We made a getaway and didn't open the windows again."

After the conference on Sunday, the General Authorities and their wives flew to Frankfurt, where the Packers caught a flight to Cairo and the Hunters, joined by Elder and Sister Faust, went on to Israel. In Jerusalem they paid a courtesy visit to Chaim Herzog, president of the state of Israel, and "had a pleasant conversation for over a half hour talking about the Jerusalem Center, world affairs, the peace meetings and many other subjects." They gave him a set of the recently published *Encyclopedia of Mormonism,* in which he seemed to be very interested, having been chairman and editor of a similar work,

At the Jerusalem Center in February 1992: Ruth Faust, Elder James E. Faust,
President Howard W. Hunter, Inis Egan Hunter

the *Encyclopedia Judaica.* The two apostles also visited the Dead
Seas Scrolls Foundation, where they were briefed on the work
of the foundation in translating and preserving the scrolls and
fragments and preparing them for publication.

At a luncheon at the Jerusalem Center attended by Mayor
Kollek and officials of the Jerusalem Symphony Association
and the Jerusalem Foundation, an invitation was extended for
the Tabernacle Choir to perform in Israel. Mayor Kollek
agreed to prepare an official invitation, which President
Hunter and Elder Faust would take back to the First Presidency. (The invitation was accepted, and on December 26
choir members flew to Israel for their first appearances in the
Holy Land, an area so rich in Old and New Testament history.[2])

On April 12, 1992, his wedding anniversary, Howard
wrote in his journal: "Two years ago today Inis and I were
married and sealed in the Salt Lake Temple. These two years
have been happy ones. She has been a sweet companion and
we have enjoyed being together, traveling together, and our
home is a place of delight." A month later they flew to Los
Angeles for a reunion of the Garvanza Ward, which Inis had

attended for many years in her youth. They went early so Inis could show him the homes where she had lived, the schools she had attended, and other places associated with her childhood. "About 80 former members of the ward came to the reunion," he wrote. "Inis knew nearly everyone. I knew many of them because I was bishop of the El Sereno Ward which adjoined, and some of them had moved back and forth. . . . This was an enjoyable day."

May found the Hunters in England again, to participate in a regional conference in Merthyr Tydfil, Wales. Then, accompanied by Elder Jeffrey R. Holland, the area president, they drove to Scotland to visit Hunterston Castle.

The couple's traveling slowed down in June when Inis underwent surgery to have a knee-joint replacement. Howard was lonely for the ten days she was in the hospital. The first evening he wrote: "The house seemed empty and cold without Inis." Another day, "After getting home and fixing dinner, I commenced to appreciate how good affairs are when Inis does all the things that are essential to everyday living, for which gratitude is not always expressed." Six days after her surgery, he commented: "It is a serious handicap to not be able to drive a car. I wanted to go to the hospital to see Inis, but I had no way of getting there. I talked with her on the telephone off and on all day, which was not as good as being able to see her." He was relieved when she came home from the hospital, on crutches, and her daughter Elayne Allebest arrived from California to help out for a few days.

By early September, Inis had recovered enough to be able to accompany Howard on a trip to Russia, Armenia, Ukraine, and Austria. Within four and a half hours after their plane touched down in Moscow, he met with priesthood leaders of the six Moscow branches of the Church and, after speaking, answered their questions for an hour. The next day a large gathering of members, investigators, and missionaries attended a conference of the Moscow District. President Gary

Browning of the Moscow Mission described the experience in a Christmas 1992 letter to family and friends:

> In September Elder and Sister Howard W. Hunter visited Moscow and spoke to five hundred gathered at a Sunday service. The meeting went well and was fulfilling from the standpoint of spiritual nourishment. But what I will recall occurred after the meeting when hundreds quietly filed past Elder Hunter and shook his hand. No one took much of his time, but all wished him good health and joy. I stood next to Elder Hunter, translating for him, and had the unforgettable experience of looking into our members' eyes as they spoke to Elder Hunter. I wish I could convey the nonverbal expressions of faith, purity, and human warmth that flowed from their smiles and gaze. To think that a few months ago most of them were just learning of the gospel and Church, and that a few years ago they would have had great difficulty professing any religious conviction. Now they radiated gratitude and love for an apostle and prophet that was both inspiring and confirming.

Four days later the Hunters were in Kiev, the capital of Ukraine, where President Hunter and Elder Robert K. Dellenbach of the Europe Area presidency spoke at a fireside at the October Palace. "There are 400 members of the Church in Kiev," President Hunter noted, "and there was an attendance of 1200 at the fireside." He was thrilled with the response of the Saints and investigators to the gospel message, the glad tidings of peace. From there, his party flew to Austria.

Early in the morning on Saturday, September 12, 1992, a group of mission, stake, and ward leaders went to the top of a hill overlooking Vienna, the Vienna Woods, and the Danube River, and President Hunter dedicated Austria for the preaching of the gospel. That afternoon he went to the Munich regional conference, which began with a priesthood leadership meeting in Linz, an Austrian city halfway between Vienna and Munich. The next day some four thousand people from Austria and eastern Germany crowded into a sports arena for the general session. Afterwards President Hunter shook hands with several hundred people.

A month later the Hunters were back in Europe, this time to attend the London regional conference and rededication sessions for the London Temple. Howard spoke at four of the sessions, and Inis was invited to speak at one.

Their last overseas assignment for 1992 took them to Tahiti and other destinations in the South Pacific. They returned just in time for Thanksgiving, and a few days later Howard entered the hospital because of internal bleeding. He was hospitalized two weeks, and his recovery was slow.

"Life Has a Fair Number of Challenges"

THE YEAR 1993 brought more ups and downs. Now eighty-five years old, many years past retirement for most persons, President Hunter—like his brethren in the First Presidency and the Twelve—continued to push himself to keep up with the rapid growth of the Church. By now, each recovery seemed to take longer, but he refused to stay down any longer than absolutely necessary. This was certainly evident in the aftermath of a bizarre incident early in the year.

On February 7 the Hunters went to the Brigham Young University campus, where President Hunter was scheduled to speak at a nineteen-stake fireside. Nearly twenty thousand young adults poured into the Marriott Center on campus, and thousands more gathered at Church buildings throughout North America for special transmission of the fireside via satellite.

After the invocation and introductions, President Hunter went to the microphone and began to speak. Suddenly a voice yelled out, "Stop right there!" A man carrying a briefcase in one hand and a black object in the other rushed out of the audience and onto the stage. Declaring that he had a bomb and a detonator, he ordered everyone except President Hunter to leave.

Most of the officials and guests quickly left the stage, but

President Hunter remained, with two personal security guards who refused to leave his side. Waving the so-called detonator, which many spectators feared was a gun, the man handed a prepared statement to President Hunter and demanded that he read it. President Hunter calmly but firmly refused to do so.

In areas where audiences had assembled to watch the fireside telecast, the screens suddenly went black and a "technical difficulties" notice replaced the image and sound. At the Marriott Center, members of the audience sat stunned momentarily. Then some broke into tears; others began moving toward the exits; and a few angrily converged toward the stage area, where they tried to get the man to surrender. A modicum of calm was restored when a few students, soon joined by the entire audience, began to sing "We Thank Thee, O God, for a Prophet" and then "I Am a Child of God."

On the stage an older man tried to distract the assailant but was pushed back into a row of chairs. Then one of the angry students near the front sprayed the intruder with a can of mace, and security officers managed to wrestle him off the stand, where other students helped to subdue him.

In the confusion, President Hunter's grandnephew, Corey Child, rushed from his seat in the fifth row to the opposite side of the stand, put his hand on his uncle's chest from behind, and, whispering reassurances, helped the security officers lower him to the floor. Corey, who cracked some ribs and pulled muscles in his shoulder and knee in the confusion, looked around to see what had happened to his date. A nurse, she had followed him to the stage, and he was surprised to see her kneeling beside President Hunter.

The entire incident took about ten minutes, but to many it seemed much longer. Finally, after resting for a few moments, President Hunter again went to the microphone and began reading his prepared talk. "Life has a fair number of challenges in it," he read. Looking out at the audience, he added,

*Members of the family in Howard's office between sessions
of general conference, April 1992*

"as demonstrated." And he continued on, speaking calmly and deliberately, as though nothing had happened.[3]

That week President Hunter carried on with his usual schedule of meetings and other work at the office, and six days after the fireside, he and Sister Hunter left on an assignment to Australia, Singapore, and Japan. After a few weeks at home, they went to Brazil in March, and in April they attended the San Diego Temple dedication.

In early May, Howard entered the hospital for gall bladder surgery. Because of scars and scar tissue from previous surgeries, the doctors couldn't use newer surgical procedures; they had to operate the old-fashioned way, making a large incision in the abdomen. Howard usually experienced adverse reactions to medications, and this time was no exception. After the surgery, which was expected to be fairly routine, he went into a deep sleep from which he couldn't be roused. At least once the doctors thought he wouldn't survive the night.

On Memorial Day, twenty days after the surgery, Howard still hadn't responded. Dorene Beagles, his faithful secretary, visited him that morning, and though his eyes were open, there was no sign that he recognized her or that he knew anyone was even in the room. The next morning when she stopped by just to check on him, she was amazed to find him sitting up in bed, alert and ready to be filled in on what had happened and what needed to be done at the office. Robert, Howard's oldest grandson, had a similar experience. He had visited the hospital regularly and had seen no response—but that morning his grandfather greeted him with a cheerful "Hello, Robert!" Four days later Howard was released from the hospital.

With summer vacation coming, he recuperated at home, but he also went out occasionally, such as to the dedication of the Joseph Smith Memorial Building, formerly the Hotel Utah, which had now been remodeled and converted to a Church office building and community center. In early September he was back in the hospital for tests, and nine days later he went to Los Angeles for the fortieth anniversary of the Southern California Mormon Choir, which he had been instrumental in helping to organize for the 1953 Los Angeles Temple dedication when he was serving as regional council chairman of stake presidents in the area.

The last weekend in September, Howard participated in a regional conference in Hattiesburg, Mississippi, where he spoke extemporaneously and with strong conviction for thirty minutes at the Saturday priesthood leadership session and again at the Sunday morning general session. But the next week he was ill and unable to attend sessions of the October general conference.

And so it went, up and down. But typically, he refused to stay down any longer than necessary. His recoveries were taking longer, but just as soon as he was able, he would go back into the office, for a few hours at first and gradually building back up to fulltime. When he had been given his charge as a new apostle, he had pledged his all to the Church, and he was determined to keep that pledge. He was happiest when he was doing the Lord's work.

Honors and Accolades

THROUGH THE YEARS many honors came to President Hunter, a man of accomplishment who went about his work quietly, efficiently, and with intense dedication and desire to do what the Lord would have him do. He never sought the limelight or drew attention to himself, preferring to give credit to others. But his efforts and the example he set did not go unnoticed, and recognition came.

Among the numerous awards and special recognitions he received through the years were these:

• Honorary membership in the Blue Key service organization at Brigham Young University in April 1966. John and Richard Hunter had both been active in Blue Key as undergraduates.[4]

• Honorary membership in the Young Men organization of BYU in April 1968.[5]

• Distinguished Citizen Award from business, industry, and church leaders in Southern California, "for having achieved distinction as Attorney, Civic Worker, Church Leader." This was presented "in connection with the appearance of the Utah Symphony Orchestra, Hollywood Bowl, June 22, 1968," according to the report in his journal.

• The honorary degree of doctor of laws from BYU on August 13, 1976, "for the excellence of his example and for his distinguished service to the profession of law, to his community, to his Church and to higher education."

• The name of Howard Hunter given by Latter-day Saint law students to their student organization at Southwestern University in Los Angeles in February 1977.

• Another Distinguished Citizen Award, presented at a dinner in Los Angeles in April 1977 to "Elder Howard W. Hunter, a native Californian adopted by the State of Utah, for having achieved distinction as attorney, civic worker, church leader."

• The Distinguished Eagle Award, presented by the Great Salt Lake Council of the Boy Scouts of America in November

President Hunter pets "Moe" at the California home of James K. Watson, an associate on the Watson Land Company board of directors

1978. This award particularly pleased Elder Hunter, who had received his Eagle fifty-six years earlier. "It is given only to men who have earned the rank of Eagle and for more than twenty-five years have continued to follow the scout oath and law by serving God, country and fellowmen," he wrote in his journal. Only one other such award had been conferred in Utah. Eleven years earlier Elder Hunter had been honored at a dinner and court of honor for Scouts in the Boise Stake. One of his former scoutmasters, Idaho State Auditor Joe R. Williams, presented him with his personal Scout Handbook, which had been in a ward library in Boise for forty-five years.

• An honorary doctor of humanities from BYU–Hawaii on June 22, 1985.

• The Howard W. Hunter Professorship, established in 1989 in the J. Reuben Clark Law School at Brigham Young University. He was particularly pleased the next year when he attended a meeting of the Watson Land Company in Los Angeles and heard the following read from the minutes of the previous meeting, which he had been unable to attend: "President Huston reported that a request had been received for a donation, in an unspecified amount, for an endowment to be

used for a Howard W. Hunter Professorship in Law at the
J. Reuben Clark School at Brigham Young University. . . . In
view of Director Hunter's countless contribution to the success of Watson Land Company over his more than fifty years
as a director,[6] Management recommended a donation of
$50,000 which will be matched by others." The proposal was
unanimously approved and adopted.

• Recognition from the United States Court of Appeals for
the Ninth Circuit in Los Angeles "for fifty years of dedication
and service to the administration of justice as a member of the
bar of this court, this 26th day of November, 1990."

• The 1992–93 Exemplary Manhood Award from the
Brigham Young University Student Association.

"Thy Strength Shall Be Turned to Zion"

IN A REVELATION given through the Prophet Joseph Smith
on January 25, 1832, the Lord declared: "Hearken, O ye who
have given your names to go forth to proclaim my gospel, and
to prune my vineyard. Behold, I say unto you that it is my will
that you should go forth and not tarry, neither be idle but
labor with your might—lifting up your voices as with the
sound of a trump, proclaiming the truth according to the revelations and commandments which I have given you. And
thus, if ye are faithful ye shall be laden with many sheaves
and crowned with honor, and glory, and immortality, and eternal life." (D&C 75:2–5.)

At no time in his life has President Hunter aspired to the
honors of men; such honors have come because his eye has
been single to the glory of God and he has practiced the teachings of the Lord in his dealings with his fellowmen. He has
proclaimed the gospel in most nations of the world, but perhaps even more important, he has quietly but unequivocally
lived the gospel and set an example for the Saints.

In the patriarchal blessing he received in 1930, he was told,
"Thy strength shall be turned to Zion, and thou shalt support
her institutions and become a tie and a security to the great

church that shall shelter God's people." Like Nephi of old, he can testify to the blessings that come from saying, "I will go and do the things which the Lord hath commanded, for I know that the Lord giveth no commandments unto the children of men, save he shall prepare a way for them that they may accomplish the thing which he commandeth them." (1 Nephi 3:7.) It is a teaching that he has put into practice.

Life has not been easy for Howard W. Hunter. He has faced many illnesses and other challenges, particularly in the later years of his ministry. Such problems would defeat many individuals, but his indomitable spirit and his determination to do whatever the Lord has commanded of him have given him strength and blessings to continue serving the Church and his fellow beings.

At general conference on April 3, 1994, he challenged the Saints: "Let us follow the Son of God in all ways and in all walks of life. Let us make him our exemplar and our guide. We should at every opportunity ask ourselves, 'What would Jesus do?' and then be more courageous to act upon the answer. We must follow Christ, in the best sense of that word. We must be about his work as he was about his Father's." This might well sum up how Howard W. Hunter himself has tried to live his life. And the Church—indeed, the world—is much richer for that!

APPENDIX

Teachings and Messages of Howard W. Hunter

The Boise Temple. I was born in Boise four years after the organization of the Boise Branch, which became a branch of the Northwestern States Mission. . . . By the widest stretch of the imagination, there was no thought that this valley would someday be blanketed by wards and stakes, but this has happened. In addition, there now stands a temple as a monument to the faith and devotion of the people. How grateful I am that the Lord has permitted me to see this span of years and the growth they have produced. (Remarks at Boise Temple dedication, May 25, 1984.)

Resolving Doubts. I have sympathy for young men and young women when honest doubts enter their minds and they engage in the great conflict of resolving doubts. These doubts can be resolved, if they have an honest desire to know the truth, by exercising moral, spiritual, and mental effort. They will emerge from the conflict into a firmer, stronger, larger faith because of the struggle. They have gone from a simple, trusting faith, through doubts and conflict, into a solid substantial faith which ripens into testimony. (*Conference Report*, October 1960.)

Secretly a Disciple? The world needs men who are willing to step forward and declare themselves. The world needs men who will lift the load of responsibility to their shoulders and carry it high under the banner of Jesus Christ—men who are willing to defend the right openly. . . .

How can men of conscience ignore the teachings of the Master in their daily affairs, in business, or in government? We stand by and wink at many things because we fear to do anything about them. We may be against crime or communism, but what do we do about it?

We may be against corruption in government or against juvenile delinquency, but what do we do about it? We may have a belief in the gospel of Jesus Christ, but what are we doing about it? We need to push fear into the background and come forward with a definite, positive declaration, and assume responsibility. . . .

Now is the time for those who have been noncommittal or who have had a halfhearted interest to come out boldly and declare belief in Christ and be willing to demonstrate faith by works. (*Conference Report*, October 1960.)

Put Your Hand to the Plow. "No man, having put his hand to the plough, and looking back, is fit for the kingdom of God." (Luke 9:62.) . . . Of all the work of the field, plow-work is the heaviest labor. It is primary and fundamental—it is pioneer toil. A seed may be dropped anywhere, and there is no resistance, but put the blade of the plow into the ground and a thousand forces join to oppose the change. To disturb the conventional, to overturn the traditional, or to attempt to make changes in the deep-rooted way of doing things in the lives of individuals, requires toil and sweat. The heaviest work in the kingdom of God is to turn the hard surface of the earth which has been baked in the sun or covered by the growth of nature.

What a great change comes over land which has been cleared and plowed,—row after row of evenly spaced furrows, the subsurface loosened and exposed to the sun and air and the rains from heaven, ready to be broken up and planted to seed. The wilderness is conquered and subdued.

Those who become disciples of the Master and put their hands to the plow without turning back prove themselves to be worthy plowmen. By turning over the old surfaces of tradition, they prepare the fields for the introduction and the spread of Christianity into the world. (D&C 75:5.) (*Conference Report*, April 1961.)

An Everyday Religion. Religion is more than a knowledge of God or a confession of faith, and it is more than theology. Religion is the doing of the word of God. It is being our brother's keeper, among other things. To keep unspotted from the world does not mean that one must withdraw from all association with the world, but rather to keep away from the evils of the world. . . .

Religion can be part of our daily work, our business, our buying and selling, building, transportation, manufacturing, our trade or profession, or of anything we do. We can serve God by honesty and fair dealing in our business transactions in the same way we do in Sunday worship. The true principles of Christianity cannot be separate and apart from business and our everyday affairs. . . .

This imposes upon us a high duty and a high responsibility. If all men would live in obedience to these principles in their daily lives and in their dealings with each other, and if this same code would prevail among those who are in leadership among the peoples and nations of the world, righteousness would prevail, peace would return, and the blessings of the Lord would be showered down upon his people. (*Conference Report,* October 1961.)

An Understanding Heart. To love one's neighbor is noble and inspiring, whether the neighbor is one who lives close by, or in a broader sense, a fellow being of the human race. It stimulates the desire to promote happiness, comfort, interest, and the welfare of others. It creates understanding. The ills of the world would be cured by understanding. Wars would cease and crime disappear. . . .

We need more understanding in our relationships with one another, in business and in industry, between management and labor, between government and the governed. We need understanding in that most important of all social units, the family: understanding between children and parents and between husband and wife. Marriage would bring happiness, and divorce would be unknown if there were understanding hearts. Hatred tears down, but understanding builds up. Our prayer could well be as was Solomon's, "Lord, give me an understanding heart." (See 1 Kgs. 3:9.) (*Conference Report,* April 1962.)

To Believe Is to See. There is no positive, concrete, tangible evidence that God lives, yet millions have a knowledge that he does through that faith which constitutes the evidence of things unseen. Many say to the missionaries, "I would accept of baptism if I could believe that Joseph Smith was visited by the Father and the Son." For this fact there is no positive, concrete, tangible evidence, but to those who are touched by the Spirit, faith will stand in the place of such evidence of things unseen. Remember the words of the crucified Master as he stood before Thomas: " . . . blessed are they that have not seen, and yet have believed." (John 20:29.) To believe is to see. (*Conference Report,* October 1962.)

Prophets in This Dispensation. To peoples of past dispensations and ages, the most important prophet was the one then living, teaching, and revealing the word of the Lord in their time. In each of the past dispensations, prophets have been raised up by the Lord as his spokesmen to the people of that particular age and for the specific problems of that age.

It is our present living prophet who is our leader, our teacher. It is from him we take direction in the modern world. From all corners of the earth, we who sustain him as a prophet of the Lord, express our appreciation for this source of divine guidance. We are grateful for his life, his example, his teachings, his leadership. . . .

As the prophets from the beginning to the present day pass in review before our memory, we become aware of the great blessing which comes to us from the influence of a living prophet. History should teach us that unless we are willing to heed the warnings and follow the teachings of a prophet of the Lord, we will be subject to the judgments of God. (*Conference Report,* October 1963.)

Where Is Peace? The peace for which the world longs is a time of suspended hostilities; but men do not realize that peace is a state of existence that comes to men only upon the terms of God, and in no other way. . . .

One may live in beautiful and peaceful surroundings but, because of inner dissension and discord, be in a state of constant turmoil. On the other hand, one may be in the midst of utter destruction and the bloodshed of war and yet have the serenity of unspeakable peace. If we look to man and the ways of the world, we will find turmoil and confusion. If we will but turn to God, we will find peace for the restless soul. . . .

This peace shelters us from the worldly turmoil. The knowledge that God lives, that we are his children, and that he loves us soothes the troubled heart. The answer to the quest lies in faith in God and in his Son, Jesus Christ. This will bring peace to us now and in the eternity to follow. (*Conference Report,* October 1966.)

Gospel Imperatives. The best goals, the best friends, and the best of opportunities are all meaningless unless they are translated into reality through our daily actions. Belief must be realized in personal achievement. Real Christians must understand that the gospel of Jesus Christ is not just a gospel of belief; it is a plan of action. His gospel is a gospel of imperatives, and the very nature of its substance is a call to action. He did not say "observe" my gospel; he said "live" it! He did not say, "Note its beautiful structure and imagery"; he said, "Go, do, see, feel, give, believe!" The gospel of Jesus Christ is full of imperatives, words that call for personal commitment and action— obligatory, binding, compulsory. . . . Merely saying, accepting, believing are not enough. They are incomplete until that which they imply is translated into the dynamic action of daily living. (*Conference Report,* April 1967.)

Is a Church Necessary? I submit that the Church of Jesus Christ is as necessary in the lives of men and women today as it was when established by him, not by passive interest or a profession of faith, but by an assumption of active responsibility. In this way the Church brings us out of the darkness of an isolated life into the light of the gospel, where belief is turned into doing according to the admonitions of scripture. This is the hope of the individual, the family, the Church, the nations of the earth. (*Conference Report*, October 1967.)

Blessed Are Those Who Have Not Seen. Our day is one in which there is a great diversity of belief with regard to many fundamental statements of scripture. Modernists deny the virgin birth of Jesus. They deny his divine power demonstrated by the many miracles he performed during his short ministry.

Modernists dispute that the Master voluntarily offered himself to atone for the sins of mankind, and they deny that there was in fact such an atonement. It is our firm belief that it is a reality, and nothing is more important in the entire divine plan of salvation than the atoning sacrifice of Jesus Christ. We believe that salvation comes because of the atonement. In its absence the whole plan of creation would come to naught. . . . Without this atoning sacrifice, temporal death would be the end, and there would be no resurrection and no purpose in our spiritual lives. There would be no hope of eternal life. (*Conference Report*, October 1968.)

Ethics Alone Is Not Sufficient. There is a great difference between ethics and religion. There is a distinction between one whose life is based on mere ethics and one who lives a truly religious life. We have a need for ethics, but true religion includes the truths of ethics and goes far beyond. True religion has its roots in the belief in a supreme being. Christian religion is based upon a belief in God the Eternal Father and in his Son Jesus Christ and in the word of the Lord as contained in scripture. . . .

True religion to the Christian is demonstrated by real belief in God and the realization that we are responsible to him for our acts and conduct. The person who lives such religion is willing to live the principles of the gospel of Christ and walk uprightly before the Lord in all things according to his revealed law. This brings to a man or a woman a sense of peace and freedom from confusion in life and gives an assurance of eternal life hereafter. (*Conference Report*, October 1969.)

The Reality of God. It is the general rule that we do not get things of value unless we are willing to pay a price. The scholar does not become learned unless he puts forth the work and effort to succeed. If he is not willing to do so, can he say there is no such thing as scholarship? Musicians, mathematicians, scientists, athletes, and skilled people in many fields spend years in study, practice, and hard work to acquire their ability. Can others who are not willing to make the effort say there are no such things as music, mathematics, science, or athletics? It is just as foolish for man to say there is no God simply because he has not had the inclination to seek him.

History tells us there is a God. Science confirms the fact there is a Supreme Being. Human reasoning persuades us that there is a God. His own revelations to man leave no doubt as to his existence. In order for an individual to obtain unwavering knowledge of the reality of God, he must live the commandments and the doctrines announced by the Savior during his personal ministry. . . .

Those who are willing to make the search, apply themselves, and do God's will, will have the knowledge come to them of the reality of God. When a man has found God and understands his ways, he learns that nothing in the universe came by chance, but all things resulted from a divinely prearranged plan. What a rich meaning comes into his life! Understanding which surpasses worldly learning is his. The beauties of the world become more beautiful, the order of the universe becomes more meaningful, and all of God's creations are more understandable as he witnesses God's days come and go and the seasons follow each in their order. If all men could find God and follow his ways, the hearts of men would be turned in love toward their brothers, and nations would be at peace. (*Conference Report*, April 1970.)

Where, Then, Is Hope? There are those who declare it is old-fashioned to believe in the Bible. Is it old-fashioned to believe in God, in Jesus Christ, the Son of the Living God? Is it old-fashioned to believe in his atoning sacrifice and the resurrection? If it is, I declare myself to be old-fashioned and the Church is old-fashioned. In great simplicity the Master taught the principles of life eternal and lessons that bring happiness to those with the faith to believe. It doesn't seem reasonable to assume the necessity of modernizing these teachings of the Master. His message concerned principles that are eternal. . . .

In this world of confusion and rushing, temporal progress, we need to return to the simplicity of Christ. We need to love, honor, and worship him. To acquire spirituality and have its influence in our lives, we cannot become confused and misdirected by the twisted teachings of the modernist. We need to study the simple fundamentals of the truths taught by the Master and eliminate the controversial. . . .

The Church stands firmly against relaxation or change in moral issues and opposes the so-called new morality. Spiritual values cannot be set aside, notwithstanding modernists who would tear them down. We can be modern without giving way to the influence of the modernist. If it is old-fashioned to believe in the Bible, we should thank God for the privilege of being old-fashioned. (*Conference Report,* October 1970.)

A Teacher. It was on a summer day early in the morning. I was standing near the window. The curtains obstructed me from two little creatures out on the lawn. One was a large bird and the other a little bird, obviously just out of the nest. I saw the larger bird hop out on the lawn, then thump his feet and cock his head. He drew a big fat worm out of the lawn and came hopping back. The little bird opened its bill wide, but the big bird swallowed the worm.

Then I saw the big bird fly up into a tree. He pecked at the bark for a little while and came back with a big bug in his mouth. The little bird opened his beak wide, but the big bird swallowed the bug. There was squawking in protest.

The big bird flew away, and I didn't see it again, but I watched the little bird. After a while, the little bird hopped out on the lawn, thumped its feet, cocked its head, and pulled a big worm out of the lawn. God bless the good people who teach our children and our youth. (*Conference Report,* April 1972.)

Of the World or of the Kingdom? Society has made a great effort to modernize the world in education, communication, travel, health, commerce, housing, and in many other ways, so as to increase the standard of living; but what has this socialization and modernization done to the family—the basic institution of society? Never before has there been greater instability. The divorce rate is higher now than at any time in history. Modernization has transferred the responsibility of education from the family to public institutions where modern thought has become paramount and moral principles have been abandoned. The crime rate has increased alarmingly. Drug addiction, disobedience to law, increase in venereal disease, and corruption in all forms seem to be accepted. In this day of modernization, freedom of thought and action is sponsored and promoted without consideration of the responsibilities that must accompany such freedom if society is to be stabilized. Surely we would agree that the family institution has been seriously, if not irreparably, damaged in our society. . . .

Where, then, is hope in this world of frustration and moral decay? It lies in the knowledge and understanding of the truths taught by the Master, which must be taught by the Church of Christ without deviation and believed in and lived by its membership. These are eternal truths and will be so in perpetuity regardless of changing circumstances in society, development of new scientific achievements, or increase of man's knowledge. (*Conference Report,* October 1973.)

Paying Our Debt. How can we really pay the debt of gratitude we owe to our parents, brothers and sisters, teachers, and those who have served us in so many ways? How can we show appreciation for good homes, husbands and wives who are true and faithful, children who have the desire to live righteously and serve the Lord? How do we express thankfulness for our baptisms, for the privilege of partaking of the sacrament and renewing our covenants, for the priesthood we bear, for the light of the restored gospel, for the program of the Church devised to help us make progress toward exaltation and eternal life?

We pay our debt of gratitude by living in such a way as to bring credit to our parents and the name we bear, by doing good to others, by being of service, by being willing to share the light and knowledge we have received so that others will also have joy and happiness, by living the principles of the gospel in their fulness. (Stockholm Area Conference, August 1974.)

To Know God. With the advance of knowledge has come a reliance upon scientific principles of proof, and as a consequence, there are some who do not believe in God because his existence cannot be substantiated by such proof. In reality, scientific research is an endeavor to ascertain truth, and the same principles which are applied to that pursuit are used in the quest to establish the truth of religion as well. . . . As important as scientific research may be, the greatest quest is a search for God—to determine his reality, his personal attributes, and to secure a knowledge of the gospel of his Son Jesus Christ. It is not easy to find a perfect understanding of God. The search requires persistent effort, and there are some who never move themselves to pursue this knowledge. (*Conference Report,* October 1974.)

Faith—the First Step. There is no tangible, concrete evidence of the existence of God or the divinity of the Master in the legal sense, but not all inquiry for truth results in proof by real or demonstrative evidence. It is fallacious to argue that because there is no demonstrative evidence of the existence of God he does not in fact exist. In the absence of evidence often thought necessary by the scientific world for positive proof, our search may take us into the realm of circumstantial evidence. We could spend hours describing the wonders of the universe, of the earth, of nature, of the human body, the exactness of the laws of physics, and a thousand things, all of which dictate to the conscience of a truth seeker that there is a creator and one who rules over the universe. . . .

Suppose that all things could be proven by demonstrative evidence. What then would become of the element of faith? There would be no need for faith and it would be eliminated, giving rise then to this query: If faith is the first step or principle of the gospel and is eliminated, what happens to the gospel plan? The very foundation will crumble. I submit that there is a divine reason why all things cannot be proven by concrete evidence. (*Conference Report,* April 1975.)

That We May Be One. As we think of the great growth of the Church, the diversities of tongues and cultures, and the monumental tasks that yet lie before us, we wonder if there is any more important objective before us than to so live that we may enjoy the unifying spirit of the Lord. As Jesus prayed, we *must* be united if the world is ever to be convinced that he was sent by God his Father to redeem us from our sins. It is unity and oneness that has thus far enabled us to bear our testimonies around the globe. . . .

It is unity that has thus far enabled the Church, its wards and stakes, branches and districts, and members, to construct temples and chapels, undertake welfare projects, seek after the dead, watch over the Church, and build faith. More must be done. These great purposes of the Lord could not have been achieved with dissension or jealousy or selfishness. Our ideas may not always be quite like those who preside over us, but this is the Lord's church and he will bless each of us as we cast off pride, pray for strength, and contribute to the good of the whole.

By the same token, I know of no stronger weapons in the hands of the adversary against any group of men or women in this church than the weapons of divisiveness, faultfinding, and antagonism. . . . The key to a unified church is a unified soul—one that is at peace with itself and not given to inner conflicts and tensions. (*Conference Report,* April 1976.)

"Hallowed Be Thy Name." There are wide areas of our society from which the spirit of prayer and reverence and worship has vanished.

Men and women in many circles are clever, interesting, or brilliant, but they lack one crucial element in a complete life. They do not look up. They do not offer up vows of righteousness. . . . Their conversation sparkles, but it is not sacred. Their talk is witty, but it is not wise. Whether it be in the office, the locker room, or the laboratory, they have come too far down the scale of dignity who display their own limited powers and then find it necessary to blaspheme those unlimited powers that come from above.

Unfortunately we sometimes find this lack of reverence even within the Church. Occasionally we visit too loudly, enter and leave meetings too disrespectfully in what should be an hour of prayer and purifying worship. Reverence is the atmosphere of heaven. Prayer is the utterance of the soul to God the Father. We do well to become more like our Father by looking up to him, by remembering him always, and by caring greatly about his world and his work. (*Conference Report,* October 1977.)

Basic Concepts of Honesty. If we are sensitive to our relationship to the Savior, we must be honest in little things as well as the big. We should always remember that we are never alone. There is no act that is not observed; there is no word spoken that is not heard; there is no thought conceived in the mind of man that is not known to God. There is no darkness that can conceal the things we do. We must think before we act. . . . If we would have the companionship of the Master and the Spirit of the Holy Ghost, we must be honest with ourselves, honest with God, and with our fellowmen. This results in true joy. (*New Era,* February 1978, 5.)

Developing Spirituality. None of us has attained perfection or the zenith of spiritual growth that is possible in mortality. Every person can and must make spiritual progress. The gospel of Jesus Christ is the divine plan for that spiritual growth eternally. It is more than a code of ethics. It is more than an ideal social order. It is more than positive thinking about self-improvement and determination. The gospel is the saving power of the Lord Jesus Christ with his priesthood and sustenance and with the Holy Spirit. With faith in the Lord Jesus Christ and obedience to his gospel, a step at a time improving as we go, pleading for strength, improving our attitudes and our ambitions, we will find ourselves successfully in the fold of the Good Shepherd. (Philip. 4:13.) (*Conference Report,* April 1979.)

"All Are Alike unto God." As members of the Lord's church, we need to lift our vision beyond personal prejudices. We need to discover the supreme truth that indeed our Father is no respecter of persons. Sometimes we unduly offend brothers and sisters of other nations by assigning exclusiveness to one nationality of people over another. . . . Imagine a father having many sons, each having different temperaments, aptitudes, and spiritual traits. Does he love one son less than another? Perhaps the son who is least spiritually inclined has the father's attention, prayers, and pleadings more than the others. Does that mean he loves the others less? Do you imagine our Heavenly Father loving one nationality of his offspring more exclusively than others? As members of the Church, we need to be reminded of Nephi's challenging question: "Know ye not that there are more nations than one?" (Fourteen-stake fireside at Brigham Young University, February 4, 1979; *Ensign,* June 1979, 74.)

Reading the Scriptures. When we follow the counsel of our leaders to read and study the scriptures, benefits and blessings of many kinds come to us. This is the most profitable of all study in which we could engage. The portion of scripture known as the Old and New Testaments is often referred to as the great literature of the world. These books have been regarded as scientific treatises, as philosophic dissertations, and also as historical records; but if we understand the true purpose of these and other scriptures, we realize that they are really the fundamental literature of religion.

The scriptural library contains the basic declarations concerning God and his children and the interrelationship between them. Throughout each of the books there is an appeal to believe and have faith in God the Eternal Father and in his Son, Jesus Christ; and from the first to the last of these books of scripture is the call to do the will of God and keep his commandments. Scriptures contain the record of the self-revelation of God, and through them God speaks to man. Where could there be more profitable use of time than reading from the scriptural library the literature that teaches us to know God and understand our relationship to him? (*Conference Report,* October 1979.)

True Greatness. We have an unlimited number of opportunities to do the many simple and minor things that will ultimately make us great. To those who have devoted their lives to service and sacrifice for others and for the Lord, the best counsel is simply to do more of the same. To those who are doing the commonplace work of the world but are wondering about the value of their accomplishments; to those who are the workhorses of this Church, who are furthering the work of the Lord in so many quiet but significant ways; to those who are the salt of the earth and the strength of the world and the backbone of each nation—to you we would simply express our admiration. If you endure to the end, and if you are valiant in the testimony of Jesus, you will achieve true greatness and will live in the presence of our Father in Heaven. (*Conference Report,* April 1982.)

Parents' Concern for Children. There are many in the Church and in the world who are living with feelings of guilt and unworthiness because some of their sons and daughters have wandered or strayed from the fold. . . . We understand that conscientious parents try their best, yet nearly all have made mistakes. One does not launch into such a project as parenthood without soon realizing that there will be many errors along the way. Surely our Heavenly Father knows, when he entrusts his spirit children into the care of young and inexperienced parents, that there will be mistakes and errors in judgment. . . .

A successful parent is one who has loved, one who has sacrificed, and one who has cared for, taught, and ministered to the needs of a child. If you have done all these and your child is still wayward or troublesome or worldly, it could well be that you are, nevertheless, a successful parent. Perhaps there are children who have come into the world that would challenge any set of parents under any set of circumstances. Likewise, perhaps there are others who would bless the lives of, and be a joy to, almost any father or mother. My concern today is that there are parents who may be pronouncing harsh judgments upon themselves and may be allowing these feelings to destroy their lives, when in fact they have done their best and should continue in faith. (*Conference Report,* October 1983.)

The Pharisee and the Publican. Humility is an attribute of godliness possessed by true Saints. It is easy to understand why a proud man fails. He is content to rely upon himself only. This is evident in those who seek social position or who push others aside to gain position in fields of business, government, education, sports, or other endeavors. Our genuine concern should be for the success of others. The proud man shuts himself off from God, and when he does he no longer lives in the light. . . . From the beginning of time there have been those with pride and others who have followed the divine admonition to be humble. History bears record that those who have exalted themselves have been abased, but the humble have been exalted. On every street there are Pharisees and publicans. It may be that one of them bears our name. (*Conference Report,* April 1984.)

"Master, the Tempest Is Raging." We will all have some adversity in our lives. I think we can be reasonably sure of that. Some of it will have the potential to be violent and damaging and destructive. Some of it may even strain our faith in a loving God who has the power to administer relief in our behalf. To those anxieties I think the Father of us all would say, "Why are ye so fearful? how is it that ye have no faith?" And of course that has to be faith for the whole journey, the entire experience, the fulness of our life, not simply around the bits and pieces and tempestuous moments. . . .

Jesus was not spared grief and pain and anguish and buffeting. No tongue can speak the unutterable burden he carried, nor have we the wisdom to understand the prophet Isaiah's description of him as "a man of sorrows." (Isa. 53:3.) His ship was tossed most of his life, and, at least to mortal eyes, it crashed fatally on the rocky coast of Calvary. We are asked not to look on life with mortal eyes; with spiritual vision we know something quite different was happening upon the cross.

Peace was on the lips and in the heart of the Savior no matter how fiercely the tempest was raging. May it so be with us—in our own hearts, in our own homes, in our nations of the world, and even in the buffetings faced from time to time by the Church. We should not expect to get through life individually or collectively without some opposition. (*Conference Report*, October 1984.)

An Apostle's Witness of the Resurrection. Alexander the Great, king of Macedon, pupil of Aristotle, conqueror of most of the known world in his time, was one of the world's great young leaders. After years of exercising military pomp and prowess and after extending his kingdom from Macedonia to Egypt and from Cyprus to India, he wept when there seemed to be no more world to conquer. Then, as evidence of just how ephemeral such power is, Alexander caught a fever and died at thirty-three years of age. The vast kingdom he had attained virtually died with him.

Quite a different young leader also died at what seems such an untimely age of thirty-three. He likewise was a king, a pupil, and a conqueror. Yet he received no honors from man, achieved no territorial conquests, rose to no political station. So far as we know, he never held a sword nor wore even a single piece of armor. But the Kingdom he established still flourishes some two thousand years later. His power was not of this world.

The differences between Alexander and this equally young Nazarene are many. But the greatest difference is in their ultimate victories. Alexander conquered lands, peoples, principalities, and earthly kingdoms. But he who is called the Perfect Leader, he who was and is the Light and Life of the world—Jesus Christ the Son of

God—conquered what neither Alexander nor any other could defeat or overcome: Jesus of Nazareth conquered death. Against the medals and monuments of centuries of men's fleeting victories stands the only monument necessary to mark the eternal triumph— an empty garden tomb. (*Conference Report,* April 1986.)

What Is True Greatness? True greatness is never a result of a chance occurrence or a one-time effort or achievement. Greatness requires the development of character. It requires a multitude of correct decisions in the everyday choices between good and evil. . . .

As we evaluate our lives, it is important that we look not only at our accomplishments but also at the conditions under which we have labored. We are each different and unique; we have each had different starting points in the race of life; we each have a unique mixture of talents and skills; we each have our own set of challenges and constraints with which to contend. Therefore, our judgments of ourselves and our achievements should not merely include the size or magnitude and number of our accomplishments; it should also include the conditions that have existed and the effect that our efforts have had on others. . . .

It appears to me that the kind of greatness our Father in Heaven would have us pursue is within the grasp of all who are within the gospel net. We have an unlimited number of opportunities to do the many simple and minor things that will ultimately make us great. To those who have devoted their lives to service and sacrifice for their families, for others, and for the Lord, the best counsel I can give is simply to do more of the same.

To those who are furthering the work of the Lord in so many quiet but significant ways, to those who are the salt of the earth and the strength of the world and the backbone of each nation—to you we would simply express our admiration. If you endure to the end, and if you are valiant in the testimony of Jesus, you will achieve true greatness and will one day live in the presence of our Father in Heaven. (*Ensign,* September 1987, 72.)

Blessed from On High. Sometimes we may feel that our spiritual edge has grown dull. On some very trying days, we may even feel that God has forgotten us, has left us alone in our confusion and concern. But that feeling is no more justified for the older ones among us than it is for the younger and less experienced. God knows and loves us all. We are, every one of us, his daughters and his sons, and whatever life's lessons may have brought us, the promise is still true: "If any of you lack wisdom, let him ask of God, that giveth to all men liberally, and upbraideth not; and it shall be given him." (James 1:5.) (*Conference Report,* October 1988.)

We Ought to Know the Scriptures. We ought to have a church full of women and men who know the scriptures thoroughly, who cross-reference and mark them, who develop lessons and talks out of the Topical Guide, and who have mastered the maps, the Bible Dictionary, and the other helps that are contained in this wonderful set of standard works. . . .

Not in this dispensation, surely not in *any* dispensation, have the scriptures—the enduring, enlightening word of God—been so readily available and so helpfully structured for the use of every man, woman, and child who will search them. The written word of God is in the most readable and accessible form ever provided to lay members in the history of the world. Surely we will be held accountable if we do not read them. (Satellite address to religious educators, February 10, 1989.)

Our Responsibility as Teachers. Give your students truth powerfully taught; that is the way to give them a spiritual experience. Let it come naturally and as it will, perhaps with the shedding of tears, but perhaps not. If what you say is the truth, and you say it purely and with honest conviction, those students will feel the spirit of the truth being taught them and will recognize that inspiration and revelation has come into their hearts. That is how we build faith. That is how we strengthen testimonies—with the power of the word of God taught in purity and with conviction.

Listen for the truth, hearken to the doctrine, and let the manifestation of the Spirit come as it may in all of its many and varied forms. Stay with solid principles; teach from a pure heart. Then the Spirit will penetrate your mind and heart and the mind and heart of every one of your students. (Satellite address to religious educators, February 10, 1989.)

The Church Is for All People. This is the church of Jesus Christ, not the church of marrieds or singles or any other group or individual. The gospel we preach is the gospel of Jesus Christ, which encompasses all the saving ordinances and covenants necessary to save and exalt every individual who is willing to accept Christ and keep the commandments that he and our Father in Heaven have given.

How foolish we would be to fail to enjoy the rich gifts of God to us! We could well miss opportunities for providing needed blessings to others because we felt personally deprived of some hoped-for blessing and were blinded by our own self-pity. Not only should we be careful not to deprive others of blessings because of our wanderings in the wastelands of self-pity or self-recrimination, but we should be careful not to deprive ourselves of other blessings that could be ours. While waiting for promised blessings, one should not mark time, for to fail to move forward is to some degree a retrogression. Be anxiously engaged in good causes, including your own development. (Satellite address to single adults, February 26, 1989.)

The Golden Thread of Choice. God's chief way of acting is by persuasion and patience and long-suffering, not by coercion and stark confrontation. He acts by gentle solicitation and by sweet enticement. He always acts with unfailing respect for the freedom and independence that we possess. He wants to help us and pleads for the chance to assist us, but he will not do so in violation of our agency. He loves us too much to do that, and doing so would run counter to his divine character. . . .

To countermand and ultimately forbid our choices was Satan's way, not God's, and the Father of us all simply never will do that. He will, however, stand by us forever to help us see the right path, find the right choice, respond to the true voice, and feel the influence of his undeniable Spirit. His gentle, peaceful, powerful persuasion to do right and find joy will be with us "so long as time shall last, or the earth shall stand, or there shall be one man upon the face thereof to be saved." (Moro. 7:36.) (*Conference Report*, October 1989.)

Standing As Witnesses of God. If we can pattern our life after the Master, and take his teaching and example as the supreme pattern for our own, we will not find it difficult to be consistent and loyal in every walk of life, for we will be committed to a single, sacred standard of conduct and belief. Whether at home or in the marketplace, whether at school or long after school is behind us, whether we are acting alone or in concert with a host of other people, our course will be clear and our standards will be obvious. We will have determined, as the prophet Alma said, "to stand as witnesses of God at all times and in all things, and in all places that [we] may be in, even until death." (Mosiah 18:9.) (*Conference Report*, April 1990.)

Walls of the Mind. As the walls in Eastern Europe, the Soviet Union, Africa, China, India, South America, and many other parts of the world come tumbling down, the corresponding need for more missionaries to fulfill the divine commission to take the gospel to all the earth will certainly go up! Are we ready to meet the contingency?

To satisfy the new demands being made upon us in this great

missionary work of the last days, perhaps some of us (particularly the older generation whose families are raised) need to take stock to determine whether "walls" that we have built in our own minds need to come down. For example, how about the "comfort wall" that seems to prevent many couples and singles from going on a mission? How about the "financial wall" of debt that interferes with some members' ability to go, or the "grandchildren wall," or the "health wall," or the "lack of self-confidence wall," or the "transgression wall," or the walls of fear, doubt, or complacency? Does anyone really doubt for a minute that with the help of the Lord he or she could bring those walls crashing down?

We have been privileged to be born in these last days, as opposed to some earlier dispensation, to help take the gospel to all the earth. There is no greater calling in this life. If we are content to hide behind self-made walls, we willingly forgo the blessings that are otherwise ours. (*Ensign*, September 1990, 10.)

Come unto Me. Why face life's burdens alone, Christ asks, or why face them with temporal support that will quickly falter? To the heavy laden it is Christ's yoke, it is the power and peace of standing side by side with a God that will provide the support, balance, and strength to meet our challenges and endure our tasks here in the hardpan field of mortality. Obviously, the personal burdens of life vary from person to person, but every one of us has them. Furthermore, each trial in life is tailored to the individual's capacities and needs as known by a loving Father in Heaven. Of course, some sorrows are brought on by the sins of a world not following the counsel of that Father in Heaven. Whatever the reason, none of us seems to be completely free from life's challenges. To one and all, Christ said, in effect: As long as we all must bear some burden and shoulder some yoke, why not let it be mine? My promise to you is that my yoke is easy, and my burden is light. (See Matt. 11:28–30.) (*Conference Report*, October 1990.)

The Gospel—A Global Faith. In the message of the gospel, the entire human race is one family descended from a single God. All men and women have not only a physical lineage leading back to Adam and Eve, their first earthly parents, but also a spiritual heritage leading back to God the Eternal Father. Thus, all persons on earth are literally brothers and sisters in the family of God. It is in understanding and accepting this universal fatherhood of God that all human beings can best appreciate God's concern for them and their relationship to each other. This is a message of life and love that strikes squarely against all stifling traditions based on race, language, economic or political standing, educational rank, or cultural background, for we are all of the same spiritual descent. We have a divine pedigree; every person is a spiritual child of God. (*Conference Report*, October 1991.)

A More Excellent Way. The world in which we live, whether close to home or far away, needs the gospel of Jesus Christ. It provides the only way the world will ever know peace. We need to be kinder with one another, more gentle and forgiving. We need to be slower to anger and more prompt to help. We need to extend the hand of friendship and resist the hand of retribution. In short, we need to love one another with the pure love of Christ, with genuine charity and compassion and, if necessary, shared suffering, for that is the way God loves us. (*Conference Report*, April 1992.)

An Anchor to the Souls of Men. In my lifetime I have seen two world wars, plus Korea, plus Vietnam and all that you are currently witnessing. I have worked my way through the depression and managed to go to law school while starting a young family at the same time. I have seen stock markets and world economics go crazy, and have seen a few despots and tyrants go crazy, all of which causes quite a bit of trouble around the world in the process. So I am frank to say tonight that I hope you won't believe all the world's difficulties have been wedged into your decade, or that things have never been worse than they are for you personally, or they will never get better. I reassure you that things have been worse and they will always get better. They always do, especially when we live and love the gospel of Jesus Christ and give it a chance to flourish in our lives. (Nineteen-stake fireside for college-age young adults, Brigham Young University, February 7, 1993; *Ensign*, October 1993, 70.)

An Apostle's Witness of Christ. As an ordained Apostle and special witness of Christ, I give you my solemn witness that Jesus Christ is in fact the Son of God. He is the Messiah prophetically anticipated by Old Testament prophets. He is the Hope of Israel, for whose coming the children of Abraham, Isaac, and Jacob had prayed during the long centuries of prescribed worship. . . . It is by the power of the Holy Ghost that I bear my witness. I know of Christ's reality as if I had seen with my eyes and heard with my ears. I know also that the Holy Spirit will confirm the truthfulness of my witness in the hearts of all those who listen with an ear of faith. (Friendshipping and fellowshipping fireside satellite broadcast, October 30, 1983; *Ensign*, January 1984, 70.)

What Manner of Men Ought Ye to Be? The great standard! The only sure way! The light and the life of the world! How grateful we should be that God sent his Only Begotten Son to earth to do at least two things that no other person could have done. The first task Christ did as a perfect, sinless Son was to redeem all mankind from the fall, providing an atonement for Adam's sin and for our own sins if we will accept and follow him. The second great thing he did was to set a perfect example of right living, of kindness and mercy and compassion, in order that all of the rest of mankind might know how to live, know how to improve, and know how to become more godlike. . . .

We must know Christ better than we know him; we must remember him more often than we remember him; we must serve him more valiantly than we serve him. Then we will drink water springing up unto eternal life and will eat the bread of life.

What manner of men and women ought we to be? Even as he is. In the name of Jesus Christ, amen. (General conference address, April 3, 1994.)

Notes

CHAPTER 1: BORN OF GOODLY PARENTS

1. When President Hunter visited Hunterston Castle on June 2, 1992, he picked up a booklet with a history of the family and estate and had it typed into his journal under that date. This quotation is taken from that transcript.

2. "President Howard W. Hunter Honored by Scottish Clan," *Ensign,* January 1988, 75.

3. In about 1939, Howard's grandfather John Hunter, who was then living in San Francisco, wrote his life story, titled "To the Children: Early Life of Your Father." This quotation and other information that follows concerning the Hunter family is taken from that document and from a summarized version written by Howard. Both manuscripts, undated and unpublished, are in possession of family members.

4. Nancy F. Nowell, *Testimony of Nancy Nowell. A Copy of My Journals. Commenced in Lapeer, Michigan. A Daily Account of the Devotional and Devout Exercises of My Heart and the Testimony of the Truth* (Salt Lake City: George Q. Cannon and Sons, 1892). Nancy had the manuscript published as a legacy for her descendants.

5. Little is known about what happened to Nancy and Silas in Nauvoo. Silas apparently opposed going west with the Saints, but Nancy was determined to go and to take with her two of their children. She had just boarded a boat to cross the Mississippi when some men who had helped her yelled out that Silas was coming. Before they could shove off, Silas reached the dock and grabbed one of the children out of the boat. Both he and the child disappeared, and descendants have been unable to learn what became of them.

6. LeRoy R. Hafen and Ann W. Hafen, *Handcarts to Zion* (Glendale, California: The Arthur H. Clark Company, 1960), 193. This source gives Anders's age as twenty-nine; he was actually twenty-one. It also gives Nilla's name incorrectly as Nellie.

7. In some family and Church records, Nilla's name is listed as Nilla Torgersen.

8. Nicoline's name is also spelled in various family and Church records as Nicholine, Nicolene, and Nicolina. Her family called her Lena.

9. Nicoline's sons lived for a time with their father and then moved in with their grandparents in Mount Pleasant.

10. Andrew Jenson, *Encyclopedic History of The Church of Jesus Christ of Latter-day Saints* (Salt Lake City: The Church of Jesus Christ of Latter-day Saints, 1941), 75–76.

11. Howard Hunter kept a diary from August 5, 1918, three months before his eleventh birthday, until January 6, 1919. When his dance orchestra, Hunter's Croonaders, went on a cruise to the Orient January 1, 1927, he kept a detailed journal of each day's activities. He wrote in this journal until the end of that year. Through the years he kept meticulous records of important dates and events in his life; and in the early 1970s, using these records and the reminiscences of family members, he wrote a history of his life up to October 1959, when he was called to the Quorum of the Twelve. From that period on, he made notes on each day's activities and then dictated them for his secretary to transcribe. The typescripts of these journals total nearly three thousand pages in four bound volumes. With President Hunter's permission, quotations throughout this biography have been taken from both his history and his journals. Additional quotations attributed to him come from newspaper and magazine articles, with the sources identified in endnotes, and from personal interviews.

CHAPTER 2: A HAPPY CHILDHOOD IN BOISE

1. In this excerpt and subsequent excerpts from Howard's childhood diary, the original spelling has been retained. Some punctuation marks have been inserted and words capitalized to facilitate understanding; otherwise the diary entries follow the style of the original transcript.

2. Kellene Ricks, "Friend to Friend," *Friend*, April 1990, 6.

3. Meridian was originally named Hunter, after Howard's grandfather John Hunter.

4. Ricks, "Friend to Friend."

5. J M. Heslop, "He Found Pleasure in Work," *Church News*, November 16, 1974.

6. Howard had hoped to be the first Eagle Scout in Idaho, and in later years some newspaper and magazine articles about him reported that he was the second one. However, since the Church had strong wards and stakes in southeastern Idaho, north of Utah's Cache Valley, he believes it is possible that one or more Scouts from that area achieved the rank before he did. But it is certain that he was the second Eagle Scout in Boise, if not the state.

CHAPTER 3: HIGH SCHOOL, WORK, AND A CRUISE

1. In 1976 Howard and Dorothy returned to Boise for the fiftieth anniversary of his high school graduation, to which Dorothy's class, the class of 1928, had also been invited. Two days of activities were capped by a banquet at a local inn. After the dinner and program, Howard wrote, "many

of [the guests] danced to the music of an orchestra that played the tunes we danced to fifty and more years ago. Those who are not so nimble visited with old friends. . . . This was a delightful, nostalgic occasion and everyone seemed to thoroughly enjoy themselves. I was glad we came. It was long after midnight when we got home."

2. Howard golfed occasionally after he moved to California, up to the time he became a bishop in 1940. After his release, he claims, he went golfing once with his wife, Claire—and she beat him.

3. Many years later Elder Neal A. Maxwell visited the Philippines and went to the Manila Hotel, where he saw what was known as the General MacArthur Suite, named after General Douglas MacArthur. When he returned to Salt Lake City and learned that Elder Hunter was also going to Manila, he said, "You really ought to go see that suite in that hotel. Have you ever been there?" "Yes," was the response. "When?" Elder Maxwell asked. "In 1927" was the response. Elder Maxwell, in an interview for this book, commented, "It isn't just that Elder Hunter has a different milieu of growing up—he ties into an era that we don't really think of his belonging to."

4. In May 1983, Howard accompanied the International Folk Dancers of Brigham Young University on a sixteen-day tour of China. While in Shanghai on May 24, he revisited the dinner club. He described this experience in his journal: "When I was in Shanghai in 1927 the city was divided into sections—the French Concession, the British Concession, Japanese Concession and Old City. I asked the guide about the French club where I was, and he told me it was only a ten-minute walk and he would take Fred [Schwendiman] and me there. . . . We walked down Mao Ming Road to No. 58 and there was the club, now named the Jing Jiang Club, still the most exclusive dinner club in the city. We walked through the gardens and then talked with the doorman. He took us inside and up the beautiful staircase to the dining and dancing room. It has been changed a little but the dance floor and ceiling lights are still the same and the orchestra stand is in the same place. I could hardly believe my eyes to stand in the place where I was 56 years ago, not realizing at that time that I would ever return."

5. When Howard revisited Kobe in 1979 for conference sessions of the Osaka Japan North Stake, he wrote: "On the way back to the mission home [of the Japan Kobe Mission] we took Brother and Sister [Yoshihiko] Kikuchi to the Oriental Hotel in Kobe, a new hotel replacing the one by the same name where I played fifty-two years ago when my orchestra was touring on the *S.S. President Jackson*. President [Robert T.] Stout drove us down the street and onto the same pier [where] we docked at that time. We stopped to look at a ship from Shanghai, and I read from my journal of coming to Kobe, February 10, 1927. It was interesting to see the pier, the old custom house, and the place where I was many years ago. It looked the same but the hundreds of rickshaws were gone." The next day, "after dinner, President Stout took Brother Kikuchi and me for a ride to the peak of Mt. Rokko and also to the top of Mt. Maya where I went in 1927. The rope cable-way and the shrines are still there."

6. After his baptism, Will continued to encourage his family's participation in the Church, but he himself was not fully active for many years. In 1953 he and Nellie received their endowments in the Arizona Temple at Mesa and Howard was sealed to them. See chapter 7.

CHAPTER 4: CALIFORNIA, HERE I COME!

1. Mildred Adams, as quoted in Carey McWilliams, *Southern California: An Island on the Land* (Santa Barbara and Salt Lake City: Peregrine Smith, 1973), 135.

2. Missionary efforts in Sorau are described briefly in Gilbert W. Scharffs, *Mormonism in Germany: A History of The Church of Jesus Christ of Latter-day Saints in Germany Between 1840 and 1970* (Salt Lake City: Deseret Book, 1970), 41–43. The area was first visited in 1892 by missionaries Hugh and David Cannon, sons of President George Q. Cannon, first counselor in the First Presidency. They "had been working only a brief time in an untrodden mission area of Prussia in the town of Sorau . . . when suddenly David Cannon died on October 17, 1892. . . . By the end of 1893, there were 262 in the [Swiss-German] mission, most of them (181) in Germany. The new Sorau Branch led with 37 baptisms." The following year, 1894, "Sorau had more baptisms than any town in Europe at this time. . . . The mission was now visited by European Mission President, Apostle Anthony H. Lund. At Sorau a wealthy farmer who was branch president had invited 200 people to his home, since public meetings were forbidden. Two city officials and a minister's son attended. After the meeting several saints who had to travel fifteen miles were stoned on their way home." That part of Prussia, near the border of Poland and Germany, was ceded to Germany after World War I, became part of the Russian zone of occupation after World War II, and then was ceded to Poland. The area was devastated during the two wars and many vital records were destroyed, making it virtually impossible to trace the Reckzeh family line.

3. Maria Emilie lived the rest of her life in Salt Lake City, where she was active in the Church and did considerable work in the Salt Lake Temple. By the time she passed away—on May 21, 1942, at age eighty-three—she had done over five hundred endowments in the temple.

4. Richard Hunter recently commented, "I have always been struck with Dad's determination to follow a course of action he thought was best. When he decided to pack up his saxophone and clarinet, it's always seemed to me that was an incredible decision. Ever since he was a young man, he had loved music and entertaining people. He was a good musician, and music was very much a part of his life. To shut the case on his instruments seems to me to be a remarkable decision, but, nonetheless, he had decided that there was a better course in life he needed to follow. When I was in high school we had a jazz band. The band needed a saxophone player. I asked Dad if he still had his saxophone around, and he said that it might be in the attic. I soon found the saxophone the way it had been shut up in 1931. I got it out, had it repadded, and played it myself for some time. Indeed, it looked

to me as though . . . the saxophone case hadn't been opened by him for twenty-five years."

5. Doyle L. Green, "Howard William Hunter, Apostle from California," *Improvement Era* 63 (January 1960): 36.

CHAPTER 5: HUSBAND, FATHER, LAWYER, BISHOP

1. The Tabernacle Choir was on a tour that included appearances at the World's Fair in San Diego, "The California Pacific International Exposition." See "The Church Moves On," *Improvement Era* 38 (October 1935): 621.

2. According to Leo J. Muir, *A Century of Mormon Activities in California* (Salt Lake City: Deseret News Press, n.d.), 1:252–53, "Again on July 24, 1936, the ward presented in the bowl a continuation of the first pageant, 'The March of the Battalion.' This pageant was again presented at the World's Fair in San Diego, also under the auspices of Inglewood Ward."

3. "The chapel was begun in December 1937 and was dedicated July 24, 1938, by Elder Melvin J. Ballard. Cost of the building and grounds exceeded $50,000." Muir, *A Century of Mormon Activities in California* 1:252.

4. Several years later the university decided to confer the degree of doctor of laws, or juris doctor, instead of the bachelor of laws. The decision was made retroactive, and in 1971 Howard applied for and received the doctor of jurisprudence degree to replace the bachelor of laws he received earlier.

5. John Hunter died the next year, on August 10, 1941, in San Francisco.

6. All sixteen members of Howard's genealogy class, as far as can be determined, later married in the temple. Green, "Howard William Hunter, Apostle from California," 36.

7. A few months later, when Frank Brundage moved from the area, Richard M. Bleak became first counselor and James A. Rawson, second counselor. When Brother Bleak moved from the area in 1943, Brother Rawson became first counselor and George C. Rands was called as second counselor. These men served with Bishop Hunter until his release in November 1946.

8. Nelle Hedtke, "History of the South Pasadena Ward Sunday School, Pasadena Stake of Zion, 1938–1950," unpublished manuscript.

9. Charles C. Pulsipher, "My Most Influential Teacher," *Church News*, January 10, 1981, 2.

CHAPTER 6: FAMILY LIFE AND LAW PRACTICE

1. Sixteen years later, in August 1970, the Explorers and their leaders held a reunion in Pasadena. "Of the fourteen boys who made the trip, most of them have been on missions, completed their education, some have served in the military, and all have married," Howard reported.

2. Green, "Howard William Hunter, Apostle from California," 37.

3. As of early 1994, Howard was still a member of the Watson board. Nearly every month for half a century, except when he was on Church

assignments or ill, he attended the monthly board meetings, often flying to Los Angeles on Sunday evening or early Monday morning, attending the Monday meeting, and returning home later that day.

4. In November 1989 Richard Hunter's fine short biography of his father was published in a booklet entitled "The Howard W. Hunter Professorship in the J. Reuben Clark Law School, Brigham Young University." The booklet was given to guests attending a special program honoring Elder Hunter in connection with the establishment of the endowed professorship in law at BYU.

5. John S. Welch, remarks at a special program honoring Howard W. Hunter, sponsored by the United States Court of Appeals for the Ninth Circuit in Los Angeles, November 26, 1990.

6. Cree-L Kofford, remarks at a meeting sponsored by the Southern California chapters of the J. Reuben Clark Society in honor of Howard W. Hunter, Hilton Hotel, Los Angeles, May 6, 1989.

CHAPTER 7: PRESIDENT OF PASADENA STAKE

1. Bruce Henstell, *Los Angeles: An Illustrated History* (New York: Alfred A. Knopf, 1980), 186.

2. The name Hollywood Stake was discontinued at this time, and thereafter the stake was known as the Los Angeles Stake. What was formerly known as the Los Angeles Stake was renamed South Los Angeles Stake.

3. Daken Broadhead was released from the stake presidency on March 1, 1953, after accepting a position as executive assistant to the new U.S. Secretary of Agriculture, Ezra Taft Benson. A. Kay Berry, who had been serving as second counselor, was sustained as first counselor, and J. Talmage Jones was called to serve as second counselor in the stake presidency. President Berry was later released and President Jones became first counselor, with Richard S. Summerhays as second counselor. In September 1959, President Jones was released as first counselor, and President Summerhays was sustained in that position. Daken Broadhead was once again sustained as a member of the stake presidency, this time as second counselor.

4. William A. Pettit, unpublished manuscript history of the Pasadena Stake, September 1966, p. 21.

5. James B. Allen and Glen M. Leonard, *The Story of the Latter-day Saints*, 2nd ed., revised and enlarged (Salt Lake City: Deseret Book, 1992), 599.

6. According to Daken Broadhead, by the 1990s the property was worth at least ten times that amount. Because of the steep hill behind the back parking lot, the property is surrounded by a natural greenbelt. For an additional $5,000, the stake purchased a field east of the building and developed recreational facilities, including a softball field, a picnic area, and a playground for younger children.

7. For additional information on the introduction of the early-morning seminary program in Los Angeles, see Allen and Leonard, *The Story of the Latter-day Saints*, 2nd ed., 575–76.

8. "Welfare and the Relief Society," *Relief Society Magazine,* April 1962, p. 238.

9. Pettit, unpublished manuscript history of the Pasadena Stake, p. 20.

10. "Make Us Thy True Undershepherds," *Ensign,* April 1986, 7.

11. Green, "Howard William Hunter, Apostle from California," 37. The individual quoted is not named in the article.

12. Betty C. McEwan, "My Most Influential Teacher," *Church News,* June 21, 1980, 2.

CHAPTER 8: CALLED TO THE QUORUM OF THE TWELVE

1. "For the three semesters she attended Pasadena City College, her work resulted in A's except for the B she received in Composition II," Howard noted in his history. "I was proud of her scholastic record."

2. *Journal of Discourses* 9:86.

3. With Howard's ordination, the Quorum of the Twelve on October 15, 1959, was comprised of President Joseph Fielding Smith, 83, and Elders Harold B. Lee, 60; Spencer W. Kimball, 64; Ezra Taft Benson, 60; Mark E. Petersen, 61; Delbert L. Stapley, 62; Marion G. Romney, 62; LeGrand Richards, 73; Richard L. Evans, 53; George Q. Morris, 85; Hugh B. Brown, 75; and Howard W. Hunter, 51.

4. Allen and Leonard, *The Story of the Latter-day Saints,* 2nd ed., 591, 593.

5. Richard Summerhays, who had served as a counselor in the stake presidency, was sustained as the new stake president, with James C. Ellsworth and Clifford I. Cummings as counselors.

6. Until 1977, the annual general conference in April was held for three days and included two sessions on April 6, the anniversary of the 1830 organization of the Church. If April 6 fell on Thursday or Friday, the other sessions would usually take place the following Saturday and Sunday. If April 6 fell on Monday, Tuesday, or Wednesday, conference began the preceding weekend. There were six general sessions, a Saturday evening priesthood session, often an early-morning welfare session, and a Sunday evening meeting for Sunday School officers and teachers. Since April 1977, general conference sessions have been held on the first Saturday and Sunday in April and the first Sunday in October and the preceding Saturday (when the first Sunday falls on October 1, conference begins Saturday, September 30).

7. Though he no longer practiced law, Elder Hunter still had numerous business interests, some in partnership with Gilles DeFlon and some with John and Richard. One of his interests was investing in cattle. For several years Elder Hunter and his sons owned cattle, which they kept at a feedlot in Lancaster, California. Elder Hunter and Mr. DeFlon purchased a 24,000–acre cattle ranch west of Promontory, Utah, in June 1961. Elder Hunter enjoyed visiting the ranch periodically, and for many years he helped prepare the taxes and took care of other business in connection with it. After Mr. DeFlon's death in 1966, his son, James DeFlon, took over his share of the property. After a visit to the ranch with James DeFlon in 1991,

Elder Hunter wrote: "Counting the cows, bulls, and heifers, we have about 1800 head on the ranch and 20 men were doing the branding and vaccinating. Jim took me for a ride around the ranch to see the watering tanks and the windmill and solar pumps that feed the pipelines. It has been a long time since I have seen the ranch and I was amazed at the size of the operation."

8. On February 9, 1973, Elder Hunter wrote: "The work of this [personnel] committee has increased substantially the past few years as the departments have been enlarged because of the growth of the Church. Many employees, such as those in the temples, building department, foreign offices, and other operations, have been brought under the committee. We determine salaries, increases, employee benefits and determine policy for standards." When he was released from the committee on June 15 that year, he wrote: "I was appointed to this committee on January 17, 1963, and have served since that time. LeGrand Richards and I have been the only members for several years during which time we engaged the services of Russell Williams as personnel director and established an efficient operating department."

9. Under date of Tuesday, April 17, 1973, Elder Hunter wrote: "I walked to the Missionary Home in the rain this morning and gave my last lecture. On November 11, 1960, I was appointed to the teaching staff to lecture on the subject of the Apostasy and Restoration, and since that time I have spoken to several hundred classes of missionaries." The Missionary Home during those years was half a block from the Church Administration Building. Beginning in 1961, missionaries called to non-English-speaking areas went to the Language Training Center north of the BYU campus in Provo, and in 1976, after that facility was substantially enlarged, missionaries called to English-speaking areas also went there for instruction.

CHAPTER 9: BEARING WITNESS TO THE WORLD

1. Printed in *Church News*, January 20, 1962, 5. See also Edward L. Kimball and Andrew E. Kimball Jr., *Spencer W. Kimball* (Salt Lake City: Bookcraft, 1977), 336. Camilla Kimball wrote of their Christmas experience in Jerusalem in *This People*, December 1985, p. 41, and in a letter to the editor, *This People*, February/March 1986, 6.

2. Remarks by President Thomas S. Monson at funeral services for Claire Jeffs Hunter, Monument Park Stake Center, Salt Lake City, October 12, 1983.

3. "Elder Hunter Reports So. Pacific Missions," *Church News*, June 9, 1992, 3.

4. Kava, a pepper grown in the islands, is crushed to make a beverage.

5. *Church News*, September 24, 1966, 15.

CHAPTER 10: THE APOSTOLIC MINISTRY, PART 1

1. Bruce R. McConkie, *Mormon Doctrine* (Salt Lake City: Bookcraft, 1966), 47.

2. Conference Report, September 30, 1961, 79, 81.

3. Some information on the history of the Genealogical Society during the 1960s has been drawn from James B. Allen and Jessie Embry, "Hearts Turned to the Fathers: A History of the Genealogical Society of The Church of Jesus Christ of Latter-day Saints," unpublished manuscript, 1991. Copies may be found in the Harold B. Lee Library at Brigham Young University in Provo, Utah, and the Church Historical Library and Family History Department Library in Salt Lake City. See also several articles on genealogy in *Improvement Era*, July 1969.

4. Management Systems Corporation (MSC), a Church-owned entity, was organized in 1968 to handle computer needs of the Church and also contract for commercial work. The Information Systems Department was established in 1974 to handle all internal computer functions, and in 1979 the MSC was dissolved. See Allen and Embry, "Hearts Turned to the Fathers," chapter 10.

5. Douglas D. Palmer, "The World Conference on Records," *Improvement Era*, July 1969, 7. As of 1993, more than two thousand family history centers had been established to serve the Saints and nonmembers.

6. Regional Representatives Seminar, Salt Lake City, Utah, 1968.

7. Jay M. Todd, "Elder Howard W. Hunter, Church Historian," *Improvement Era*, April 1970, 27.

8. *Church News*, February 14, 1970, 3.

9. Background information on the New World Archaeological Foundation has been drawn from John L. Sorenson, "Brief History of the BYU New World Archaeological Foundation," unpublished paper prepared for the Centennial Symposium on Mesoamerica Archaeology at Brigham Young University in 1975.

10. Ibid.

CHAPTER 11: THE APOSTOLIC MINISTRY, PART 2

1. Information on Laie, the college, and the Polynesian Cultural Center appears in the following sources: Robert O'Brien, *Hands Across the Water: The Story of the Polynesian Cultural Center* (Laie: The Polynesian Cultural Center, 1983); R. Lanier Britsch, *Unto the Islands of the Sea: A History of the Latter-day Saints in the Pacific* (Salt Lake City: Deseret Book, 1986); Craig Ferre, "A History of the Polynesian Cultural Center's 'Night Show': 1963–1983," Ph.D. dissertation, Brigham Young University, August 1988; Alton L. Wade, devotional address delivered at Brigham Young University–Hawaii January 7, 1993, and published in *Profile Magazine* (BYU–Hawaii), Summer 1993, pp. 4–8.

2. "All Are Alike unto God," address delivered at a fourteen-stake fireside at the Marriott Center, Brigham Young University, February 4, 1979, and reprinted in *Ensign*, June 1979, 72–74.

3. At a reception in Jerusalem in October 1975, Elder Hunter met Premier Yitzhak Rabin, who in 1993 would travel to the United States to sign a

peace accord with Yasir Arafat, head of the Palestinian Liberation Organization.

4. A letter from Elder Hyde, describing his missionary experiences and including a copy of his prayer, was published in *Millennial Star* and is reprinted in Joseph Smith, *History of the Church* 4:454–59.

5. Steven W. Baldridge, with Marilyn N. Rona, *Grafting In: A History of the Latter-day Saints in the Holy Land* (Israel: The Jerusalem Branch of The Church of Jesus Christ of Latter-day Saints, 1989), 19–21. According to this book, the monument had been suggested earlier by Jerusalem mayor Teddy Kollek.

6. "President Kimball Dedicates Orson Hyde Memorial Garden in Jerusalem," *Ensign*, December 1979, 67–68. For additional information on the memorial project, see Lucile C. Tate, *LeGrand Richards: Beloved Apostle* (Salt Lake City: Bookcraft, 1982), 284–85, 299–301. That book states that the dedication was held on a Sunday; however, the 1979 calendar shows that October 24 fell on Wednesday.

7. The million-dollar contribution was to pay for the construction and landscaping of the garden. The Jerusalem Foundation, which developed the green-belt area, agreed to maintain the garden for the 999 years of the lease.

8. Baldridge, *Grafting In*, 53–54.

9. Naomi Shepherd, *Teddy Kollek, Mayor of Jerusalem* (New York: Harper & Row, 1988), 102–3. See also Baldridge, *Grafting In*, 76–81.

10. *Church News*, July 28, 1985.

11. The modifications included the guarantee that no one who was in any way associated with the center would ever proselyte in Israel.

12. Baldridge, *Grafting In*, 94.

CHAPTER 12: "WE TOOK SWEET COUNSEL TOGETHER"

1. Spencer W. Kimball, *Instructor*, August 1960, 256–57, as quoted in an article by Ezra Taft Benson on the 150th anniversary of the organization of the Twelve, *Church News*, January 27, 1983, 3.

2. Will Hunter had been in good health until shortly before his death, when he suffered a cerebral hemorrhage. He died peacefully, without regaining consciousness. He was eighty-three years of age.

3. Bruce R. McConkie, "The New Revelation on Priesthood," *Priesthood* (Salt Lake City: Deseret Book, 1981), 126.

CHAPTER 13: FAMILY AND NEIGHBORS

1. Carma Wadley, "Utahns Share Memories of Mother," *Deseret News*, May 8, 1983.

2. Muir, *A Century of Mormon Activities in California* 1:447.

CHAPTER 14: "A FULL SHARE OF UPS AND DOWNS"

1. "The Opening and Closing of Doors," *Ensign*, November 1987, 58.

2. Spencer W. Kimball, *Faith Precedes the Miracle* (Salt Lake City: Deseret Book, 1972), 98.

3. In a general conference address in April 1991, Elder Rulon G. Craven of the Seventy, the former executive secretary to the Quorum of the Twelve, talked about President Hunter's struggles to walk and the triumphant day when he walked to the temple: "Many will remember a number of years ago President Hunter was informed that he would not walk again. However, his faith and determination was greater than that message. Daily, without fanfare and the knowledge of others, he went through some very strenuous physical therapy exercises with determination, faith, and the vision that he would walk again. During those difficult months, his Brethren of the Twelve were praying for him daily in their quorum meetings and in their private prayers.

"Months later, on a Thursday morning, I went to President Hunter's office to discuss an agenda item for the temple meeting that morning. I found he left early and was informed that he was walking to the temple. I questioned that information and then hurried to catch up with him. When I caught up with him, he was walking with the help of a walker. We walked together to the elevator and then up to the fourth floor. We went down the hall to the upper room of the temple. When their president walked into that room, the Twelve stood and began to clap their hands. They tenderly watched him walk over to his chair and let his body down into the chair. Then with magnificent love, honor, and tenderness, each of the Twelve went up to him and extended to him an affectionate touch, kiss on the forehead, and a hug, showing their great love and admiration for him. They all sat down, and President Hunter thanked them and said, 'I was not supposed to walk again, but with the Lord's help and my determination and, most important, the faith of my Brethren of the Twelve, I am walking again.'" Rulon G. Craven, "Prophets," *Ensign*, May 1991, 28–29.

4. Dell Van Orden, "Exciting Time in Church History," *Church News*, June 25, 1988, 6.

CHAPTER 15: PRESIDENT OF THE QUORUM OF THE TWELVE

1. Van Orden, "Exciting Time in Church History," 6.

2. The Tabernacle Choir was in Israel from December 27, 1992, to January 6, 1993. Their tour and concert appearances are described in detail in LaRene Gaunt, "One Voice," *Ensign*, April 1993, 34–49. President Hunter had planned to be in Israel for this historic tour, but because of ill health, he had to cancel his trip.

3. Cody Judy, a twenty-seven-year-old man from Bakersfield, California, was booked into the Utah County jail for investigation of aggravated assault, disorderly conduct, and unlawful detention. He was identified as having also placed guns and ammunition in Temple Square a week earlier

(no charges were filed in that incident). Asked why he had threatened President Hunter, he claimed he had received visions from God, who wanted him to be the next prophet of the Church. He was sent to the Utah State Hospital for psychiatric evaluation, and on March 23 he escaped from that institution by jumping from a third-story window. Three days later he turned himself in at a Salt Lake City television station. On June 2, 1993, he pleaded guilty in Fourth District Court in Provo to one count of aggravated burglary, a first-degree felony; one count of assault, a third-degree felony; and one count of escape, a class B misdemeanor, and was sentenced to prison. See "Suspect Linked to Guns Left at Square," *Deseret News*, February 8, 1993, A-1; "Suspect in Fireside Bomb Threat Says He Is Fulfilling Prophecies," *Deseret News*, February 9, 1993, B-1; "Judy Pleads Guilt to 'Bomb' Threat," *Deseret News*, June 3, 1993, B-2; "California Man Threatens President Hunter, Fireside Audience with Fake Bomb," *Brigham Young Magazine*, February 1993, 15–16.

4. "Y. Honors Elder Hunter," *Church News*, April 16, 1966.

5. "Students Honor Elder Hunter," *Church News*, April 27, 1968.

6. President Hunter was actually elected to the board on July 10, 1944, forty-six years—not fifty years—before the company made its contribution in his name to the BYU law school.

Bibliography

Allen, Frederick Lewis. *Only Yesterday: An Informal History of the 1920's.* New York: Harper & Row, 1931.

Allen, James B., and Glen M. Leonard. *The Story of the Latter- day Saints.* Second ed., revised and enlarged. Salt Lake City: Deseret Book, 1992.

Baldridge, Steven W., with Marilyn M. Rona. *Grafting In: A History of the Latter-day Saints in the Holy Land.* Israel: The Jerusalem Branch, 1989.

Bitton, Davis. *Guide to Mormon Diaries and Autobiographies.* Provo: Brigham Young University Press, 1977.

Britsch, R. Lanier. *Unto the Islands of the Sea.* Salt Lake City: Deseret Book, 1986.

Cowan, Richard O. *The Church in the Twentieth Century.* Salt Lake City: Bookcraft, 1985.

Dew, Sheri L. *Ezra Taft Benson, a Biography.* Salt Lake City: Deseret Book, 1987.

Doctrine and Covenants of The Church of Jesus Christ of Latter-day Saints. Salt Lake City: The Church of Jesus Christ of Latter-day Saints, 1979.

Durham, G. Homer. *N. Eldon Tanner: His Life and Service.* Salt Lake City: Deseret Book, 1982.

Esshom, Frank. *Pioneers and Prominent Men of Utah.* 1913. Reprint. Salt Lake City: Western Epics, Inc., 1966.

Gibbons, Francis M. *David O. McKay: Apostle to the World, Prophet of God.* Salt Lake City: Deseret Book, 1986.

Gibbons, Francis M. *Harold B. Lee: Man of Vision, Prophet of God.* Salt Lake City: Deseret Book, 1993.

Gibbons, Francis M. *Joseph Fielding Smith: Gospel Scholar, Prophet of God.* Salt Lake City: Deseret Book, 1992.

Gibbs, Rafe. *Beckoning the Bold: Story of the Dawning of Idaho.* Moscow, Idaho: University Press of Idaho, 1976.

Goates, L. Brent. *Harold B. Lee, Prophet and Seer.* Salt Lake City: Bookcraft, 1985.

Hafen, LeRoy R., and Ann W. Hafen. *Handcarts to Zion.* Glendale, California: The Arthur H. Clark Company, 1960.

Henstell, Bruce. *Los Angeles: An Illustrated History.* New York: Alfred A. Knopf, 1980.

Hill, Napoleon. *Think and Grow Rich.* New York: Fawcett Crest, July 1960.

Howard, F. Burton. *Marion G. Romney: His Life and Faith.* Salt Lake City: Bookcraft, 1988.

Idaho: An Illustrated History. Boise: The Idaho State Historical Society, 1976.

Jenson, Andrew. *Encyclopedic History of the Church of Jesus Christ of Latter-day Saints.* Salt Lake City: The Church of Jesus Christ of Latter-day Saints, 1941.

Journal of Discourses. 26 vols. London: Latter-day Saints' Book Depot, 1854–1886. Vol. 9.

Kent, Zachary. *America the Beautiful: Idaho.* Chicago: Children's Press, 1990.

Kimball, Edward L., and Andrew E. Kimball Jr. *Spencer W. Kimball.* Salt Lake City: Bookcraft, 1977.

Kimball, Spencer W. *Faith Precedes the Miracle.* Salt Lake City: Deseret Book, 1972.

Ludlow, Daniel H., ed. *Encyclopedia of Mormonism.* 4 vols. New York: Macmillan Publishing Company, 1992.

McConkie, Bruce R. *Mormon Doctrine.* Salt Lake City: Bookcraft, 1966.

McWilliams, Carey. *Southern California: An Island on the Land.* Santa Barbara and Salt Lake City: Peregrine Smith, 1973.

Muir, Leo J. *A Century of Mormon Activities in California.* 2 vols. Salt Lake City: Deseret News Press, 1951–52.

Nowell, Nancy F. *Testimony of Nancy Nowell. A Copy of my Journals. Commenced in Lapeer, Michigan. A Daily Account of the Devotional and Devout Exercises of My Heart and the Testimony of the Truth.* Salt Lake City: George Q. Cannon and Sons, 1892.

O'Brien, Robert. *Hands Across the Water: The Story of the Polynesian Cultural Center.* Laie, Hawaii: Polynesian Cultural Center, 1983.

Orton, Chad M. *More Faith than Fear: The Los Angeles Stake Story.* Salt Lake City: Bookcraft, 1987.

Peterson, F. Ross. *Idaho, a Bicentennial History.* The States and the Nation Series. New York: W. W. Norton & Co., Inc., and Nashville: American Association for State and Local History, 1976.

Priesthood. Salt Lake City: Deseret Book, 1981.

Richards, LeGrand. *Israel! Do You Know?* Salt Lake City, Deseret Book, 1954.

Rolle, Andrew F. *From California: A History.* 2nd ed. New York: Thomas Y. Crowell Company, 1969.

Scharffs, Gilbert W. *Mormonism in Germany: A History of the Church of Jesus Christ of Latter-day Saints in Germany Between 1840 and 1970.* Salt Lake City: Deseret Book, 1970.

Shepherd, Naomi. *Teddy Kollek, Mayor of Jerusalem.* New York: Harper and Row, 1988.

Smith, Joseph. *History of the Church.* 7 vols. Salt Lake City: Deseret Book.

Talbot, Wilburn D. *The Acts of the Modern Apostles.* Salt Lake City: Randall Book Co., 1985.

Tate, Lucile C. *David B. Haight: The Life Story of a Disciple.* Salt Lake City: Bookcraft, 1987.

Tate, Lucile C. *LeGrand Richards: Beloved Apostle.* Salt Lake City: Bookcraft, 1982.

Top, Brent L., Larry E. Dahl, and Walter D. Bowen. *Follow the Living Prophets.* Salt Lake City: Bookcraft, 1993.

World Almanac and Book of Facts. New York: Pharos Books, 1993.

PERIODICALS

Brigham Young Magazine

Conference Report of The Church of Jesus Christ of Latter-day Saints

Deseret News

Church News section of the *Deseret News*

Ensign

Friend

Idaho Statesman

Improvement Era

Los Angeles Times

New Era

Profile Magazine (BYU–Hawaii)

Relief Society Magazine

Salt Lake Tribune

This People

UNPUBLISHED MATERIALS

Allen, James B., and Jessie Embry. "Hearts Turned to the Fathers: A History of the Genealogical Society of The Church of Jesus Christ of Latter-day Saints." Unpublished manuscript, 1991. Copies on file at the libraries of Brigham Young University, the Church Historical Department, and the Family History Department.

Dedication program of the South Pasadena Ward and South Pasadena Second Ward meetinghouse, August 30, 1970.

Ferre, Craig. "A History of the Polynesian Cultural Center's 'Night Show': 1963–1983." Ph.D. dissertation, Brigham Young University, 1988.

Hedtke, Nelle, "History of the South Pasadena Ward Sunday School, Pasadena Stake of Zion, 1938–1950," n.d.

Hunter, Richard. "Hunter." Biography written for pamphlet introducing the Howard W. Hunter Professorship in the J. Reuben Clark Law School, Brigham Young University, 1989.

Lofthouse, Merrill S. "A History of the Genealogical Society of The Church of Jesus Christ of Latter-day Saints to 1970." Master's thesis, Brigham Young University, 1971.

Pettit, William A. A history of the Pasadena Stake, manuscript completed in September 1966.

Sorenson, John L. "Brief History of the BYU New World Archaeological Foundation." Unpublished paper, April 1975.

Index

281–83; gives advice to grandchildren at birthday dinner, 282;
marries Inis Egan Stanton,
291–93; enjoys travels with Inis,
295–96, 297–98, 300; celebrates
eighty-third birthday in Australia, 296; goes with Inis to
ward reunions in California, 297,
301–2; vacations with family in
Hawaii, 299; writes about marriage to Inis, 301, 302

Claire's Death; Health Problems
consults neurologists about
Claire, 265; decides to allow surgery on Claire, 265–66; learns to
perform tests for Claire's diabetes, 266; cares for Claire at
home, 267; travels with others as
Claire's condition deteriorates,
267; dances, talks with Claire,
268; resists putting Claire in care
center, finally capitulates, 268;
visits Claire often, 268–69;
removes Claire's rings, 268; is
told of Claire's death, 269;
returns home to cold house, 270;
takes comfort from funeral talks,
270; consults doctor first time for
illness, 271; contracts mumps,
271–72; has surgery to remove
tumor, 272; suffers heart attack,
272–73; is bored with recuperation, 273; is not enthusiastic
about walking, 273; New Year's
Eve reflections, 274; loneliness
without Claire, 275–76; undergoes coronary bypass surgery,
276; has surgery for bleeding
ulcer, 277–78; undergoes surgery
on back, 278–79; is cared for during summer by family, 279;
independence of, described by
Richard, 279; rehabilitation after
back surgery, 279, 283, 284;
addresses general conference
from wheelchair, 280–81; goes to
temple meeting using walker,
284, 343n.3 (chap. 14); practices
standing at Tabernacle pulpit,

284; falls while speaking in
Tabernacle, 285; teased by
family after fall, 285; suffers
from broken ribs, 285–86; on
intravenous feeding, 289; has
pneumonia, 296; chokes on food
at dinner, 298; treated for internal bleeding, 304; gall bladder
surgery, 306–7

*Quorum of the Twelve (see also
    Quorum of the Twelve,
    Miscellaneous Activities)*
receives call from David O.
McKay, 144; is shocked by call,
145; is sustained in conference,
145; speaks at conference,
146–47; learns about new duties,
147; is ordained an apostle,
147–48; position of, in Twelve,
148; reactions of others to call,
151; begins commuting between
California, Utah, 151–53, 155;
ends law career, 153; is admitted
to Utah Bar, 154; committee and
board assignments, 155, 184,
287; reviews divorce clearances
and sealing cancellations, 156;
plans own travel itinerary, 162;
associates in Twelve describe
HWH, 185; president of
Genealogical Society, 186–94;
learns to use computers, 189;
dedicates record vault, 190;
changes made in genealogy and
temple work, 190–92; challenged
to prepare family records by
home teachers, 192; presides at
World Conference on Records,
193; attends international
genealogical conferences, 193;
Church Historian, 194–98; surprised at call, 195–96; reorga-
nizes Church Historical
Department, 197; chairman of
board of New World Archaelog-
ical Foundation, 198; visits
archaeological sites, 199–201;
organizes fifteen stakes in Mexico, 202–3; president of Polyne-